Cult of Analytics

Cult of Analytics

Driving online marketing strategies
using web analytics

Steve Jackson

AMSTERDAM • BOSTON • HEIDELBERG • LONDON • NEW YORK • OXFORD
PARIS • SAN DIEGO • SAN FRANCISCO • SINGAPORE • SYDNEY • TOKYO

Butterworth-Heinemann is an imprint of Elsevier

Butterworth-Heinemann is an imprint of Elsevier
Linacre House, Jordan Hill, Oxford OX2 8DP, UK
30 Corporate Drive, Suite 400, Burlington, MA 01803, USA

First edition 2009

British Library Cataloguing in Publication Data
A catalogue record for this book is available from the British Library

Library of Congress Cataloguing in Publication Data
A catalogue record for this book is available from the Library of Congress

ISBN: 978-1-85617-611-8

For information on all Butterworth-Heinemann publications visit
our web site at books.elsevier.com

Typeset by Macmillan Publishing Solutions
(www.macmillansolutions.com)

Printed and bound in Great Britain
09 10 11 12 13   10 9 8 7 6 5 4 3 2 1

Contents

Praise for Cult of Analytics

Steve has spent years down in the weeds, talking to executives and meditating on a mountain. That unique perspective is the main reason *Cult of Analytics* is such a unique book. Easy to read, easy to follow, easier still to find relevant ideas you can implement in your company.

> *Avinash Kaushik*
> *Author of* Web Analytics: An Hour A Day

Web analysis is central to the success of most modern organizations. However, operationalizing the insights gleaned and the next actions to take are what hold back many from reaping the benefits of web analytics. *Cult of Analytics* is a must read from someone who is not just sharing hope and theory but someone who has actually done it for others and is willing to show you the way.

> *Bryan Eisenberg*
> New York Times *bestselling author of* Waiting For Your Cat to Bark

A great read! I wish I had read this 3 years ago – it would have saved me a lot of time (and pain) at Google! I must admit I was initially not enthused at reading another potentially dry analytics book, but this is really engaging right from page 1.

> *Brian Clifton*
> *Author of* Advanced Web Metrics. *Senior Strategist, Omega Digital Media;*
> *Former Head of Web Analytics Google EMEA*

When I first wrote *Web Analytics Demystified* and *The Big Book of Key Performance Indicators* it was difficult to tell how deeply engrained in business culture web analytics would eventually become. Now, nearly five years later, the question has been answered and the best companies around the world are actively working to better understand the online opportunity through better measurement. Steve Jackson in *Cult of Analytics* has provided a necessary update to much of my work, providing one of the most broad views of analytics in the Enterprise available in print. Steve covers the topic of analytics at a variety of levels – from corporate adoption of analytics down into the depths of key performance indicators – providing clear explanations throughout.

I have always known that Steve is one of the best and the brightest in our industry, *Cult of Analytics* will clarify that for the rest of the world.

Eric T. Peterson
Author of Web Analytics Demystified, Web Site Measurement Hacks *and* The Big Book of Key Performance Indicators, *founder of Web Analytics Wednesday and The Web Analytics Forum, and principal consultant at Web Analytics Demystified, Inc.*

Creating a competitive advantage based on web analytics includes a shift towards the true data driven organization. This shift demands that you master your web analytics technology, but more importantly that you understand how to derive insight from all this new data and that you have a setup and an ability to execute on the insights. For the above nirvana to happen, you need two books, one on your technology, the other, without any doubts, *Cult of Analytics*!

Dennis R. Mortensen
Author of Yahoo! Web Analytics and Director of Data Insights at Yahoo!

Great job, useful insights and smart pieces of business thinking tied to practical tips and tricks. Chapter 9 'The proliferation process' is the masterpiece of the work. The quality of chapter 9 was a pleasant and unexpected surprise at the end of your book. You have a very personal style with a strong focus on marketing, especially with the REAN and Insight models. Example 4 in chapter 4 – Quick wins shows the importance of customer process optimization and how the online channel is much more than media and marketing. Very good!

Seppo Roponen
Director Media Research/Digital, TNS Gallup Oy

The long-awaited classic. Much needed and wanted. I have been waiting for this book a long time and now I was finally given the opportunity to read Steve's first published book. *Cult of Analytics* is by definition a classic as it will become a reference book for people working with web analytics and online marketing optimization. It is required reading for those wanting to avoid the pain they would face if they didn't read *Cult of Analytics*.

The book follows its own underlying theory, the REAN model. First the book cover, name and review grab your attention, the first chapter hooks you and I promise the following chapters will keep you going. The processes, best practices and templates make you want to test them … you'll be asking do they really work, and finally, you'll see they do and will be satisfied with *Cult of Analytics*.

In *Cult of Analytics* Steve provides you with an exploration into a leading analyst's mind and reveals the diamonds he has been uncovering over many years. I honestly believe this book reveals some of the secrets of web analytics consultancy that needed to be published.

Kalle Heinonen
Has worked with ERP & BI, Online Business Optimization and Web Analytics for some 8 years. Currently executive of enterprise accounts at Omniture in Finland and Baltic area

In *Cult of Analytics*, Steve Jackson gives you an all-encompassing overview of web analytics, everything from tool selection to segmentation. This book will help you come up to speed and is the perfect guide for those new to the subject, but even experts will learn something new. Steve's work focuses on how to build an organization that will promote actions from web analytics data, how to develop KPIs, and how to combine clickstream data with other data sources. I have experience in applying several of the techniques used in the book and can testify that they work. Building on years of experience and examples from companies such as Amazon and Tesco, Steve makes the case for analytics-driven business.

Lars Johansson
Content director for Internet Marketing Conference, Web analytics blogger at WebAnalysts.Info

Steve Jackson draws on years of experience to show how to improve results from digital channels without being overly technical.

Dave Chaffey
Author and consultant. Marketing Insights

Acknowledgements

I would like to first thank my wife Tanja without whose support I would never have finished this book. She encouraged when she could have despaired, supported when she had the right to be selfish and continues to keep my feet firmly on the ground with her love and humour. I would also like to thank the rest of my family and friends. They keep it real to steal an American phrase.

Next, my friends and colleagues at Trainers' House Analytics unit. Special mention to those that have helped directly, whether they know it or not goes to Jari, Henry, Janne, Sanna, Mira, Outi, Juha, Terhi, Markus, Michael and the irrepressible Sampsa. You people are among some of the best I've worked with. I also extend thanks to Mikko Isoniemi the units' director who has supported the process and helped with marketing.

I also need to thank some former colleagues from the Satama days, most notably Xavier Blanc for his energy and inventing REAN as a concept, Leevi Kokko for calm sparring in the face of adversity, Martijn Van Welie for his design insights and Tommi Pelkonen who helped make me a better consultant.

In addition I would like to thank Omniture (Kalle Heinonen, Antoine Janning, Jesper Lindhardt, Neil Morgan, Andrew Bartlam and Jonas Damgaard Nielsen in particular) for supporting my use of their tools over the years and in the future, Google for giving us Google Analytics for free, Yahoo! For giving us IndexTools for free and Microsoft for trying with AdCenter Analytics, Ossi Hiekkala (archipictor.com) for the great front cover art and a lot more besides.

Then thanks are extended to all the countless people I have learned from. I could list the authors of the thousands of books, whitepapers or articles I've read over the years but space is limited. Special mention is due to: Sean D'Souza the guy I credit with changing the way I think about marketing; Bryan Eisenberg and John Quarto-vonTivadar for their ideas generally over the years but specifically in allowing me to document my take on their persona methodology (chapter 6); Eric Peterson for the first good tactical book *Web Analytics Demystified*, still very relevant five years since its publication and a must have for any serious analytics practitioner; Avinash Kaushik for his book *Web Analytics An Hour A Day* (another must have) as well as his blog, his humility and his attitude.

I can't thank people I have learned from without thanking Jim Sterne, an absolute gentleman in our industry, co-founder of the Web Analytics Association and true thought leader. His eMetrics summits are where his disciples congregate all over the world.

To bring the thanks to a close Dave Chaffey deserves the credit for giving me the kick I needed to write this book as well as being a sparring partner on every chapter, and also my publishers, specifically Marie Hooper and Amy Laurens, for getting me over the final hurdle.

Finally thanks to one I haven't mentioned. You are not forgotten.

Foreword

Back in the 1990s one of the common questions asked of online professionals was, 'what were you doing before the Internet?' The answers were many and varied and helped understand the drift of the ensuing conversation. Today, the most common answer is, 'I was in school', delivered with a quizzical look as if wondering what on earth people did 'before' the Internet.

By the time I met Steve Jackson he had already started Aboavista and was happily posting to the Conversion Chronicles – long before we knew it was going to be called a blog. This was after he had tackled total quality management, KAIZEN and measuring standard deviations of the processes and end products within the automobile industry. This was after he had spent the later 1990s as a freelancer designing websites for companies that wanted online brochures, and after doing A/B/C/D split test print runs of 10,000 direct marketing pieces in preparation for sending out a million letters.

Steve then shifted his focus to email marketing – a perfect melding of his previous experience. From there, he switched to the publishing world and was transformed. The telling moment in this book is where Steve tells us, 'I decided to delve into the data,' and 'I then dug deeper … and noticed a very important trend'. He was hooked.

There was no turning back for him then. He had been bitten by the data bug, he had caught the analytics virus and it would change his career, his life, his dinner table conversation. His passion for the possibilities is infectious and this book is his transmission technique.

When Steve moved to Finland (yes, there was a girl involved), he found a job with an elevator company running online lead generation tests and, by the way, increased their conversion rate by 800% – worth approximately €2 million a year in new business. From there, he created his own consulting company, started publishing the Conversion Chronicles, became a frequent speaker at my eMetrics Marketing Optimization Summit and a very active member of the Web Analytics Association.

So when I asked him what he had done before the Internet, his answer was, 'getting ready for it'.

Steve assumed nothing about the reader when he wrote *Cult Of Analytics*. But he doesn't waste any time either. He starts with the roles, responsibilities and the organizational structure of an analytics driven company. He then points the way to understanding the ins and outs of analysis by using the relationship between company and customer as a framework for collecting and examining your online success.

So if you're interested in identifying clear goals for your organization, convincing those around you that you're onto something, truly understanding where the data comes from, what the tools do, and then how to delve into the data, you've come to the right place.

But wait – there's more.

Steve doesn't stop there. He hands you the keys to the process of becoming an analytics driven company and shows you how to implement a Cult Of Analytics in your organization.

Steve has been there and done that. He's helped countless companies improve their customers' online experience, improved their conversion rates and improved their bottom line. Who wouldn't want to read this book?

Jim Sterne
Producer, eMetrics Marketing Optimization Summit
Chairman, Web Analytics Association

Introduction – The Day that Changed My Life

I made a mistake. It was a job-threatening mistake. I'd only been on the job a month and I was still on trial.

I was working for a newspaper firm running seven websites with readerships in the millions daily. The websites had a large readership and therefore we needed to control quite carefully what went online every day.

My first job was to develop an application for the websites I was in charge of. The editors had asked if I could get people to sign up to have the paper delivered. We decided to use a voucher system where people buying the paper could sign up using the voucher for daily home delivery, the idea being that people buying a newspaper could sign up online and by using the voucher could get a 10% discount.

I created the sign-up pages, seven of them, one for each website. There was a voucher form field (among five or six other fields like name, address, email, etc.). In those days we didn't have any sophisticated ideas about analytics we just measured the number of sign-ups we got. We didn't measure conversion rates.

I got a call about a month later from a colleague working in IT responsible for manually subscribing folks to the newspaper who'd signed up. He tells me, 'Hi Steve, this online subscription thing is a pain in the neck, can we automate it somehow?'; fearing the extra work involved I enquired as to why. He then told me something entirely unexpected that uncovered my mistake.

He said, 'I'm getting too many inquiries from abroad, South Africa, New Zealand, Australia, the USA, it's too much to handle credit card details by phone when I get like 10 enquires a day.' I put my head in my hands and told him I'd look into it before replacing the phone in its receiver.

I'd already realized I'd made a mistake because the form could not be completed by anyone outside of the UK. You needed a voucher from the newspaper itself and the newspaper couldn't be bought abroad. It was impossible to register unless all the form fields had been filled in. Looking at the publishing system confirmed that the voucher field was missing from one of the seven websites.

At least the problem only existed on one site I told myself. It's unlikely to be a big problem if I make the changes quietly. Then I remembered a previous conversation a week earlier from a different newspaper editor about taking the form off the site altogether. I wondered why one site outperformed the other site so greatly that one site was getting too many queries and another was getting too few to warrant marketing it in the newspaper.

I asked my boss where he got his figures, how he knew that millions of visitors a day visited the websites. 'Oh' he replies, 'Yes we have a system on our server called WebTrends, take a look if you like'.

Upon logging into the system the whole thing looked new and scary to me but being the persevering type and having enough technical knowledge to know it would be difficult for me to break, I looked for the pages in question.

I saw that each page was sorted by its address and that you could get the amount of page views over time. I decided to delve into the data looking for the form pages. Pretty quickly I had seven numbers in front of me, a number representing the amount of form pages viewed for each website. I then dug deeper and found the number of submission thank you pages and noticed a very important trend.

One site had five times more submission thanks pages in comparison to the others. It was the site I had made a mistake with. In other words the form conversion rate was five times higher without the voucher field. I still didn't understand why but remembered that the original problem was overseas visitors (South Africa, New Zealand, The USA, Australia).

I began digging again and a full day later – it was my first time with WebTrends – I found that over 60% of the visitors hitting the form pages were people living abroad who couldn't get the paper where they lived but would have liked it delivered. My hunch was that they we're ex-pats, people who had moved away from their roots. I'd also discovered that over 40% of all the visitors hitting the whole website were from abroad. To me this was huge. I didn't think anyone in the company knew this.

I asked my boss if he used WebTrends but he only ever logged in to find out the visitor counts. I asked my colleagues from each newspaper. They only measured sign-up information and relied on my boss for the weekly and monthly visitor counts. That was all that they measured at the time.

I asked all the editors how many subscribers had signed up and most of them said between two and four a day from local people, but that was about it. 'Waste of time' was a common theme throughout the conversations I had with the people who wanted the valuable newspaper voucher print space for advertising revenue.

It quickly became clear to me that this was a huge opportunity, but it didn't get around the fact I'd made a mistake and I was still worried about my job. Primarily at this point in my career I was a young web editor and I shouldn't have made a mistake of that magnitude.

TESTING?

I approached my boss with the line, '*I did a test which has uncovered some extremely interesting results. I purposely left the voucher field out of one of the forms we put online in order to compare them to the others ....*'

Self-serving? Of course but in truth no-one cared whether I'd dropped the form field by mistake or not, the main finding here was the uncovering of something important:

1. We weren't serving our overseas visitors as well as we could and there was a demand for newspaper subscriptions from them.

2. Additionally the marketing effort locally was a wasted effort according to all the data I had (and a lot of that 'data' was simply discussions I'd had with editors).

3. Newspaper advertising revenue was worth more than the voucher space in the newspapers.

4. Serving the ex-pats would be very cheap to maintain once the system to process credit cards was in place.

Once I'd explained all this to senior management everyone was impressed. We would run some phased tests dropping the offline vouchers from the newspapers and dropping the voucher form fields from the websites. If sales from ex-pats went up at the same level from the other sites we would invest in an online booking subscription system.

Dropping the newspaper vouchers delighted the editors who wanted the space for advertising and the bottom line results from the ex-pats sign-ups cleared the way from a happy senior management to invest in credit card clearing facilities online. This also pleased my boss because his unit suddenly took on new importance, having the ability to process orders online meant ideas about how to start e-commerce operations flowed through the company. Even the original colleague who complained about too much work from processing credit card orders from ex-pats was happy because he got what he wanted in the end, an automated system that saved him processing the orders manually.

I'd made my first quick win with analytics but more importantly I'd talked to the editors in a language they could understand.

I'd used analytics to change a business process. Something I was used to doing years before in my quality assurance days, but something I'd never been able to apply to online marketing and business thinking. This to me was the life-changing experience. I didn't realize then how it would change my life, but I recognized that I would never look at web marketing in the same way again and I would always use whatever tools I could to back up my arguments.

There are a number of reasons that my first quick win turned out the way it did.:

1. A lot of it was down to luck in leaving out the voucher field that started the chain reaction but I believe quick wins can and should be planned and Chapter 4 will deal with that a little later on.

2. Another reason is that everything I was doing related to the business and it was easy to explain to senior management why I wanted them to listen.

3. I was also one of the people at the centre of the business. I was running all the websites and therefore I talked to everyone involved with the online channel regularly.

4. There was a tool in place that could give me the data I needed.

5. The whole thing was a test anyway. The vouchers were just an idea the management came up with as a test to increase sales that failed locally but actually worked internationally so no one minded. Had there been someone whose 'baby' it was to come up with offline vouchers I might have had more problems.

This leads me to what I see as the biggest obstacle to getting web analytics grounded firmly into the daily lives of every company employee: **There is a fundamental lack of analytics culture and the natural forces that stand in the way of change for the better need to be addressed by your company as soon as possible before your competition do it.**

This book will guide how you integrate analytics as part of a change management programme, gaining and building the required forces and culture you need to deploy analytics strategy throughout your company.

CHAPTER 1

The Organizational Hub and Spoke Method

We must become the change we want to see.
Mahatma Gandhi

CHAPTER CONTENTS

1.1 HOW THE INTERNET HAS CHANGED YOUR WORLD

The way you do business has changed enormously since the arrival of the Internet as a practical medium in the early 1990s. There are three ways in which the Internet has had a profound impact on businesses and organizations in the world today. You will probably quickly recognize the first two ways but the third way is the biggest opportunity the Internet offers to businesses as well as, paradoxically, the biggest threat to building a strong analytics culture.

1. **Consumer empowerment.** Anyone can use the Internet to find out about products and services. This has huge implications for your business. Firstly your competition is out there. Search Engines like Google have empowered people with the ability to find out anything written that has appeared on the public domain. This includes the products and services your competition is talking about. Companies like eBay have empowered the same consumers to find pretty much any product they want to buy and demonstrated the power of online commerce (or e-commerce as it's become known). Now unlike any other time in history there is the ability to compare all this information quickly and easily. I can look at your product or service in Europe as well as a similar offering from the USA or Australia in less time than it takes to make a cup of coffee. The abundance of information available to the consumer has meant that the power has shifted from the companies who could reach the most audience via marketing channels to the consumers themselves deciding when they want to interact with your brand. The consumer is now more likely to ignore traditional push marketing methods in favour of doing online research when it suits them not when it suits you.

2. **Communication.** No aspect of the Internet has changed our lives or the way we live and work more than email. It has enabled 24-hour global business to become a reality. It has also revolutionized internal communication within companies. In addition, mobile access to email and other forms of communication has helped to make the world a smaller place. There are also public forums in which customers or competitors can openly talk about the products and services you offer in a positive and a negative way. Think for example how influential TripAdvisor (http://www.tripadvisor.com) has become when planning a holiday. The first thing a lot of people do is look for customer reviews via services like TripAdvisor before they make their bookings. In addition to being able to read

peer reviews about your products and services your customers can also publish any information they want quickly and easily via services such as Wordpress (blogs and articles), YouTube (videos) and a wide range of social media applications like Facebook. In this environment it can be easy for you to lose the control of your brand, but again this is double edged and you can use this to your great advantage.

3. **Data abundance.** The first two ways the Internet have changed your life are widely known and widely in use in business today. Everything now comes with a URL and an email address attached. What many businesses have underestimated is the abundance of data, which can be easily gathered by web analytics tools for **all marketing purposes**. It is now easier than it has ever been to track the effectiveness of a newspaper advert because of the Internet. Online you can measure clicks, visits and visitors, pages viewed, where people come from, keywords, paths, track campaigns and a whole lot more. All this is vital data that can help you improve your business.

The **amount of information** you can get is often **overwhelming** and this is the paradox. Never before have we had so much data about the behaviour of our customers and prospects. Part of the problem now is that the people who know the data is there don't know how to capitalize on it. The opportunity here is obvious, with this much data you should be able to take real advantage of it. The threat is that you can't figure it out and your competitors can.

1.2 HOW THE INFORMATION REVOLUTION CHANGED YOUR BUSINESS

Your business has adapted to massive changes in the last couple of decades. Your business has now got all the communication tools at least (email, Internet access, global networks, website) and perhaps you're even shifting the focus of your marketing to make it more and more customer centric to take advantage of the information revolution.

There are reasons why you have embraced the technology so prolifically and come to terms with it in the way that you have at the speed you have. These reasons are more to do with culture than with the actual technology.

1. **Urgency.** The mid 1990s was the Internet's 'wild west' period when everyone was rushing to be online. If you weren't online you were

missing out on the *'information superhighway'*. Companies were appearing that didn't exist before, everything from consultancies to help you get online, online marketing companies to help you get traffic and *'hits'* meant everything. You were missing out if you weren't online, thousands of people from all over the world had money to buy your goods and services so you needed to get online and quick or miss out on the gold rush. This sense of urgency was slightly misplaced but the effect was the same, people sat up, took notice and took action.

2. **Led top down.** The charge wasn't led by a geek in glasses. The charge was led by people with titles like CEO, Founder, Chairman of the Board of Directors. These folks understood the sense of urgency and had built up enthusiastic executive teams to make the changes happen.

3. **Vision.** The vision was there that the Internet could cut costs and open up new markets for a lot of businesses, and there were some extremely big successes to look at as proof (for instance Amazon in 1996/7). The vision of the success you *might* or *could* achieve existed in the mind of every leader of every business and that was enough to get them excited enough to invest and use the technology.

4. **Internal communication.** The practical communication aspect of the Internet cannot be overstated. The fact that you could communicate easily over large distances via email and get the message in seconds meant the vision of the Internet was a very easy sell. A CEO could now email the same message to everyone in his business, essentially for free. This was probably the biggest catalyst for change, the fact that the communication medium was so strong. The vision was easy for the management to communicate because everyone could easily understand the benefit.

5. **Actionable.** Many of the Internet's tools actually fitted in nicely with the way most businesses worked. Communication for instance was made easier by email, chat rooms, bulletin boards and later things like video satellite links, SKYPE and other VoIP (Voice over Internet Protocol) technology. Marketing had the potential to improve – but it took longer to work in the way it does now because people had to learn a new way to do things. Cost-cutting happened very quickly: administrative procedures which required routine and expensive fax transmissions were quickly replaced by email; telephone bills

were considerably lower, why speak to the guy at the other side of the world when you could drop him a line? The Internet was very quickly actionable and effective in a business sense and therefore very quickly adopted.

6. **Quick wins.** Most businesses could quickly produce short-term wins based around the communication power of the Internet. Cost-cutting could quickly be produced as proof that the people leading the charge were right. Every time a new deal was signed from somewhere abroad it was hailed as a 'victory for the online strategy'. Because of the new communication ability these quick wins were often communicated by email to all staff and so the march toward a cultural change continued.

7. **Continuous organizational improvement.** Because the Internet worked so well all the changes were built upon. Systems got better, suppliers got slicker, employees who learned quickly and were positive got moved up the ladder often to new positions created by the management leading the charge. Roles like web designer, digital marketing manager, online marketing manager, search engine marketing specialist, VP online sales, director of online research, chief information officer and many more appeared as the new roles were required. These new roles meant that even more culture was built around the Internet tools being used in the business.

8. **Routinely used.** When was the last time you can remember that you have not been online, sent an email or at least thought about checking your email? It is simply a part of your daily life, accepted and normal. Actually the thought of not being able to access this routine is now worrying to us. Unless you live in a remote part of the world that is not yet developed and has no Internet access the thought of a few days without net access is at the very least an inconvenience.

Looking at these powerful cultural drivers it's easy to see why the Internet has been so successfully integrated into most businesses in the developed world today. Without the cultural drivers behind the adoption of the Internet as a business tool we might still have a small network that existed for the use of governments and military.

In order to fully benefit from web analytics you need to change the culture in your company to that of a web analytics culture. In order to do that you should follow the eight steps that you've just seen demonstrated that worked for the Internet.

1.3 THE CULTURAL CHANGE MODEL

FIGURE 1.1 *The cultural change model*

Let's look at the first example described in the introduction to this book. How many of the eight steps described in Figure 1.1 had I needed to go through to make the change?

1. **Urgency.** Newspaper sales were going down because web readership was going up. This was – and still is – a huge threat and had blasted away the complacency in the publishing industry. Later when I discussed the 'test' I had made to my boss I talked about how much it was costing us and how much we could benefit by testing take up from ex-pats. He passed this on to senior management that meant point 2 (below) was initiated.

2. **Led top down.** The managers and senior guys after seeing my results made the decision to test and spend resources to see if they could improve their business results. They understood the urgency and had the vision already.

3. **Vision.** The vision was to get the online channel working for the business so that losses from sales of newspapers to the online channel could be re-claimed. Because my findings fit with that vision it was an easy decision to continue with the testing. The vision was NOT about analytics it was about the bottom line.

4. **Internal communication.** I was right at the heart of the business in a central role. I took advantage of this by communicating with everyone involved. I knew for instance that one website was ready to drop the coupon idea and knew that others were saying they could get more money from the advert space in the publication.

I also knew that one site was vastly out-performing the others in subscription sales from overseas. There is something you can learn from this. A central unit functioning for the business as a whole but independent of the business units can be very useful in breaking down information silos.

5. **Actionable.** One of the most important things I did was to go to the management team with an actionable plan. It was very easy for them to say yes to a phased roll out of dropping the coupon fields on each website. I was playing every positive I had to get them to agree. I knew that some parts of the business were dissatisfied so we could start roll outs with them. I didn't communicate the plan with technical jargon, I communicated it by saying 'because of the figures I'm seeing I think we can bring "x" amount of extra revenue through each site and return to our original adverting revenues in the print publication'. They liked that because my plan was simple and easy to understand.

6. **Quick win.** The whole thing would be proved as a quick win in one month or else we would scrap the idea. I had given them a timeframe to prove my findings and the whole win was very low risk from a cost point of view. I had 'planned' the quick win and everyone was waiting for me to produce the results.

7. **Organizational improvement.** The management elevated my position and also elevated the status of the online team because we now had more e-commerce functionality in house because of the credit card capabilities.

8. **Routinely used.** Web analytics became one of my weekly tasks and reporting/actions were part of the process. I promised editors one insight a month that they could use.

I didn't recognize it at the time but as you can see every part of the eight-step process was followed. I believe the vision and the leadership were the biggest factors in helping the analytics culture develop roots in the organization. For more information on change processes within your company I recommend you read a book called *Leading Change* by John P. Kotter (Harvard Business School Press, 1996). He goes into a lot more depth about an overall change process. I've integrated his eight-step process to work with building an analytics culture inside your company. *I call it the hub and spoke method of analytics.*

1.4 THE HUB AND SPOKE METHOD

Figure 1.2 shows the model you should try to create internally for your business. At the centre of the organization is the analytics hub, a combination of tools, process and people. If you remember from my introductory example I1 was at the centre of the organization. I was in the information 'hub' somewhere where I could know all the different perspectives.

On the outside are the spokes. The spokes are the different business units, areas or competences that your business has. They could be called marketing, sales, support and corporate for instance. Each has different underlying goals and objectives that require different things from their analytics. The job of the hub is to supply the spokes with the information they need via processes designed to get the most out of the tools.

This hub and spoke model is one of the key strategies your leadership should try to create in your business.

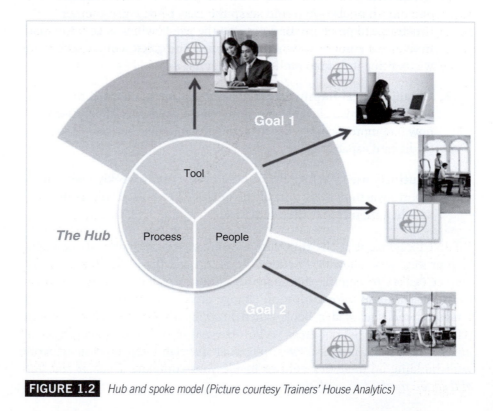

FIGURE 1.2   *Hub and spoke model (Picture courtesy Trainers' House Analytics)*

The Hub People

The hub includes people like senior business analysts, technical specialists, data miners, business intelligence people, marketing analysts and web analytics specialists, who report directly to someone like a chief analytics officer (CAO) who reports directly to the CEO and the executive steering group.

Two models can be adopted for the hub and spoke. The first model, the enterprise model, typically has a lot of different divisions, product or service portfolios, or has a number of markets all over the world, with employees usually in the thousands. The second type of model is more suited to the smaller business that has less to deal with internationally and doesn't need such a complex hierarchy. Either way the idea remains the same – the hub people are responsible for breaking down the information silos, analysing data and serving spokes, steering groups or people who can take decisions on recommendations.

A hub hierarchy in a large enterprise might look like Figure 1.3. The size of the hub depends on the size of your organization.

It may be that there are a dozen different spokes to collate data for, analyse, report and make recommendations, or it may be that there are only two major spokes and lots of minor ones. It may even be that you have more than one hub if your company is big enough, serving particular markets for instance, however if at all possible, centralization should be enabled meaning even if you do have multiple hubs, they should communicate with one central 'super hub' reporting direct to the executive board.

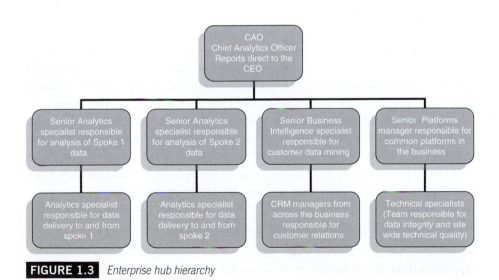

FIGURE 1.3 *Enterprise hub hierarchy*

The Hub as an Exclusive Division

It makes more sense especially in larger enterprises to separate the hub from the various business spokes. The hub's core function is to serve all spokes to the best of its ability without being affected by politics that may exist in each business spoke. If a hub analytics specialist is part of a business spoke then he effectively reports to the spoke manager, not the CAO or senior analytics specialist as shown in Figure 1.3. This may lead to conflict of interests. The analytics hub's primary purpose is to be the intelligence for the whole business and give the spokes the most factual data they can so that business decisions can be taken.

Chief Analytics Officer

This person focuses on building the vision or aligning the company vision to allow it to generate and analyse information. The CAO focuses on providing input into company-wide operational decisions on the basis of the analysis. As such, the CAO requires experience in analysis and marketing, finance or operations. The CAO may be a member of the board of directors of the organization, but this is dependent on the type of organization. In the ideal scenario the CAO should report directly to the CEO or executive steering group. The person in this role will also require a great deal of inter-personal skills as he/she will be dealing with executives, business managers and leaders in the company and guiding them in analytics best practices.

Senior Analytics Specialist

Senior analysts responsible for the spokes are there to run strategic workshops and analyse data collected by less senior analytics specialists to find business insights. It is also their job to make recommendations based on KPIs they are reviewing (there is more about KPIs in Chapter 3). Their key role is to find out what stops marketing campaigns working as well as they should and help build performance benchmarks. Because they also sit in the same unit as the business intelligence senior specialist they can combine information and come up with new ideas based on what customers actually do and not just how prospects behave online. All information is fed up and down. The CAO finds out about all the things going on in each spoke and the spokes get recommendations and actions based on the results of the analysts.

Business Intelligence (BI) Specialist

In BI, competent specialists are able to quickly compile reports from data for forecasting, analysis and business decision-making. By helping to predict what the customer will do, or predict when and how the best time to contact an old customer is, the BI competence is a vital part of any large enterprise, especially those serving the consumer. By putting BI and analytics specialists together you create a very empowering and exciting environment where ideas spark off each other. The BI specialist typically covers the field known as customer analytics, or the Nurture phase as described in the REAN model in Chapter 2.

Platforms Manager

There should be someone in charge of the platforms that the business uses to measure the online and offline activity. This function is extremely important from a quality control perspective. Data integrity (see Chapter 5) is vital if the data is to be believed. It is the platform manager's responsibility to make sure that the data coming in hits the standard it is supposed to. The platform manager's responsibility is to make sure that the platform(s) is suitable for the purpose of tracking all the online activities being run around the enterprise.

Analytics Specialists, Customer Relationship Managers and Technical Specialists

Sitting underneath these three senior staff levels are the supporting crews. They are responsible for actually providing the data requested by the spokes, by the senior analysts and by BI, as well as ensuring the data integrity through careful quality control.

In smaller organizations the roles should still be quite similar with all the aspects covered and the hub sitting centrally. It may be that you ask people to multi-task but the hub/spoke principle remains the same. For instance, you may have something that looks like Figure 1.4.

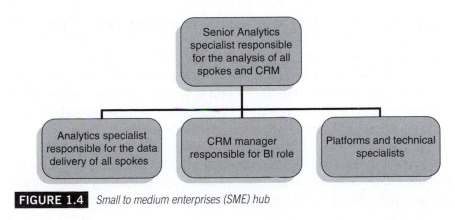

FIGURE 1.4   *Small to medium enterprises (SME) hub*

The difference here is the resources required are either not needed or not available. Overall the structure is the same with analytics covering all the analysis bases, customer relationship managers (CRMs) covering customer analytics and platforms combined in one unit. The senior analyst in this case is responsible for the whole unit and also for giving the CEO or company founder the best information possible to make better decisions.

Spoke People

The spokes are your people at the business end. They are your marketing managers, your sales people, your communications division, your e-commerce managers and people responsible for online lead generation. All these people are directly responsible for a specific part of your company's function and they are in a high-pressure position. The spokes are vitally important to building a successful hub and spoke strategy and building an analytics culture throughout your business. You must involve senior spoke people in the executive steering group decisions so that they are in control of their business.

Spoke people are the ones responsible for the success of their initiatives, therefore your hub must allow them to retain control unless the senior analyst backed by the CAO have better company-wide intelligence. The hub's job is to understand the bigger picture and give each spoke that information; it's not to alienate the spokes into not trusting the hub and interfering with their business strategy.

Suffice to say that each spoke is as vital to the business as the analytics hub and each has a separate function all aiming toward the same end goal, higher profitability and better decision-making. It's vital that each hub and each spoke work together and not let political/social/demographic differences get in the way. This of course requires strong leadership and vision.

1.5 LEADERSHIP, VISION AND STEERING THE SHIP

Every company has a CEO and quite often some remarkable things are attributed to these mystical beings. For instance, it's often reported in the press how a CEO has turned things around in less than 5 years. This is never a one-man effort. Most successful CEOs organize a team of enthusiastic individuals to successfully communicate a vision, but it's unlikely he or she was the sole factor behind the success. Assembling this team is vital.

While discussing building a culture of analytics throughout the book I refer to teams like the steering group. There could be lots of steering groups in the company especially around the spokes that take low-budget, tactical decisions.

However the first job of the CAO, the person who leads the hub, should be to create an executive steering group that can help make the message stick in the company. Usually their role is to make things happen at the *company* level rather than just at the *hub and spoke* level. The CAO needs to be part analytics specialist and part politician but he needs to be successful in developing a strong executive understanding to make vital budget decisions and keep leading with the analytics vision.

Creating an Executive Steering Group

The CAO can't make expensive decisions alone. He or she shouldn't be allowed to go out and spend millions on the best analytics system in the world without really defining if they need it, or if it truly suits the company's best interests. The CAO should not be allowed to order a new online shopping cart for the entire company without understanding the needs of the e-commerce organization. They shouldn't be allowed to stop marketing initiatives even if they're failing without the full consent and knowledge of the spoke director. They shouldn't be allowed to change software or systems or anything at all without backing from a majority in a steering committee. The point of the steering group is twofold:

1. By inviting other executives to the analytics party you encourage buy in and help the executives understand why the analytics push is happening. You help the executives to fully understand the vision and help them to build the analytics culture.

2. By bringing in all the key people that have a real vested interest in certain areas your CAO can tackle head on any challenges that the company may face.

I have see executives talking about millions of euros as if it were small change. *'If it's a seven-figure number then I don't have a problem. I only look twice when it goes to eight figures.'* In some cases the seven-figure number could be a five- or six-figure number if tackled early enough and the CAO should be able to prove that. He/she needs political support to change things from top management across the company.

It's impossible to say who exactly should be in this team. However one definite person is the chief analytics officer. The other people should have some defining characteristics that make them useful to have in this steering group.

1. **Passion.** They are passionate about improving the business and if analytics helps that then they're all for it.

2. **Position.** Are the key people involved? The main spoke directors/executives should be included so that decisions affecting them take their point of view into account. This means things are likely to go more smoothly.

3. **Expertise.** Various points of view need to be represented in terms of areas of expertise covered by the spokes, central IT people (CIO?), countries, nationality, work experience.

4. **Credibility.** Do the people in this group have enough reputation to command the respect of the employees at large and foster the vision?

5. **Leadership.** Include proven leaders (CEO/vice president level) that back the process to make the steering group effective and accountable.

The job of the steering group should be to take decisions on the overall vision. This is a company goal that includes analytics at its core. If the goal is increasing sales by 50% in 3 years in a particular market, it's fair to say that lead generation tactics are involved.

If the hub has proved that the online lead generation process across three major divisions has critical usability problems meaning people abandon in droves, the CAO should come armed with the cost of that, discuss it with the steering group and then start discussions about alternative systems. Once employees see changes coming as a result of steering group efforts then they will truly see leadership in action.

The steering group should meet as necessary but at least once per quarter to discuss the things (at the very least) that need to be communicated to the employees. It is quite possible that the analytics is showing you some great things and you're doing a lot right already. If that's the case it needs communicating within the company.

In order to 'see' leadership in action the changes need to be clearly communicated. This is where the executive steering team needs to start delegating.

Leadership and Management

The process of leadership and management should follow a simple route of delegation. Figure 1.5 illustrates the way the executive steering group should delegate.

Vision

The white parts of this model show the responsibilities of the executive steering group. They should come up with the company vision and how it

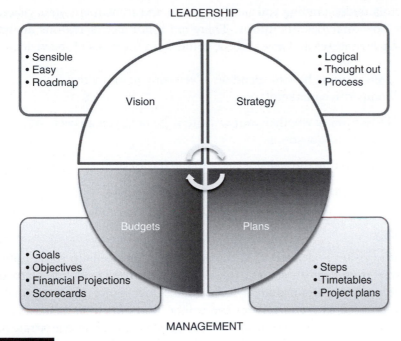

LEADERSHIP

- Sensible
- Easy
- Roadmap

Vision

- Logical
- Thought out
- Process

Strategy

Budgets

Plans

- Goals
- Objectives
- Financial Projections
- Scorecards

- Steps
- Timetables
- Project plans

MANAGEMENT

FIGURE 1.5   *The leadership and management relationship*

is to be communicated internally. It should be a sensible easy vision understood by all with a date of delivery.

A simple vision like 'Relentlessly focus on customer experience by offering our customers low prices, convenience, and a wide selection of merchandise.' (Amazon)

The vision to offer Earth's biggest selection and to be Earth's most customer-centric company is a grand goal everyone can understand, how they get there is down to the spoke plans. You should always suggest why the vision is appealing and why it's sensible to follow this course of action, but the vision statement should be simple.

In order to create an internal vision around analytics that works and is understood there are two things that can help:

1. Firstly, the urgency of the situation needs to be clearly communicated. Building Cult of Analytics itself is not usually the entire reason for change; it's more likely to be part of some wider change process that might last a number of years.

2. Secondly, as shown in Figure 1.5, the vision needs to be actionable and sensible. If your staff can't do things that help make the vision a reality then it's simply a fancy idea.

With this understanding you need to create and implement your vision to decide how analytics fits into it. There are a number of reasons analytics can help businesses and any of these could form the basis of the vision;

1. Determining how to spend on advertising in an increasingly competitive marketplace.
2. Determining whether your website is helping you answer your customers' questions.
3. Determining the website value to the business.
4. Determining the customer value to the business.

Strategy

Once the vision is defined then the steering group needs to come up with the strategy to help implement the vision. They need to define plans that get the company from point a to point b. Once those plans are defined they then need to set targets and spending limits for their spokes so that the company doesn't invest in the wrong things. While the strategy is discussed at a high level in the executive steering committee they never execute it.

Final planning and budgeting with be left to each spoke. The size of the spoke depends on the business, however the spokes are ultimately responsible for the strategy being carried out and therefore the vision being delivered. They are the ones who need to define the plans that will work on a tactical level. They are the people at the business end who deliver on the KPIs that mean they hit the targets the business has set.

The Spoke Management Role

The management group would be made up of spoke people who plan, manage, set budgets and develop tactics to execute strategy. They make up the grey segment of Figure 1.5 and are responsible for the success or failure of the leadership strategy.

The spoke actors should have defined KPIs (see Chapter 3) that they can act on and which should have targets set. Figure 1.6 shows the process of deciding on the results of a KPI.

Once the KPIs are defined (see Chapter 3) then the hub should send the KPIs as results to the individual actors charged with taking action on flagged challenges. The spoke actor should make a decision, based on whether they can take action or not.

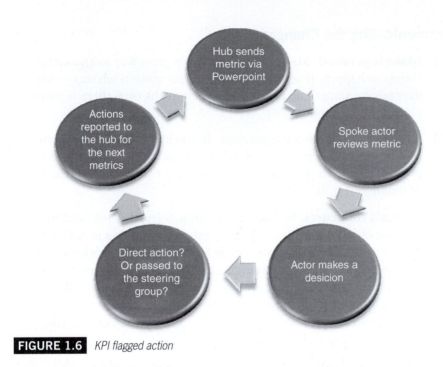

FIGURE 1.6   *KPI flagged action*

The spoke actors can take actions on the things that they can affect such as marketing campaign spend, vendor selection, consultancy requirements and other relatively low tactical costs that the spoke can handle alone. The tactical plans the spoke make to fulfil strategy also may mean re-setting objectives and applying for new budgets, hence the central arrow in Figure 1.5.

If there is no direct action the spoke actor should tell the hub who will then raise the point to the CAO for the next executive steering group session.

The executive steering groups decisions will affect the more major decisions like should we change our shopping cart provider or change our website content management system. If these kinds of decisions are made then the entire business will be affected.

1.6 COMMUNICATION

There are a number of plans to be created in the hub and spoke change programme. These are some tactics to help you communicate. The way you should communicate this is to focus on the bigger vision and come up with analytics as one of the keys to the success of the strategy laid out by the executive steering group. It's your hub's job to do the analytics parts for you and it's your spokes job to execute business strategy.

Communicating the Changes

1. **Make it personal.** Making it personal is a great way to encourage things to happen. If your peoples bonus/promotion/job/way of life depends on something happening in 3 months then there is more chance it will happen.

2. **Urgency.** Deadlines are important. In the above example 3 months makes the change urgent. Regular meetings on progress should be pre-agreed within those 3 months. Urgency could also take the form of required results.

3. **External influences.** Is your competition doing this well and thriving because of it? If so there is nothing wrong with trying to achieve similar results yourself if you think the strategy will work for you. Is there a change in the marketplace? It could be a consolidation, merger, new competitor or even the threat of a recession. All of these factors often affect the urgency of the situation and it's worth taking these into account when trying to think of ways to improve your situation including by using analytics.

4. **Actionable plans.** It's no good making personal demands with tight deadlines and describing external scenarios to people if you don't have an executable plan to go forward with. Draw up a roadmap with actionable tasks. Draw up an action plan and set timescales that show the each phase timeline (See Figure 1.7 overleaf). Your hub and spoke managers need to own and project manage this.

Actionable Plans

The principle is that the 'analytics hub' serves the spokes by actually setting up the tools and doing the analysis. The spoke people have to be aware of what they can ask the hub to deliver The steps are described below with the area of responsibility shown in parenthesis.

Awareness Generation (Hub and Spokes)

If your staff doesn't fully understand analytics then you need to start from the beginning and to teach them what the benefits are. You need to show them the way to achieve wins in their own line of work. They have to understand how they can benefit on a daily basis. If you require a little coaching it's worth using a little time to get an expert in to show you what you can get and how you can get it. Any external consultant you bring in should be made fully aware of your business model and requirements and

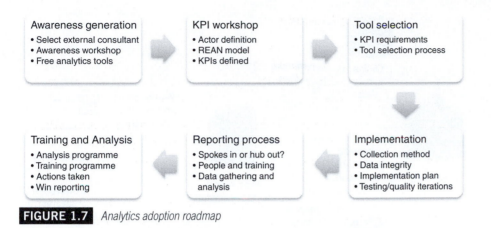

FIGURE 1.7   *Analytics adoption roadmap*

level of understanding. The consultant should ask to send the participants a short survey before doing any workshop so that he or she knows whom they are dealing with as well as at least one pre-workshop interview with the leader of the exercise.

KPI Workshop (Hub and Spokes)

KPIs are the foundation of any major web analytics process. A full description of how to do a KPI workshop is described in Chapter 3. The objective is to have metrics that will allow you to take actions on the data you see rather than simply have numbers in front of you.

Tool Selection (Hub – with Spoke KPIs)

Without a good analytics tool you will fail. Chapter 5 discusses free tools in depth as well as what to look for when paying for a more robust solution.

Implementation (Hub)

Chapter 5 will also deal with implementation, data integrity and quality issues you should not overlook. Implementation is critical to get right even if the process you decide on is in iterations, at least you should have a plan which rolls out the iterations sensibly and is based on your KPIs.

Reporting Process (Hub Delivers to the Spokes)

Usually the spokes would much prefer to simply receive the insights from the data and act on them rather than have to go and find out themselves. One way that can work across channel is using spreadsheet software to compile data. In Figure 1.8 you see a data integration and reporting process mapped out.

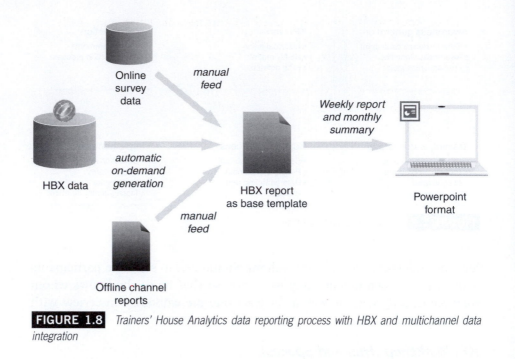

FIGURE 1.8 *Trainers' House Analytics data reporting process with HBX and multichannel data integration*

Firstly you have the data from the web analytics tool (in this case Omniture's HBX) generating on-demand data into Excel using the report builder tool. You could also add relevant offline data. For instance lets say 1000,000 leaflets were passed out with coupon codes around a similar offer you were selling online (and measuring with HBX). You could add your offline channel data to the Excel sheets coming direct from HBX. Finally you could add qualitative survey data, for instance let's say that HBX reports one of your KPIs (bounce rate) is losing you a lot of traffic from a certain page. When people leave that page you could open an exit survey for them with a very good incentive to fill in the survey. Once compiled the insights and various graphs required can be shared with the spokes via Powerpoint. Ideally this would then be acted upon or sent back to the steering group for further analysis.

For more information on the structure and type of reporting and analysis see Chapter 8.

Training and Analysis (Hub and Spokes)

Once you have got your process together you may require a little training to do on the job analysis. A lot of the things you do in the beginning will be trial and error but remember when you win communicate the success as best you can. See Chapter 4 on planning your quick wins.

Once your spokes have managed to understand what your KPIs are telling them then you're halfway there. That is why Chapter 3 discusses the KPIs in so much depth and Chapter 8 covers business dashboards and scorecards.

The hub are the ones responsible for analysing the data and finding insights, which is covered in Chapters 6 and 7.

CHAPTER 2

Understanding Reach, Engage, Activate and Nurture (REAN)

If we plan, then we can effectively measure; and if we measure, we can effectively improve.
John Quarto-vonTivadar (FutureNow Inc.)

CHAPTER CONTENTS

2.1 DEVELOPING A REACH, ENGAGE, ACTIVATE AND NURTURE (REAN) MODEL

Before you set goals, objectives, define KPIs and start using web analytics, you need to understand what marketing methods you're going to employ and how you're going to effectively plan and measure these activities.

In 2006 a model was created by Satama (now Trainers' House) called REAN. It's an acronym that stands for Reach, Engage, Activate and Nurture.

The reason you should use REAN in the hub and spoke method is because it's important to visualize what you're measuring and why for planning purposes. All KPIs and metrics should fall into at least one of the four dimensions.

Introducing REAN

In developing this model you could use existing and well-known marketing terms, for instance AIDA (Awareness, Interest, Desire and Action). However semantically AIDA is not very good for measurement. Measuring something like 'Desire' can't be measured with web analytics alone, you need to have qualitative data (face to face interviews, surveys, market research) in order to gauge the desires and motivations of the prospect.

Awareness is a difficult term to define when you consider the word from a measurement perspective. How do you measure the awareness of your brand in someone who has never contacted, visited, purchased but has been exposed to your logo? Again it's very difficult without qualitative data from other sources than web analytics.

Also the word 'Interest' in the AIDA model isn't exactly right either. If we you use 'interest' as a term for people visiting your websites, you're assuming they are interested in something on the site.

Actions can be measured but you should be able to plan the other three dimensions much more clearly. The REAN model gives you more concrete terms to help us visualize and measure marketing activities.

The history of this model goes back a few years when a smart guy and ex-colleague of mine Xavier Blanc, then a senior planner at Satama (now Trainers House'), came up with the REAN framework with help from one of his colleauges, Leevi Kokko.

Xavier Blanc's Comments

I came up with this loose framework while I was working at Satama. The basic point was to get a large client of mine grasp the very simple idea that there's no point at all in investing a lot of money in creating cool websites if no one was looking at building traffic for these sites in the first place, if no one was then defining what to do with these hard-won contacts, how to leverage them as part of an entire branding, marketing or sales effort, now and in the future, online, but and this is very important, also offline … (because as much as it hurts to recognize when you're working in a web agency, there IS life outside the web and guess what, most of it still happens THERE!).

In other words, the two messages I wanted to deliver were:

1. **Break the silo walls.** it's not SEM + website + CRM, it's about creating EXPERIENCES that flow from the very first moment a contact is established down the lifecycle of that contact. This often implies, especially in large companies, difficult organizational alignment efforts and clear leadership challenges.

2. **Define KPIs.** Define what your business goals and objectives are. Think hard, before you do anything and invest any dollars. Only then does it become possible to design effective and efficient marketing ARCHITECTURES. Creatives are cool and certainly needed, but without a good, solid architecture, they're pointless.

Initially, this framework was more educational material than anything else. However, we instantly started to use it as a tool to structure our work and ground our metrics. This was my contribution.

Xavier Blanc – Fjord
http://www.fjord.co.uk/

Leevi Kokko's Comments

Having seen Steve present the KONE case at eMetrics Stockholm, I was impressed by how the initial REAN model was improved and how it was utilized very cleverly in the analytics process.

I remember the first realization very well, and from the very first project it was created for it really turned out to be an invaluable tool in customer communications and planning in many ways. I'm personally using a variant of the model with practically all of my clients now.

Leevi Kokko – Ego Beta
http://www.ego.fi/

REAN Definition

Every business website is affected by REAN. They all need to reach their potential customers, they then need to engage with them, activate them (get them to convert to your goal) and finally you need to nurture them, in other words encourage them to come back. We define these four factors in the following way:

Reach sources, the methods you use to attract people to your offer. It also includes how you raise awareness among your target audience

Engage, is how people interact with your business. Engage is essentially the process before a point of action that helps your prospect come to a decision

Activate means a person has taken a preferred point of action. Typical examples include a person purchasing a product, a newsletter subscription or a sign-up

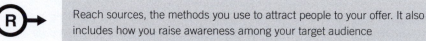

Nurture describes the method of retaining and re-engaging with activated consumers. The consumer is a person who has already taken at least one preferred point of action

The Main Point of REAN Planning

Planning using the REAN model and utilizing the measurement tools available to measure your online activities gives you a method to measure every marketing euro you spend. This organizational improvement means you can allocate yearly budgets based on the ROI of marketing activity.

You can use web analytic tools to measure the marketing effect of everything from a brochure, fliers, TV and radio commercials, corporate events as well as online marketing. All you need is tactical planning to do so.

By understanding all the places that customers or prospects might come from you can develop a solid understanding of how to begin thinking about your measurement strategy.

Once you understand how the REAN model works you can easily visualize what you need to do in terms of tactical operations like website tagging requirements, campaign measurement requirements and combining platforms to, for instance, be able to combine CRM systems with web analytics systems.

REAN allows you to quickly develop visualizations within your organization that both marketers and technicians understand. Utilizing REAN can help any business visualize and plan their marketing and measurement activities.

2.2 THE TYPICAL REAN PLANNING SCENARIOS

Figure 2.1 shows some ways in which visitors might act in a typical scenario between their reach source, through to engagement, activation and then nurture phases. For instance a search keyword in Google may attract a visitor to click which would then lead to an info rich product page. This may then lead to a spares for sale process (spares cart process) which might then lead to a spare sold. Once the customer is in your database CRM marketing begins in the hope that more sales are made at a later date meaning a new REAN model is required (for after the purchase lifecycle).

Reach

As you can see on the left hand side of Figure 2.1, there are a number of reach touch points. These are some ways that you can potentially touch your prospect or customer with your advert. The list of reach sources is by

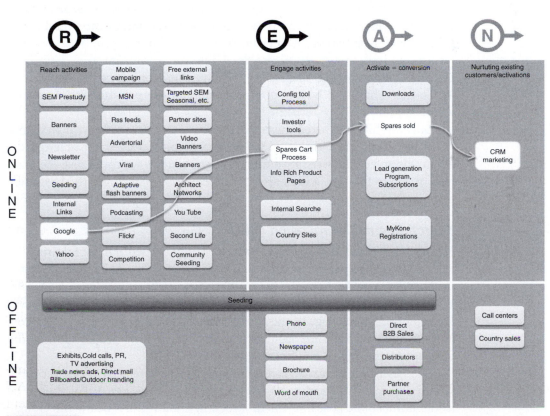

FIGURE 2.1   *Online and offline REAN model*

no means comprehensive. However you can see a number of traffic sources everyone will be able to relate to and can easily associate to the reach touch point.

For example, Google, Yahoo and MSN (online reach touch points) are often used to find people that are searching for your products. You advertise on the Google network using a set of keywords and phrases that relate to your product or service.

Search Engine Marketing (Pay Per Click or PPC)

When a potential customer goes to a search engine, types in a keyword or phrase that matches your keyword, your advert appears. That is an online touch point because potentially your prospect could then visit your website by clicking your advert. This is often termed PPC or pay per click.

Listed in Figure 2.1 are some things which you may not have heard of before, like the SEM pre-study.

Search Engine Marketing Pre-study

This was a study that measured the most successful keywords in relation to their particular campaign. We only used a small portion of the overall campaign spend as a testing budget and then focused our efforts on the higher return on investment (ROI) traffic when the campaign was launched. Figure 2.2 shows where these ads typically appear on a search engine such as Google. The black boxes show whereabouts the pre-study paid adverts would appear.

Once we had measured the performance of the pre-study with web analytics we would then direct spend to the highest converting or engaging ad-groups and campaigns. By doing these pre-studies we could test the position of ads to find out which areas we needed to be in to get the best click through for the right price.

Search Engine Optimization (SEO)

Figure 2.3 overleaf shows a now famous study carried out by Enquiro – a leading Canadian search engine marketing company. They carried out a series of eye tracking tests in June 2005 showing how people used Google, Yahoo and MSN search engines. The black overlay is a heat map laid over the top of the home page of the search engines query results page. The now famous and much quoted 'golden triangle' shows how people look at the different search engine results.

The triangular heat map represents the most valuable real estate on the search engine. This means that to get good visibility your links should be in the number one position (the first rectangle shown just below the Google

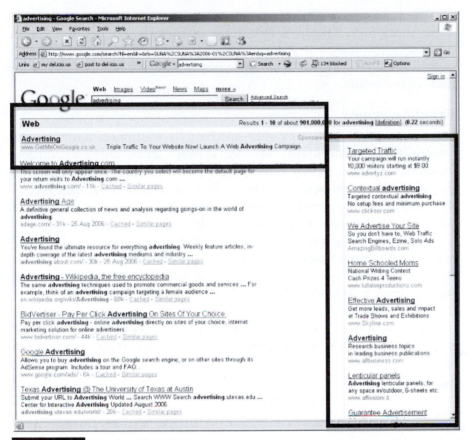

logo in Figure 2.2). This position is typically the most expensive to buy from search engines on a cost per click basis.

This is why it's becoming increasingly important to develop good search engine optimization practices into your website. By doing this you can appear in the top free listings meaning that you get the same exposure in the golden triangle and not have to pay the search engine for it.

FIGURE 2.3 *The search golden triangle*

To find out whether you need to do SEO or stick with SEM (search engine marketing) you need to figure out how much it's all going to cost and weigh up your options.

This is of course all measurable with web analytics. You can get the white paper from Enquiro's website at http://www.enquiroresearch.com/eyetracking-report.aspx if you're interested in this very useful qualitative study carried out on three of the most important reach sources you're ever likely to use online.

Brand Awareness

Whenever a person visits you after searching for your brand name you can refer to it as a branded visit. Branded keyword terms might be someone searching for your company name or your product names. You can also say that when there is no referring domain that this is a branded visit, because the user has either typed in your website address (i.e. they knew your brand) or they had bookmarked it previously.

Adaptive web pages are applications developed for campaigns. They were planned with Reach, Engage and Activate as key elements – not nurture for these particular campaigns – in order to measure and test which elements were the most successful. This is a form of A/B split testing (see Chapter 7).

We used three different campaigns, each campaign having a different theme.

As you can see from the Conversion Chronicles example in Figure 2.4, we chose themes in which we looked to attract people from three different

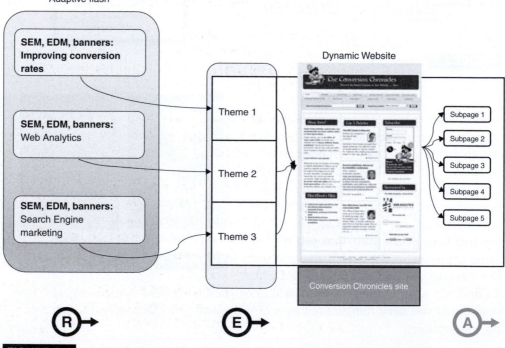

FIGURE 2.4 *Adaptive flash campaigns planned with Reach, Engage and Activate as elements*

Web

How To **Reduce Single Page Accesses** Or Bounce Rates On A Content ...
How To **Reduce Single Page Accesses** Or Bounce Rates On A Content Website Website
conversion improvement resources from Conversion Chronicles.
www.conversionchronicles.com/How_To_**Reduce_**
Single_Page_Accesses_Or_Bounce_Rates_On_A_Content_Website.html - 24k -
Välimuistissa - Samankaltaisia sivuja - Tee merkintä

FIGURE 2.5   *Google SERP (search engine)*

reach sources, SEM (search engine marketing as described earlier),
EDM (electronic direct mail) and banners across different keywords and
messages.

The first theme was 'improving web conversion', the second 'web analytics' and the third theme was 'search engine marketing'. We would measure with web analytics tools how each theme and specific type of reach
source drove the most traffic. Then we would compare each source and
theme combination across how many activations we got – in the Chronicles
case it was sign-up subscriptions. So for instance if the web analytics
theme drove the most traffic that converted then we could re-direct our
efforts there.

The engage part of this scenario is interesting because it adapted
to what the user had seen in an interactive manner. If a flash banner
on a media site was the reach source we were using to attract a visitor our website dynamically changed its content to reflect the colour
schemes and messaging found on the banner. This we believed would
improve landing page relevance to the visitor. If a visitor finds one of
the Conversion Chronicles pages using a keyword typed into Google
then we display something that might help them find what they were
looking for if the article they read didn't immediately hit the mark. For
instance try going to Google and typing 'reduce single page accesses'
and a link to the Conversion Chronicles will appear (Figure 2.5).

When you click on this link and get to the Chronicles page the page
dynamically appears with a link box field called 'Did you Google?' as
shown in Figure 2.6. This dynamic approach was designed to try and
help the visitor by searching our article database for relevant content.

We measured these link clicks with web analytics to see if the
clicks drove higher levels of engagement than traditional search engine
marketing.

We also used this method with EDMs. When someone had used
a link in an email to get to the Chronicles site we would display our
page with slightly different content, likely to be more relevant to the

FIGURE 2.6   *Did you Google?*

link the visitor clicked. We did this with some success, and found by using web analytics to test and compare offers that we got higher click through and response than in other campaigns.

Seeding

This is a form of viral marketing which if done well can be very successful in terms of reaching your desired target market. Seeding is essentially giving samples of your product to thought or opinion leaders in your target market. They review, use and write about your product or services features, good and bad. This not only allows you to modify your product or service in response to feedback, but also generates a lot of free publicity. Opinion leaders generally blog or write articles about products and services they like, often feeling flattered by the seeding company, which usually gets a lot of goodwill.

Offline Seeding

The following campaign was carried out by the company 3M. Dr Paul Marsden, a UK-based market researcher, identified and illustrated a seeding campaign carried out by 3M in the 1970s.

Seeding Trials in Action: Post-it Notes

The power of seeding trials in transforming the fortunes of a brand is no better illustrated than through the intriguing history of Post-it Notes, the little yellow stickies from the office supplies company 3M. The story started in 1968, when 3M asked one of its researchers, Dr Spence Silver, to develop a new super-sticky adhesive. Unfortunately Dr Silver failed, and did so quite spectacularly. What he came up with was super-weak glue that wouldn't stay stuck. Consigned to the back shelves of 3M's R&D lab for six years, the fruits of the failed innovation project were virtually forgotten.

Then on one Sunday in 1974, Art Fry, a new product development researcher for 3M, had a 'Eureka' moment whilst cursing scrap paper bookmarks that kept falling out of his church choir hymnal. Perhaps the un-sticky glue could be used to make bookmarks? The idea of Post-it Notes was born. Unfortunately, when this concept of temporary sticky paper bookmarks was tested in research, it bombed. Nobody could see a use for them. However, and despite 'kill the program' calls from management, Fry convinced 3M to run a limited test launch of Post-it Notes. Unfortunately, that failed too. Post-it Notes were doomed.

Before pulling the plug on the whole sad affair, 3M decided to run a seeding trial with opinion leaders in its target market – a sampling initiative conducted in the name of research. The company identified secretaries to CEOs in large companies all across America as opinion leaders for office supply products, and sent them boxes of Post-it Notes, inviting them to come up with ideas for how the little yellow stickies could be used. Flattered by the invitation to be involved in the development and commercialization of a new product, the seeding trial generated goodwill and advocacy among these opinion-leading secretaries, transforming them into Post-it Notes brand champions. The 'useless' Post-it Notes soon started appearing on memos, desks, diaries, drafts, reports and correspondence and spread like an infectious rash through and between companies. The rest is, as they say, history. Post-it Notes had been saved by a seeding trial, transformed from failure to a multi-million dollar and highly profitable brand by a group of opinion-leading secretaries.

Dr Paul Marsden
Director of the Crowd Sourcing Agency
clickadvisor.com

Offline Reach

Offline reach touch points are things like (but again not limited to) in-store advertising such as posters, leaflets or other point of sale materials. However you could include adverts on the side of a bus with your web address posted on the side, adverts in newspapers, in fact anything you can think of which has enough room to host an advert on it seems to have a URL on the side these days. All of these touch points can be measured to a far greater extent than was possible 10 years ago.

For instance you could use marketing URLs in your newspaper ads which re-directed to your campaign pages but passed a 'newspaper parameter' to your tracking system which then knew the visitor must have seen your newspaper ad rather than arrived from elsewhere. In fact any printed advert could have the same kind of parameter applied to it. Domain names cost €10 these days, so it is not expensive to even buy new domain names to run specific offline branding campaigns, nor is it unusual.

Mobile phone campaigns are another Reach touch point that are considered 'online' but actually fall into a grey area in many cases. One mobile campaign I was involved with saw customers using GPS navigation systems to find a physical location as part of a competition. To win they had to register their position online. All measurable by cleverly planned mobile website registration and task completions.

What's important to understand about the REAN model in relation to reach is you map all the potential ways a customer can discover you with your marketing efforts. By visualizing your REAN model in a similar way to the way shown in Figure 2.1 you can start to understand what you have as a measurement challenge. You should ask yourself if you can take advantage of the analytics tools you have to more effectively measure and combine on- and offline data.

Engage

Engagement in the REAN model is not about engaging with customers, it's simply about observing how people interact with your marketing and figure out what the best ways are to measure this activity.

You might want to include specific campaign landing pages tracked from offline sources. Additionally you might include third party partner sites that sell the same or related products to your own and so you ask those partners to affiliate with you to allow you to tag their pages in relation to your campaigns (like Amazon for instance).

Figure 2.1 lists some common engagement points but there could also be processes like online shopping carts, self-service processes, lead generation forms, search results pages, etc. Anything, usually something marketers call a 'creative', that engages your visitor in some way and asks your visitor to do something other than leave the site is an engaging factor.

For instance in a typical 'shopping cart' you might measure engagement by using a process funnel. The process funnel measures how many people have started at the beginning of the process and got through to the end. The idea behind this is to see if there are any obvious places that could be optimized.

In Figure 2.7 the process funnel shows each step from the shopping cart (the top of the funnel), through the shipping address (step 2), to the order summary (step 3) and finally the order confirmation (step 4 at 1.44%). This is taken from the Omniture HBX suite and shows a clear problem between moving from the shopping cart to the shipping address page. When only 8.17% of your visitors go from one part of the process to the next there could be a fundamental problem.

This would be the first place I would look to improve the purchase process in this particular case and perfect to create a quick win (see Chapter 4). Measuring engagement in this way allows you to find usability problems that might be a big opportunity for you to improve your visitors' user experience. See Chapter 7 on the Insight model for more information.

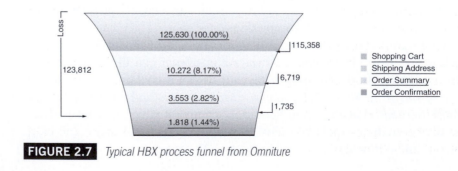

FIGURE 2.7 *Typical HBX process funnel from Omniture*

Engage – Segmentation

There is another more important side to this coin however when it comes to measuring engagement. Session length and depth is very important, so when you can segment the visitor audience based on their behaviour you have a very powerful way to optimize campaigns, especially those websites that don't physically sell anything online.

Not all tools will allow you to do this easily, however it's definitely worth taking the effort to learn how your tool can be set up to measure visitor behaviour as a segment. By segment I mean you want to be able to separate visitors who have behaved in a way that you like (or dislike) from the general visitor population. This gives you much more insight into everything that works from a reach perspective.

For instance, let's say that you define an engaged visitor as someone who has stayed on your website for at least two minutes and looked at five pages (or in the rich media environment clicked five times). This would allow you to optimize your reach sources. The reach sources that have a higher percentage of visitors becoming engaged are the sources of traffic you spend more of your marketing euros with.

Those traffic drivers which don't engage as well with your website either need optimizing at the reach source or dropping altogether so that you can re-direct your money to the higher engaging campaigns. If you have the resources I would advise getting user experience data in the form of customer surveys, heuristic analysis (talked about later in Chapter 7) or usability studies. This data might help you understand **why** people aren't engaging.

It's rare that web analytics will ever tell you why people don't engage, but it will certainly tell you how they interact with you. We'll discuss defining your ideal engagement a little later as we come to the method behind designing your KPIs (in Chapter 3).

The following things should be taken into account when designing your KPI's later on for what we call the 'engage' dimension.

Engage – Click-depth

This is simply the amount of times your visitors click when they move through your website. It may be flash events you measure or the amount of page impressions viewed to quote the web analytics terminology. Click-depth is an engagement measure because it shows on average or individually how each visitor has 'engaged' with your site.

Engage – Duration

Duration is simply the length of time that the visitor stays on your website. I've very often used session time or time spent on site (as duration is also known as) to set up segments as I discussed earlier with varying levels of success. When used in combination with activation or nurture data it can be very actionable and insightful.

Offline Engagement

Offline engagement is a place where the customer can touch, see, hear, smell and taste your product or service. It's when potentially all your five senses come into play when experiencing the product or service. It's talking to a representative, seeing a demonstration, playing with a product, experimenting with a device, eating the new type of cookie sample!

Typically in the consumer environment offline engagement happens in a retail store where there are samples, product demos, interactive videos, customer service agents or places where you can try things out. In a business to business environment it is seeing a presentation, being educated by a consultant, being sold an idea, meeting the sales person for the first time, seeing the service unfold on video.

You should map your own engagement model and again in Chapter 3 (KPIs) you'll learn how to do this.

How you might go about measuring offline engagement is again quite simple and very often underutilized. In all the scenarios I have discussed you could be giving the people you have met any number of specific 'campaign type vouchers' which direct the visitor back to your online marketing. For instance, let's say for a moment you're selling furniture at a store. If the customer doesn't purchase immediately, you could give the person a voucher with a special code that gives them a 10% discount if they buy the specific product they were interested in within 'x amount' of days by visiting your website and inputting the voucher number. It's a simple case to tie in the voucher codes to specific stores. In this way you find out all sorts of priceless information about the purchase decision-making process.

To summarize, engagement in all forms is what has to happen before activation, therefore it makes sense to optimize all the engagement elements.

Activation

Activation is the most important of the four elements. Activation occurs when your visitor has 'acted in the manner you desired'. This is also called a conversion, a call to action or a business outcome. It's when your consumer buys something from your shopping cart, when your prospect becomes a lead filling in a form for more information, when the visitor signs up for your newsletter, when your customer successfully finds what she was looking for from your self-service website. Activation is typically what reach, engagement and nurture KPIs are measured against.

Offline Activation is No Different

Again it's typically what you want your prospect to do but in the offline arena conversion is typically higher.

Activation is always (**ALWAYS**) the end goal in business. You might have dozens of things at any given time that you're measuring, but when it comes down to it your business exists to make money. Reach, Engage and Nurture elements all support the process of activating your prospect. It doesn't matter what kind of sales you're in.

- **Business to business.** You want leads (visitor to prospect **activations**) that turn into sales (prospect to customer **activations**).

- **Business to consumer.** You want purchases (visitor to customer **activations**) that turn into loyal customers (nurturing to result in customer to repeat customer **activations**).

- **Media (advertising business model).** You want more visitors (reach and nurture) to click banners and advertising mediums (visitor **activation**) in order to sell more advertising space (nurturing and encouraging more **activation** from existing advertisers and new customers).

- **Customer service website.** You want more customers to be satisfied by finding a successful answer to their question (**activation**) so that they will buy more (nurturing to result in customer to repeat customer **activations**).

- **Branding website.** You want more customers to be engaged by your brand so that more of the visitors are encouraged to buy your product or service (**activation**).

In order to truly understand how to activate your visitor you need to learn how to do three things well and measurement is key to understanding whether you're on the right track or not. The three things you need to do are:

1. Reach the right people (find or be found by people that you can help by solving their problem).

2. Engage with those people in a way which helps them achieve **their goals** (not necessarily your goals).

3. Nurture them so that they seek you out the next time you can fulfill their need.

The second sentence is particularly important. Typically you activate your customer when you solve **their** problems and help them achieve **their goals**, but the goal of your customer is not always the goal of your business. Aligning customer needs with your business goals is the trick to succeeding online and doing so can be very challenging.

This is why analysis of the data is very important. The hub and spoke approach has at its core the principle of increasing activation or improving conversion rates. When the hub and spoke is implemented in your organization you will have a process which allows you to **learn how** to target the right people, engage with them in the right way and nurture them so they continue to come back until they reach the end of their customer lifecycle with you.

Nurture

The nurture phase comes after the activation has initially happened. Nurturing often online includes CRM marketing, newsletter marketing, follow up emails, online support and community membership. The idea is to get people to become loyal to the brand, or at least value the brand for a specific need that you as a business fill in the mind of the customer.

A good example of an online nurturing program is Amazon.com.

Because Amazon know who I am (by using cookies – see section 5.3 data collection methods) they can tailor the content that appears on the pages for me specifically based on my preferences and recent purchases. When you sign up with Amazon they ask your interests and when you go back to their website they present you with offers you may be interested in. Also when you make a purchase they offer books that other people have bought that are related to the subject of your purchase. For instance a few months ago I bought some books on web analytics. When I return to the Amazon site they remember I was interested in analytics but also predict what else *I might* be interested in.

As you can see in Figure 2.8 books discussing web analytics (specifically Google analytics) and search engine marketing books appear when I arrive at Amazon. I haven't bought any of the books featured in Figure 2.8, I bought some books related to the web analytics subject, but because Amazon know that I am interested in web analytics and that search optimization is related to web analytics they have tailored my experience. They have even made it more personal by saying '**Hello Steve Jackson**. *We have recommendations for you.*' Clicking that link brings up even more books which are relevant to me (Figure 2.9). Amazon even reminds me why it recommends the books it does. I bought 'Avinash Kaushik's *Web Analytics – An hour a day* and *Eric Petersons Web Analytics Demystified* to see what my peers have to say about web analytics.

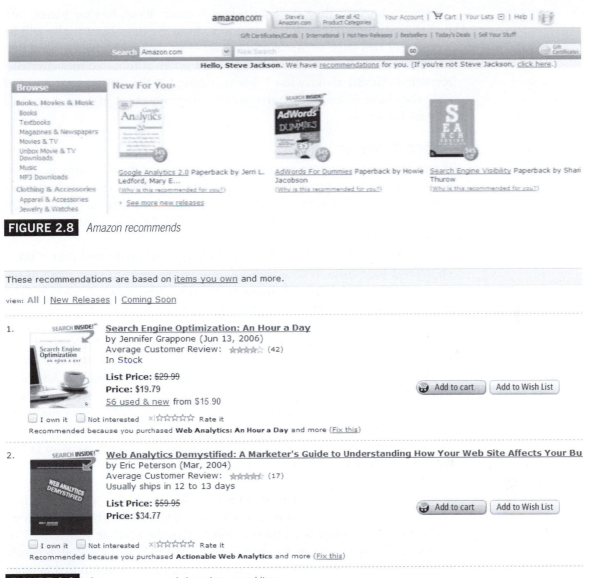

FIGURE 2.8 *Amazon recommends*

These recommendations are based on <u>items you own</u> and more.

view: **All** | <u>New Releases</u> | <u>Coming Soon</u>

FIGURE 2.9 *Amazon recommends based on owned items*

Amazon has learned how to use its database to match certain things to each other. In this case the 'hour a day' series has been shown as well as tying in search marketing to web analytics. In other words the Amazon system has learned that these industries are related and that recommendations of this kind are more likely to bring results.

Simply because they do this, when I think about buying books, the first thing I think is 'check out Amazon'. Even the searches I make will be logged and tied back to Amazon's database so looking for something will likely mean that in a couple of days I would get an automated message with recommendations about what I was searching for. From Amazon's point of view they have successfully nurtured me. From my point of view they are a very useful service.

Offline Nurturing

When you call a service representative, a complaints department, go to physically meet a representative of the company either in a store or at a company that is offline nurturing. Vouchers and discounts via offline methods (such as direct mail) is offline nurturing. Call centres are offline nurturing organizations.

Over time and with clever CRM techniques, you might find that it takes on average four visits to your website, at least one visit to your store to see the item before purchasing it. Imagine if you had thousands of visitors simply looking for guidance to an offline store from your website on the third or fourth visit. It could reap handsome rewards. The time between and frequency of customer visits are vitally important and are called recency and frequency in most web analytics tools.

A lot of smaller retailers don't measure that kind of thing at all. Even some of the bigger retailers don't take advantage of what they know about their customers online. According to *The Guardian* (a UK newspaper) in 2005 over half of the households in Britain used a loyalty card of some nature, and at that time over 10 million Tesco store cards were in active use. Many of the websites you go to aren't proactive in offering the customers what they want.

Tesco are an example of a company that does tailor the customer offline engagement experience with their online one. Figure 2.10 shows what happens when you say you don't have a club card in their online store.

As Tesco say, when you login to their service they will place all recently bought products into a 'My Favourites' folder on a website tailored personally to you. It is about nurturing the customer primarily but also engaging in a way in which is useful for that visitor. It helps them to achieve their goals.

There is a big opportunity in doing things like this to make the customer's experience faster and much more personal. By knowing what you buy offline and presenting you with the same or similar offers online, they make your life easier.

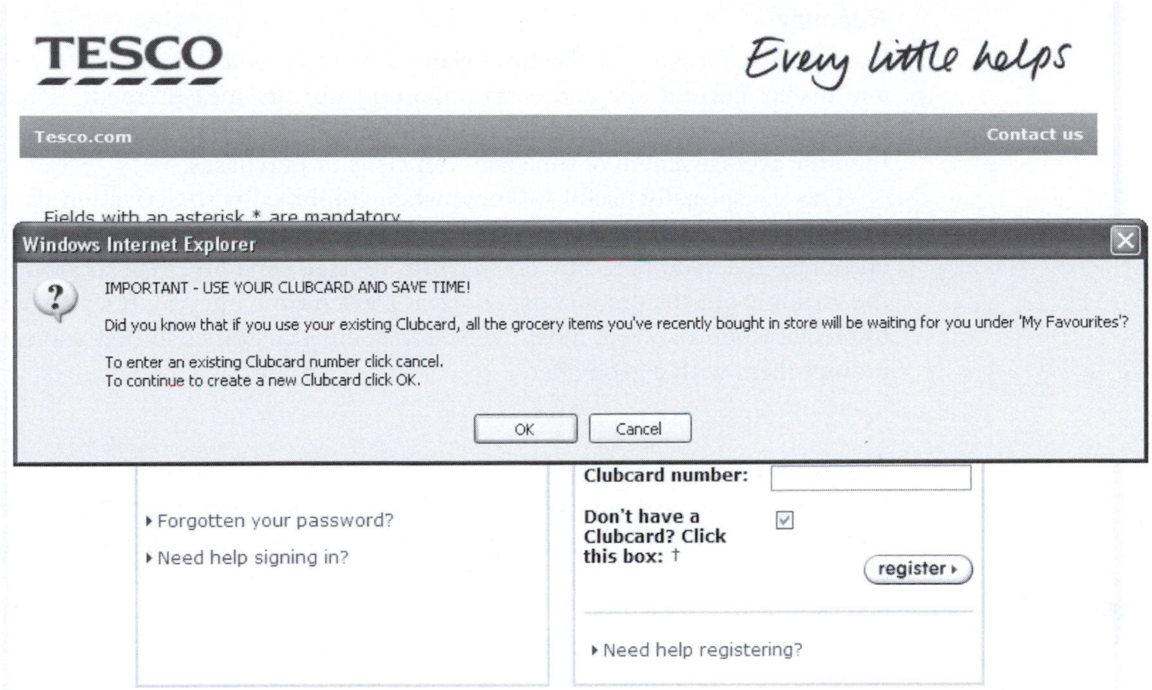

FIGURE 2.10   *Tesco Clubcard*

With business to business operations most companies have CRM systems dedicated to tracking the prospect/customer interactions.

Offline nurturing can be measured as well as online nurturing as long as it is part of the tactical plan. Thus store reps can login to their CRM system and log your query. So could the complaints department. Vouchers and direct mail can all be tracked back to origin and call centres can log and record all conversations. Then all of this data can be compared to the online channel and where possible tied back to web browsing activity. This gives you a complete picture of the customer.

You may for example find that the web is very good for a particular job like supplying information while call centres are better for others, like customer complaints. Measuring the effectiveness of how you deal with your current customers can greatly improve your chances of them becoming a repeat customer. You should also measure the time between your visitors' visits to your website as well as your customers' visits. This is called recency.

Recency

Recency is a measure of the time elapsed between your visitor's last visit and his/her current one and is an important nurture measurement. There is no better measure of knowing the likelihood of re-visit or re-purchase than the average length of time between visits or purchases.

This is especially useful to know when combined with activation data. Knowing how many times between purchases can lead to actions taken to encourage the visitors to buy on the 'nth' visit, or send an email to prompt the visitor about the product or service at a given time interval. It's an effort to predict when they will most likely stop being a customer so that you can prompt them with a good offer.

Frequency

Frequency is the amount of times the customer has 'activated'. The more frequently a visitor or customer looks at your offers the higher the likelihood that they will convert at higher levels. When used with Recency in what's called an RF model – it becomes possible to predict visitor and customer behaviour thus allowing you to react to visitor and customer trends.

KONE REAN Example

REAN should be a tool to help you form the tactics you need to measure activities going on in your organization's marketing. It allows you to visualize everything you're doing. Here as shown before is a working example from KONE (http://www.kone.com) showing their REAN model.

In this variation of the REAN model shown in Figure 2.11 KONE have the reach sources they use or plan to use on the left. The online box in the top left shows the plans they have to market their services online and reach new audiences. The box in the bottom left shows the offline sources they currently employ to reach their target markets. You can see industry-specific items there like 'Architect Networks' which basically mean that KONE plan to advertise on prominent architect networks as they have identified architects as one of their main target audiences.

Their engage elements are all specific to their website. Their activations are again all specific to KONE's business and the nurture activities are listed as they stood at the time of writing.

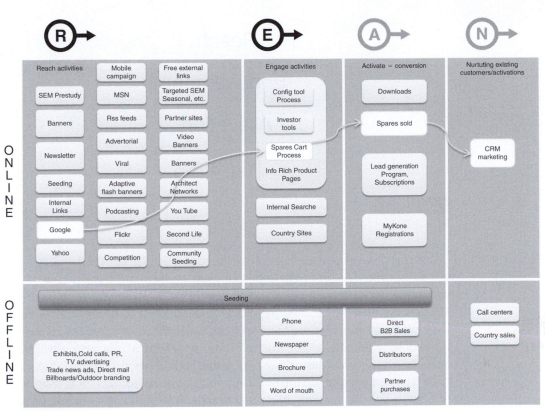

FIGURE 2.11   *KONE online and offline REAN model*

2.3 USING REAN TO HELP DEFINE YOUR BUSINESS CASE

REAN can help you define your business case by planning your marketing roadmap. The first place to start when developing any business case is to define your maximum sales potential. To do that you need to understand how many people you can market to.

The CIA have very good statistics on the world populations and their technological adoption levels. If you're in the consumer market you can determine your market size by using this kind of data. For instance, if I am a retailer selling clothes in the UK I might look at the following statistics taken from the CIA's website to determine my business case: https://www.cia.gov/library/publications/the-world-factbook/geos/uk.html

FIGURE 2.12   *REAN marketing funnel*

At the time of writing the labour force in the UK is 30.89 million. It's fair to assume that all of these people want clothes and have the resources to buy them, so this is the maximum market size for any retailer in the UK. This is however limited by market awareness. If the people don't know they can buy your clothes then you can't sell them. Awareness in turn is limited by your marketing budget. This is where media and advertising agencies come into play. They can reach your desired demographic audience that can then be defined as a feasible set of customers. You then have to determine your market share in comparison to your competition. Overall awareness then funnels into the REAN marketing funnel so you can effectively start to plan your business case (Figure 2.12).

REAN Does Two Things Very Well

Firstly it gives you a very clear indication of the measurement challenges you might have when breaking your strategy down into its component parts. Tactics can be decided from a diagram like Figure 2.11. For instance if you understand that you're going to be driving traffic via second life, you have to put tactics in place to measure it which are different to the tactics you use for measuring visitors from Google for instance.

Secondly it can be used to help you define measurement strategy. You could develop KPI's around each activity (Reach, Engage, Activate and Nurture) and then combine the metrics as matrices of each other. Best reach in terms of volume that converted best combines reach and activation for instance. We'll come to the REAN matrix in Chapter 3.

REAN Summary

Reach, Engage, Activate and Nurture are four factors that every website is affected by. If you don't reach any visitors your website has no value. If you can't effectively engage with those visitors you do reach and persuade them to take action (activate them) then you will also fail to nurture them (get them to come back and consume more). By learning how to visualize these four factors in your online strategy you can begin to understand why KPIs become important. There is no better summary than our four definitions.

Reach sources, the methods you use to attract people to your offer. It also includes how you raise awareness among your target audience about your offer.

Engage, is how people interact with your business. Engage is essentially the process before a point of action that helps your prospect come to a decision.

Activate means a person has taken a preferred point of action. Typical examples include a person purchasing a product, a newsletter subscription or a sign-up.

Nurture describes the method of retaining and re-engaging with activated consumers. The consumer is a person that has already taken at least one preferred point of action.

CHAPTER 3

How to Develop KPIs

Everything that can be counted does not necessarily count; everything that counts cannot necessarily be counted.
Albert Einstein

CHAPTER CONTENTS

3.1 WHAT ARE KEY PERFORMANCE INDICATORS (KPIs)?

Einstein understood that success is not the opposite of failure. If you're to pick out what is successful and what fails then you need KPIs. In essence you have to figure out why things fail with as much clarity as figuring out why things work and this is what KPIs help you do.

There are two types of KPI: the visionary KPI and the tactical KPI.

Visionary KPI

The visionary KPI reflects what your company is trying to achieve. It's the BHAG defined as a metric (the big hairy audacious goal as defined by Jim Collins in *Built to Last*).

In his book *The One Thing You Need To Know*, Marcus Buckingham described this as the 'Core Score'. In it he asked Sir David Ramsbotham, the chief inspector of Her Majesty's prisons, what their key metric was. It turns out that in Sir David's prison reform process he changed the metric from 'number of escapees' to 'number of repeat offenders'. In doing so he completely changed the culture of the prison system. This visionary KPI is one that drives change or helps your company build its culture. This has to be defined by your leaders as part of the strategy.

Tactical KPI

The tactical KPI depends on the goals and objectives of spokes – covered in Chapter 1 and here in Chapter 3. This chapter will cover how to develop management level KPIs starting with their goals and objectives, applying industry thinking and a workshop process.

Web Analytics Association Definition

The Web Analytics Association has developed standard terms and definitions around KPIs. Since the purpose of the WAA is to standardize the approach to using web analytics I would advise you follow their definition in your tactical workshops.

> ### Definition Framework Overview (source volume 1, Standards Analytics Definitions, WAA)
>
> There are three types of Web analytics metrics – counts, ratios and KPIs:
>
> - **Count** – the most basic unit of measure; a single number, not a ratio. Often a whole number (visits = 12,398), but not necessarily (total sales = $52,126.37.).

- **Ratio** – typically, a count divided by a count, although a ratio can use either a count or a ratio in the numerator or denominator. (An example of a ratio fabricated from ratios is 'Stickiness'.) Usually it is not a whole number. Because it's a ratio, 'per' is typically in the name, such as 'Page Views per Visit'. A ratio's definition defines the ratio itself, as well as any underlying metrics.
- **KPI (Key Performance Indicator)** – while a KPI can be either a count or a ratio, it is frequently a ratio. While basic counts and ratios can be used by all website types, a KPI is infused with business strategy – hence the term, 'Key' – and therefore the set of appropriate KPIs typically differs between site and process types.

A fourth type of definition is included for terms that describe concepts instead of numbers.

- **Dimension** – a general source of data that can be used to define various types of segments or counts and represents a fundamental dimension of visitor behaviour or site dynamics. Some examples are event and referrer. They can be interpreted the same as counts above, but typically they must be further qualified or segmented to be of actual interest. Therefore these define a more general class of metrics and represent a dimension of data that can be associated with each individual visitor. Metrics are measured across the dimensions.*

A metric can apply to three different universes:

- **Aggregate** – total site traffic for a defined period of time.
- **Segmented** – a subset of the site traffic for a defined period of time, filtered in some way to gain greater analytical insight: e.g. by campaign (email, banner, PPC, affiliate), by visitor type (new vs. returning, repeat buyers, high value), by referrer.
- **Individual** – activity of a single web visitor for a defined period of time.

---

* REAN are four such conceptual dimensions

The definitions set out by the WAA are now quite widely accepted as industry standard and you can get a copy of the whole file from the WAA website (http://www.webanalyticsassociation.com/).

REAN explained in Chapter 2 are some 'dimensions' referred to by the WAA, a conceptual way to define different counts or ratios, such as referrers (part of reach) and conversion rate (part of activate). They define the KPI as either a count or a ratio and go on to say 'KPI is infused with business strategy – hence the term, "Key" – and therefore the set of appropriate KPIs typically differs between site and process types'.

Infusing KPIs into Business Strategy

In order to infuse KPIs into business strategy four attributes are assigned to the metric that mean actions are taken depending on the performance being indicated. If you can apply all four of these attributes to your metrics then you have KPIs. If you can't then what you have is a count (number) or a ratio (a calculation of two numbers).

Every KPI should have the following attributes assigned to it:

1. The metric has a timescale associated to it (i.e. it is reported once a month).

2. The metric has a benchmark (see standard deviations later in this chapter).

3. The metric has a reason to be reported to an actor (we call them actors because they 'act' on the information).

4. The metric has an associated action surrounding it if a problem occurs. (If metric = xxx an action is taken to rectify the situation.)

The Web Analytics Association defined Unique visitor, Visit and Page views as the 'big 3' counts. This is because nearly all ratios and KPIs include at least one of these three metrics. You can also substitute page views with clicks or events in a rich media environment where pages themselves don't exist. The point that the WAA are making is that there are people (unique visitors), doing things (page views) in a time frame (session or visit).

Taking the WAA example of a ratio, **page views per visit,** a typical number reported by all web analytics tools, you can see that on its own it doesn't really help you do that much. However if you said page views per visit was a KPI the attributes and business logic would apply.

1. **Time period.** You would be looking for trends over a time period (such as a month).

2. **Benchmark.** You would start with the first Figure (5 page views per visit) and monitor the figure. If the figure deviated (depending on your standard deviation) for instance either plus or minus 20% from 4 to 6 you would be flagged to take action.

3. **Actor.** The analyst is flagged if the benchmark indicated there was a reason to investigate further.

4. **Action.** If the page views per visit have deviated you would conduct a study to examine what had occurred to make such a big difference. It may be for example that users have found some content that they were confused by and meant they were clicking through a lot more pages to find the content they were looking for. The action

then would be to fix the problem either by taking action directly or passing the information to the steering group to take a decision.

A Real Life KPI Illustration

MTV3 are a media company in Finland. They run one of the most popular websites in the country, regularly recording over 150 million page views per month. The numbers are publicly available on the TNS Gallup website (http://www.gallupweb.com/tnsmetrix/), which includes all the top media websites in Finland (the list shown gives a weekly count).

It's vitally important that MTV3 retain the high page view levels they currently enjoy so that they can sell advertising space on their website.

One of the most important things is the MTV3 front page (Figure 3.1). One of the editors of the site asked me 'How do we know **when** to change the content of our front page?' This is a great question because the front page of the site is a very important entry point for a lot of their visitors. The point is if they put content on the front page which doesn't sit well with the visitors then they need to know when to change it to try and improve click through and therefore number of pages viewed. The editors working on the page need to monitor this in real time. Because the time of the day affects the number of visits to the website ratios not counts are required.

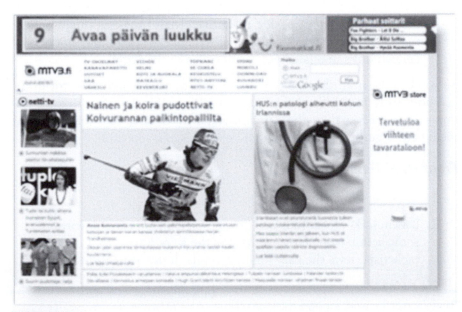

FIGURE 3.1   *http://www.mtv3.fi*

In order to answer the question on a page level, I might suggest two KPIs. Bounce ratio and Page Time Index. Bounce Ratio of the index page is the amount of visits (sessions) that visited only once and left the page without doing anything further as a ratio of total visits to the page. The page time index is a sum of the total time spent on the page divided by the total visits to the page as a ratio. Alone these numbers are just ratios as we already discussed. However if we infused business logic thus making them a KPI this example scenario might play out.

Front Page Bounce Rate (KPI)

1. Time period: Hourly.

2. Benchmark: 15%[*] and 20% deviation (deviation upwards is the action flag). This means that the actor knows that on average the page bounces at 15%. If his/her page scores below that there is no problem. If it scores above that (by more than a 20% deviation so 18% or more) he needs to take the action described.

3. Actor: Editors working on the page.

4. Action taken: Firstly look to see if the page time index is dropping at a comparable rate. If so it is time to change the content as visits looking at the page are viewing it with a worse than average time and a more than average 'lack of interest'. If the page time index is not dropping it could mean that the article needs tweaking (the headline may need to be more attractive for instance) or there may not be enough links to related pages embedded in the article.

As you can see from this the page time index is the secondary factor in the decision being made to take action and what action is taken. It's no less important however than the combination with bounce rate for answering the business question and you should use the same approach.

Front Page Time Index (KPI)

1. Time period: Hourly.

2. Benchmark: 85 seconds and 20% deviation (deviation downwards is the action flag). This means that the actor knows that on average each visit views the page for 85 seconds. If this time drops by

---

[*]These numbers are not accurate reflections of current MTV3 figures and are used for illustrative purposes only.

17 seconds or more (20%) action needs to be taken as it is deviating away from average levels. If the time spent is lower it simply means sessions are spending less time on the page but moving throughout the site, which also meets the business objective, therefore no action required. If the time spent is higher than 85 it means sessions are engaging longer than average with the page and actions described should be taken.

3. Actor: Editors working on the page.

4. Actions taken: If lower than the deviation first check to see the bounce rate. If this is deviating at similar levels then change the page content. If it is higher than 85 seconds but the bounce rate is OK (or lower) then it may indicate a usability problem. Please inform the hub analysts to investigate further.

The outcome might be that those two KPIs answer the business questions that people working for MTV3 have about their website and how they should improve it.

What follows is a full description on the KPI workshop process that will help you design tactical KPIs.

3.2 RUNNING THE INITIAL KPI WORKSHOP

What You'll Need

1. A mix of hub and spoke people who are responsible for a particular business spoke. I would advise no more than ten people. It's best with around seven.

2. A workshop facilitator who knows your business and how to run a workshop.

3. A person to compile notes of what happens in the workshop itself.

4. Flip chart/magic markers.

5. post-it notes (one pad for each person).

6. Internet connection to access the website – preferably on a big screen which everyone can easily see.

In the hub and spoke model, the people responsible for taking action and driving better online business are part of the spokes. The people responsible for data analysis, integrity, delivery and technology are part of the hub.

KPIs are equally important to both people from the hub and people from the spoke. From a business perspective the most important things in the KPI process are the actions that result from the spokes. In other words if the people in the spokes don't act on the data then the process is likely to fail.

Workshop Overview

In order to create KPIs there should first be a workshop. This will encompass the first seven of nine stages of developing your KPIs (as shown in Figure 3.2, the KPI development process). The workshop is designed as an information gathering exercise for the analyst or strategist of your choice to actually create the KPIs.

In the workshop one of the business spoke leaders, or for instance a skilled external consultant, a high level strategist or a web analyst should facilitate. It's his/her job to make sure everyone else in the room gets involved.

Once the facilitator and the actors (to be defined) have completed the first six steps of the process all the material is given to the web analytics specialist and the guys in the hub to work on the last three steps. These workshops can take anywhere from four hours to a day depending on the amount of business questions identified by your actors.

Actor Definition

Some companies call people in charge of a business function 'stakeholders'. You shouldn't in this case. You should call them actors, simply because the

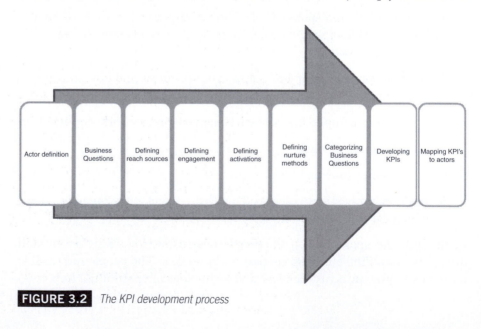

FIGURE 3.2 *The KPI development process*

word 'actor' includes the verb 'to act'. The purpose of an actor is to take action based on what the KPIs are telling them. If the KPI is flagging something bad then an actor acts accordingly. If for instance the KPI is flagging 'you're spending too much on this campaign' then the actor acts by reducing the campaign spend.

The actors in your organization should be a mix of hub people and spoke people.

Hub Actors

The people that you want from the hub are those that are mainly responsible for the technical side of getting the data, validating it and formatting it so that it is understood. You may also want technology 'owners' such as the web analytics platform manager and the content management system owner for instance. It may (depending on the size of the business you're in) mean bringing outsourced vendors into the play early.

One of my clients had their content management system company sitting through the entire KPI process so that they could know why they were tagging pages in the website the way that they were doing it.

Last but certainly not least, you need a web analytics specialist – someone who is capable of understanding what the tools can deliver in terms of KPIs and can design the metrics based on what the business questions are.

If you don't have the required actors, outsource where possible. If you have a small organization that doesn't have the resources, I would advise hiring. Failing that get Google Analytics installed as you shouldn't spend any money on tools if you don't have people, buy Eric Peterson's *Big Book of KPIs* and apply what you learn from both this book and Eric's. DIY KPIs are better than no KPIs at all and the person whose job it is to learn how to design KPIs should become your organization's web analytics specialist.

There needs to be at least one hub actor in the KPI workshop, usually at least the person responsible (or the person who will be responsible) for getting the data to the spoke actors.

Spoke Actors

The spoke actors are the business owners, the people responsible for improving the business they are involved with online. They are the campaign managers, the marketing directors, the online editors. Each particular spoke has its own business questions that need answering.

The people in the spokes are more likely to be in your organization than not. You probably already have skilled people.

There needs to be one person leading the workshop, usually this is an executive or a senior guy. It could also be the web analytics expert if they have experience running workshops.

Once you have gathered the actors you need (I'd suggest no more than seven people per spoke served) then you're ready to start.

Actor Categorization

The first thing you do is to categorize the actors in the workshop and their relation to staff in their working life.

The spokes have, depending on your business, a lot of different needs internally. It's rare that the budget owner needs the same data as the person running the day to day marketing. So we split the spokes into three simple functions like so and separate potential hub people out from the spokes (the technicians – see below):

BUDGET OWNERS

BUSINESS OWNERS

TECHNICIANS

Budget Owners

The people labelled as budget owners here may or may not be part of the KPI workshop or care particularly about how the data is collected and presented, they simply act according to what they see as good business intelligence. They might also be part of the executive steering group.

What they are in charge of is budget. Primarily what they want to know is how to allocate their yearly or quarterly spend and they expect the rest of the staff to tell them how to do it. They may, especially in smaller units, be a part of the KPI workshop and if so are generally senior people. They may even be the ones facilitating your workshop.

They are included here because no KPI workshop I've done has failed to mention these people. They generally are in some form or another omnipresent in all business operations. Somebody somewhere holds the purse strings.

Workshop Technique

On a flipchart write the word Budget Owners in the top left hand corner. Go around everyone in the room and ask if they control any budgets. Then ask everyone in the room if they can add anyone else not present at the workshop that controls their budget in relation to online resources.

Once all the people are listed write down the goal of the budget owners of each department in terms of what they want to know to allocate resources. Once these names are down and the questions are answered move onto Business owners.

Business Owners

The business owner area is generally in charge of improving online business.

In marketing for instance you want to optimize your spend, so you need to know which content works best, which campaigns convert the most sales, and which initiatives or products keep the customers coming back. Therefore marketing often needs the most KPIs and has one of the toughest jobs of all the spoke actors.

Additionally there may be a lot of specific business owner actors, such as regional coordinators or managers (in larger companies) responsible for the successful marketing in a specific area. You may also have operations within a business unit or small company that require different managers. It doesn't matter at this stage. The exercise is designed to get KPIs which then can be cultivated throughout the organization so that the rest can learn and then design their own KPIs based on their own needs.

Workshop Technique

On a flipchart write the word 'Business Owners' in the top left hand corner. Go around everyone in the room and ask if they are part of 'the business team'. Then ask everyone in the room if they can add anyone else not present at the workshop that controls their budget in relation to online resources.

Once these names are down and the questions are answered move onto technicians.

Technicians

Technicians form the part of the business that is primarily involved with the engage activities and data. They are responsible for delivering content, making sure the website does its functional job and testing things to see if improvements can be made. They are responsible for getting the data to the people that need it, ensuring that the business takes action and ensuring that the process developed by the hub works. In short these people form the hub from your organization.

It may be that these people are also heavily supported by the tool vendors and external consultants. It's important to involve externals at the KPI workshop stage if you can so that they understand what you're trying to achieve.

Workshop Technique

On a flipchart write the word 'Technicians' in the top left hand corner. Go around everyone in the room and ask if they are part of 'the technicians team'. Then ask everyone in the room if they can add anyone else not present at the workshop that is part of this team that should be here.

Once all the people are listed write down the roles they currently have and who they directly report to. Once they have been listed ask the technicians in the workshop what they have currently done regards handling data. Grade this as 0, 1, 2 or 3 where '3' is highly proficient data miner/analyst, '1' is knows Excel to a reasonable level and '2' is somewhere in the middle. '0' is no experience with data analysis or tools.

You ask this because you're trying to assess the data skills your technicians currently have. It may be if there are too many 0-1 scores that you need outsourced help or that your staff need training in something they currently don't have much experience with.

The Business Questions

Once you have defined and categorized your actors you should have someone take the actor data and put it to one side for later. You're now onto a very interesting and engaging part of the workshop.

The moderator now needs to just ask everyone in the room what business questions they have that they want answering regards the business they're in. It has to be run in a perfect world scenario. It shouldn't matter what tools you have or what kind of potential tool you could have as your analytics system. It should be phrased as, 'If there is a business question you want answered lets write it down and see if we can come up with KPIs to match it'. You might also ask something like 'What don't you know about the website traffic that you would like to know and why would you like to know it?'

The moderator has to be quite active here and get the ball rolling. In order to illustrate this process I've listed some questions from typical KPI workshops I've run.

Some Sample Business Questions

1. What is the best source of traffic in terms of volume and sales? (reach – activate)

2. Is it good or bad that the content in our site changes? (engage)

3. How can we get them to buy? (activate)

4. How many of them make the purchase decision online, but buy offline? (engage – activate)

5. Where are the visitors coming from? (reach)

6. Which channels are the most productive? (reach)

7. Which channels are overlapping – are reaching the same visitor/visitors? (reach)

8. Which landing page converts the best? (reach – activate)

9. Do the registered users buy more than others? (nurture)

10. Most searched location? (engage – activate)

11. How many downloads? (activate)

12. What is the value of a download to our organization? (activate – nurture)

13. How many leads fed to CRM system? (nurture)

14. What is the average response time for lead response? (nurture)

15. How many internal search responses do we get? (engage, activate)

16. Which is the best, getting people to buy direct or getting people to come back and buy? (activate – nurture)

17. How engaged are our visitors? (engage)

18. What arc the top paths through our site? (engage)

The idea is to get an open discussion going about what it is that your actors want to find out. Some workshops may result in 20 questions, some might result in 40 or more. It depends on the complexity of the channel strategy and what you want your visitors to do when they get there.

Workshop Technique

What you want is as many business questions as you can get.

The facilitator needs to start the ball rolling by writing a few general things down on his flipchart. I usually always start with one that every website needs to know, 'What is the best source of traffic in terms of volume and sales'.

Then the facilitator should ask for more things from everyone in the room. Go to the most vocal or senior person first, they should start the ball rolling. Once a few people have thrown in some ideas, a good facilitator will encourage the room with helpful comments. **Make sure every question is written on the flipchart.** This serves two purposes, firstly it makes sure people don't repeat the same issues in the workshop, and secondly it stimulates thinking, when people can see the progress they are making they start to feel really involved.

Once you have got all the questions down – this may take an hour or two depending on how involved people get and how much your business wants to know – you move to the next phase of the workshop. Once again, file the flipchart questions. The analyst will use these later.

Facilitating Business Questions

As a facilitator of the workshop you can do the following to help this stage of the workshop run smoothly:

1. Start off the questions. One I always ask is 'Which source of traffic is best in terms of volume (number of visitors) and cost?' I then explain the thought process behind asking this question. I'd say something like 'By knowing the answer to this question we'd be able to direct our marketing spend to the sources of traffic that were most effective in terms of value for money and numbers'.

2. Write the questions down. When you start it off, write it on the flipchart. When someone else asks a question which hasn't been asked, write it on the flipchart. This shows the people in the workshop that they are making progress and also helps to get them thinking.

3. Give the actors a benchmark. 49 questions defined is the record I have had from a workshop. When I mention that you would be surprised how many workshop teams try to beat it. Most of them don't (the average is 25–30 questions) but it really gets people going.

4. Encourage questions by agreeing with the actor and help justify the question where possible. For instance if the question 'What is the value of a download to our organization?' was asked by a workshop actor, I'd answer with 'Great question, by knowing the answer to that we can help justify our marketing spend on getting people to download as well as start monetizing our website' while writing it on the flipchart. This helps the atmosphere and also improves the chances of the shy actor asking a question.

5. If the process is slow to start, ask the senior guys in the room specifically what they think would be useful to know. You could ask open questions like 'Thomas, what's the hard part about your job? What do you want to know about the online part of your business? How could knowing something about the behaviour of our visitors online help you in your work?' The senior people are in senior positions because they have opinions and thoughts about these kinds of things. They will get the party started.

Once you have exhausted the room and they can't think of anything else then you have done a major part of the workshop. You now have a list of business requirements from your spoke.

Now you can move onto determining the most important reach factors.

Defining Reach Sources

The following method is a very simple way to figure out what everyone agrees on as the most important reach sources.

Workshop Technique

On one sheet of your flipchart draw two lines. One from the middle of the chart vertically down all the way to the bottom and one horizontally across the middle so that you have four squares on the flipchart. Write 'Reach' in the top left, 'Engage' in the top right, 'Activate' in the bottom left and 'Nurture' in the bottom right.

Next ask your actors to take the post-it note and write down the top five most important reach sources (on- or offline) for their business. This should not be a group discussion it should be an individual effort on the part of each actor. It's important that each actor only write **one reach source per post-it note**.

Each person should have five post-it notes at the end with one reach source on each note. Collect all the notes and group them together in the top left box called 'Reach'. Where similar ideas appear group them together in a list. This should allow you to see if everyone is on the same page with the most important sources of traffic.

If from your seven actors you get seven post-it notes saying for instance Google paid search campaigns were very important then this would be one of the top things to look at when determining reach KPIs. It will allow you to very quickly determine a top list as derived from your own business people.

As you can see from Figure 3.3 you split up the flipchart into four segments as shown, you call one 'Reach', one 'Engage', one 'Activate' and one 'Nurture'. Group together the post-it notes so that similar answers are bundled together. In this way you get a consensus of opinion from those in the workshop without a discussion which is more likely to be less influenced by peer pressure.

Facilitating Reach Definition

As a facilitator this is quite a simple exercise:

1. Segment the flipchart into four areas as shown in Figure 3.3, calling each segment 'Reach', 'Engage', 'Activate' and 'Nurture' respectively.

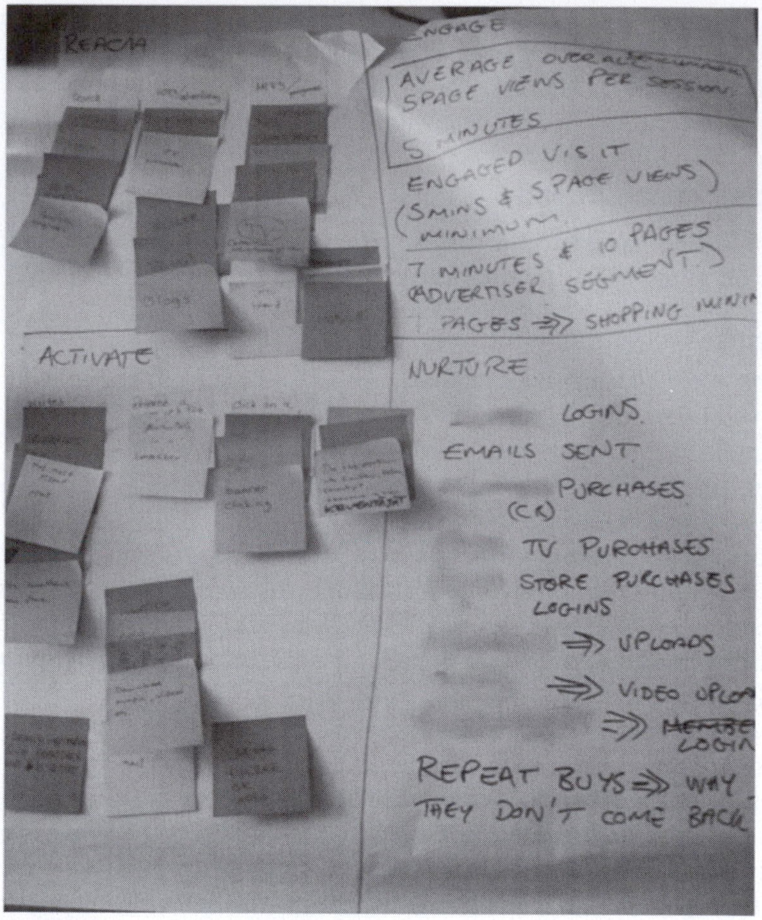

FIGURE 3.3 *REAN flipchart*

2. Ask everyone to write the five most important reach sources on a post-it note. One reach source per post-it note is required and the objective is to get each actor's opinion (not a collective discussion). So people should do this alone.

3. Collect everyone's post-it notes together and group similar sources together by sticking the post-its to each other in the 'Reach' segment of the flipchart.

What this does is determine what everyone in the room thinks are the most important sources of traffic and helps the analyst when defining the KPIs. Usually we find that between five and ten reach sources are defined with a clear top three or four that everyone agrees on. This is the point of the exercise.

Once you have run this exercise you can now move onto defining engagement.

Defining Engagement

Your objective when defining engagement is to start thinking about how to segment your website visitors. It should be based on visitor behaviour, so if you have any current statistics that allow you to make an internal benchmark (even raw log data for instance) this would be good. If you don't then you need to base it on common sense and what kinds of interactions your visitors will need to do on your site in order to complete one of your business objectives. You could use a combination of this approach, which is generally what I try to do in all cases.

For instance if you have a shopping cart in which you need to complete a five-page process before you can buy a product, it is common sense to use a five-page session as one of your engagement segments. Before you go onto the workshop technique, you need to understand what segmentation is.

Segmentation

All traffic is not equal and the better web analytics tools today can segment (examine different parts of your traffic) based on visitor behaviour.

I believe learning how to do segmentation is probably one of the things that will help you gain the most insight around clickstream data. **Please read section 5.6 for more about segmentation, as it's very important**.

Segmentation allows you to, for instance, see what people who have come from a particular reach source have done on your website as opposed to what all the visitors have done. It's extremely useful to see which sources of traffic drive 'engaged' visitors.

Those visitors that stay more than a few seconds, or move through the steps in your shopping cart, or enter your lead generation process, are more valuable to you than visitors who see your page for a few seconds and leave. What segmentation does in web analytics tools is separate the visitors based on behaviour you pre-define.

What you're looking to achieve with this part of the workshop is pre-defining what that behaviour is.

Workshop Technique

This part of the workshop is an open discussion. What you want to do is to define what 'engaged' behaviour is as opposed to less interesting traffic. From your perspective engagement could be when a visitor has potentially done enough to complete one of your processes. You could also benchmark the engagement based on average page views per visit statistics gleaned from your tool (if you have something already in place) or from raw log figures. Make sure that once again you write this down on the flipchart in the designated right hand corner.

This again is best illustrated with an example.

KONE is one of the world's leading elevator and escalator companies. It provides its customers with industry-leading elevators and escalators and with innovative solutions for their maintenance and modernization. KONE also provides maintenance of automatic building doors. In 2006, KONE had annual net sales of €3.6 billion and approximately 29,000 employees.

KONE's main website purpose is to serve existing customers and potentially provide information to new ones (Figure 3.4). I worked with KONE in a KPI workshop where we defined engagement as the following:

Lightly engaged visit = a visit which has viewed 4 pages and spent at least 60 seconds on the site.

Engaged visit = a visit which has viewed 7 pages and spent at least 120 seconds on the site.

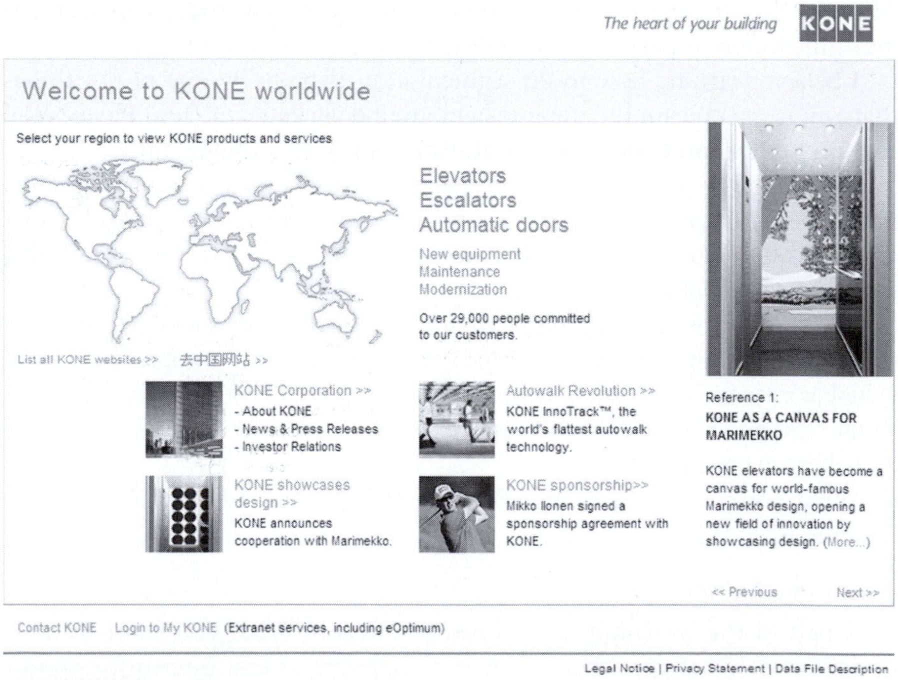

FIGURE 3.4 Kone.com

Heavily engaged visit = a visit which has viewed 10 pages and spent at least 240 seconds on the site.

Anything less than a lightly engaged visitor is not that interesting to KONE. The lightly engaged visit showed the visitors who at least viewed the average level of page views per visit and stuck around for 60 seconds. We got the average figure from the HBX system they had already in place.

The engaged visit means that a customer could have purchased a spare part online, could have registered to MyKone (a customer extranet) and were viewing more pages than the average global visitor.

The heavily engaged visit is the kind of visitors KONE needed to keep a close eye on. The segment was designed to make sure visitors were not finding it difficult to find things and were being serviced well by KONE's website.

In effect KONE have developed three engagement indexes (of which heavy users will be counted in all the statistics) but the purpose is to separate visitors that don't engage with the visitors that do.

The KONE example illustrates how they use segments. KONE have used three segments because they wanted to split their audience into four different types of traffic (all traffic, lightly engaged, engaged and heavily engaged traffic). It could be that you wanted to do something similar or it could be that your requirements are less and that you only want to use one segment.

Facilitating Engagement Definition

The purpose of defining engagement is to enable you to look at traffic that behaves in a certain manner (which you pre-define).

1. Look at the processes which exist on your website. Work out how many clicks/pages it takes to complete the process and how long this process takes in seconds. This could be one set of criteria you could define in your segment. For example if it takes five pages and 60 seconds on average to buy a product you could use this as engagement criteria, because people that stayed this long potentially could have bought a product.

2. Look at the average time spent/pages viewed on your website from the tools you have. This could be used as a benchmark for engagement.

3. Define which pages are the most important. For instance you might want to segment purely by all the folks that saw your services page. This in itself could be a segment.

4. Again write down everything on the flipchart.

This is a **vital part of the workshop**. Some of my clients have saved millions of euros by defining good engagement metrics and optimizing their campaigns based on engagement segmentation.

Once you have defined how you can segment your visitors by flagging their behavioural patterns you can move onto the next phase of the workshop, activation.

Defining Activations

At this stage of the workshop you can go back to the flipchart and do the same trick we discussed with reach and using the post-it notes. As before ask your actors to take the post-it note but this time write down the top five most important actions (conversions) that a visitor could take on the website.

This should not be a group discussion it should be an individual effort on the part of each actor. It's important that each actor only write **one activation per post-it note.** So each person should have five post-it notes at the end. Collect all the notes and group them together in the bottom left box called activations.

Where similar ideas appear group them together in a list. This should allow you to see if everyone is on the same page with the most important conversions from the point of view of the business. If from your seven actors you get seven post-it notes saying for instance PDF downloads were very important then this would be one of the top things to look at when designing the KPIs.

It will allow you to very quickly determine a top list as derived from your own business people.

Facilitating Activation Definition

As a facilitator this is quite a simple exercise:

1. In the same way as you asked with the Reach exercise earlier ask everyone to write on a post-it note the five most important activations. One activation per post-it note is required and the objective is to get each actor's opinion (not a collective discussion), so people should do this alone.

2. Collect everyone's post-it notes together and group similar activations together by sticking the post-its to each other in the 'activation segment'.

What this does is determine what everyone in the room thinks are the most important conversions and helps the analyst when defining the KPIs.

Usually we find that between five and ten activations are defined with a clear top three or four that everyone agrees on. This is the point of the exercise.

Once you have defined the activations you can move onto the last part of the activities for this particular workshop group – defining methods of nurturing your visitors so that they become loyal to your brand.

Defining Nurture Methods

Nurturing the visitor so that they value your products or services is of course vital. Your objective in the workshop is to highlight certain types of things that your business offers, which helps existing customers, improves the experience of the visitors and increases your brand's exposure in a positive way.

Workshop Technique

Much like the engagement methodology, this is an open discussion. What you're doing is simply writing a list of all the things that you consider are nurturing your visitor or customer (as we defined it earlier).

Simply write down in the bottom right hand corner of the flipchart all the relevant points. This serves the purpose of helping the rest of the team to stay focused and not repeat things that have already been discussed. It also helps refresh the memory so that nothing is forgotten.

Referring back to the KONE example we found that the following things were all related to the nurture phase of their online operations.

The number of leads that came from the web to the CRM system was interesting, as well as the response time for those leads that came from the web to actually become customers. Survey responses were also very interesting as were the amount of newsletter reads (a way in which KONE contacted existing website visitors).

Training requests which came direct from the customer extranet as well as immediate meeting requests were all things which KONE classed as nurturing activities.

Facilitating Nurture Definitions

As the facilitator of this activity there are a few simple ways to get the actors thinking about this aspect of the REAN process.

1. Go back through the business questions and pull out ones that you think might relate to nurturing. Remember that nurturing is all about helping your customer or your visitor become happy with your brand so that they buy more of your products or services.

2. Nurturing activities usually happen after 'activation' or 'conversion' of one sort or another. It may be that a visitor has subscribed to a newsletter and you are keeping in touch by sending the news for instance. It may be that you're running customer service activities, helping your customer with frequently asked questions or difficulties they have with your product/service. Both of these occasions have come as a result of an activation (a newsletter subscription and a purchase). Try to think of things that could happen after you have sold or converted someone in some way.

3. Repeat visits, purchases (or repeat activations) are also nurturing activities. Look for things that happen two or three times from the same customer/visitor as potential nurturing factors.

Once all the nurturing activities have been listed simply wrap up the workshop and explain what happens next. The actors at this stage will have been working for 2–4 hours at least and it's not necessary for them to be involved in the last stages of the KPI design.

In wrapping up you should give the information to your analyst who then should be able to use that information to design the KPIs. The next few pages show how to do this effectively, starting with categorizing business questions.

3.3 DESIGNING KPIs

The analyst or web strategist in the hub who was running or was part of the workshop should now gather all the information and get to work designing the KPIs for the spoke.

Categorizing Business Questions

The analyst should take the information provided by his actors and categorize them into reach, engage, activate and nurture questions. By doing this he/she can first reduce the amount of KPIs required by the spoke and secondly make it clearer in his/her own mind which KPIs need designing.

In order to demonstrate this effectively, I'll take two questions from some previous workshops' reach, engage, activate and nurture questions and demonstrate how to categorize them. One question will be fairly easy and probably quite a common scenario while one question will be less obvious and therefore more difficult to categorize.

Examining the REAN Technique

The next eight business questions need categorizing. The technique for doing this comes quite quickly once you have in your mind the Reach, Engage, Activate and Nurture model.

1. How do visitors find my site?

2. What is the cost per conversion per campaign?

3. What ratio of visitors can support flash?

4. Where do people come from geographically?

5. How many purchases do we get?

6. How many people from our members' area contact us?

7. Why do people buy our products?

8. How many people don't get through our shopping cart?

All of these questions could appear in KPI workshops. In order to categorize the questions you could start by re-visiting the REAN definitions.

Reach sources, the methods you use to attract people to your offer. It also includes how you raise awareness among your target audience

Reach questions are therefore questions that involve how you attract people to your offers, their areas, their locations, demographics and similar kinds of questions should be classed as reach questions.

Engage, is how people interact with your business. Engage is essentially the process before a point of action that helps your prospect come to a decision.

Engage questions are anything to do with how visitors interact with your website. How they move through processes is an engage question, the landing page they hit is the first engagement, the time they spend looking at pages is engagement, the number of pages or clicks they make are engagement questions.

Activate means a person has taken a preferred point of action. Typical examples include a person purchasing a product, a newsletter subscription or a sign-up.

Activate questions are simply those which discuss an action being taken. How many downloads, purchases, subscriptions, logins and such like are activate questions. Anything that includes some form of conversion is an activation. It should however be the **FIRST time** that the action has been recorded, otherwise it goes into the nurture category.

Nurture describes the method of retaining and re-engaging with activated consumers. The consumer is a person that has already taken at least one preferred point of action.

Nurture questions are those that generally mean that the visitor is a customer, a lead, a subscriber, or made contact with you in some way so that you know who the person is. Nurture questions generally include things like how often do our visitors login to our extranet, or how many leads become sales.

What we're trying to achieve is to group each question into one or more of these online functions.

Categorizing the Questions into the REAN Model

1. How do Visitors find My Site?

This is one I would categorize as a **reach question**. Firstly because it's asking how a visitor might find me and secondly because it's asking how they do it. Do they search online? Come from a partner link? Hit on a banner campaign you have out there? Whatever they do they are coming from somewhere and in order to answer that question you need to know where from. Where questions are very often reach questions.

2. What is the Cost per Conversion per Campaign?

This is more difficult because it fits two categories. It's asking a clear activate question (conversion) but also asking for cost per campaign. So it's two questions in one. It's asking for a list of campaigns that you're running (reach) and the cost of conversion (activation). So I would put this question into two categories, **reach and activation.**

3. What Ratio of Visitors can Support Flash?

Flash is a website technology designed to interact with people and designed to attract people to click certain things. It's an engaging website function and would go into the **engage** category.

4. Where do People Come from Geographically?

This is another 'where' question. Asking the geography of people is one of the most **obvious reach** questions that can be asked.

5. How many Purchases do we Get?

How many is a typical action question. A purchase is an action. This is a very obvious **activation question.**

6. How many People from Our Members' Area Contact Us?

This is a classic nurture question. Being a member indicates that the first activation has already happened and another activation is asked for in the contact us part of the question. I would class this as **nurture and activation.**

7. Why do People Buy Our Products?

Another thing you look for is 'why' questions. Typically these are questions that can't be answered by KPIs alone. They require qualitative data to help answer those questions. Question 7, while a superb question asked in one of our KPI workshops would need experience data (see Chapter 7) added to the equation. This question however discusses an action being carried out by the visitor so it would be grouped with the **activation questions.**

8. How many People don't Get Through Our Shopping Cart?

The shopping cart is something people have to use to buy a product in a typical e-commerce environment. Shopping cart processes are a typical engagement factor in that people have to engage with the process in order to complete it. This is a classic **engage question** and the KPI that comes to mind instantly is shopping cart abandonment rate.

Developing KPIs

When you have categorized all questions into one or more of the reach, engage activate and nurture functions, then you want to group the questions into a REAN matrix as shown in Figure 3.5.

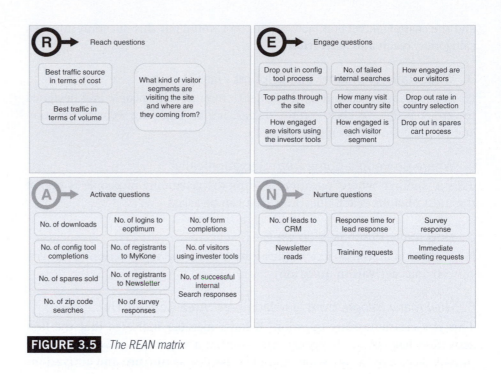

FIGURE 3.5 *The REAN matrix*

Question Grouping

The first thing the analyst needs to do is determine which questions you can group. Consider questions that were of a similar nature grouped as reach and activation, or reach and engage, or reach and nurture. This means that you can define 'best traffic in terms of cost' which can be compared to say, for instance, all different activations.

The above matrix came from around 30 business questions asked by the actors. By reducing reach to a source location and defining volume, physical location and cost as the main factors affecting all those sources, you reduce the amount of work you have to do to develop good KPIs.

For instance take the actor question *'Which source of traffic results in a contract being signed?'* The reach part of the question is 'Which source of traffic', and the 'contracts being signed' is the activation part.

By combining the traffic source questions and determining where the other factor of each question goes, you reduce the amount of metrics you need to create because we can always compare all sources of traffic to **any** activation so you don't need one KPI per question.

By developing a matrix you can answer all the business questions your actors have asked and make it easier to create KPIs.

Using the Matrix

Consider the question again. *Which source of traffic results in a contract being signed?* It isn't a perfect question when it comes to defining a KPI. All you would have is a list of sources not a benchmarked KPI. If we tried to answer that question specifically as a KPI you could quickly have 100 different sources.

The sources of traffic defined as important in your workshop could help a little with this question if we only concentrated on those sources. It's far better, however, to consider looking simply at volume and cost as your two main considerations and compare all sources in the same way, though of course first looking at the ones your workshop participants deemed the most important.

On- and offline reach sources should be compared in the matrix to firstly how well each source engages, then activates and finally nurtures. The point is not to define every source of a contract being signed, its to define the best sources in terms of cost and volume of a contract being signed.

Now consider that you had a number of questions that were of a similar nature (grouped as reach and activation, or reach and engage, or reach and nurture). For instance the reach questions we have discussed in this chapter: *How do visitors find my site? Which source of traffic results in a contract being signed? Where do people come from geographically? What is the cost per conversion per campaign?*

All of these questions can be grouped together because they can really be answered by one or two statements. For instance as in Figure 3.6 overleaf we've listed how we answered all the reach questions asked with just three statements that encompassed all of them:

1. Best traffic in terms of volume.

2. Best traffic in terms of cost.

3. What kind of visitor segments are visiting and where are they coming from.

These three statements can answer everything **when compared to engagement and activation.**

Best traffic in terms of volume answers 'How do visitors find my site?' because by definition you will be looking at the ways visitors find you in your metric. 'Which source of traffic results in a contract being signed' is answered when you cross reference the reach part (where you got the traffic) of the matrix with the activation part. So best traffic in terms of volume or cost compared to the activation (contracts signed) answers that question.

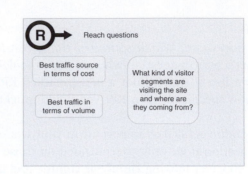

FIGURE 3.6 *Reach questions and important traffic*

Best traffic in terms of cost answers 'What is the cost per conversion per campaign' again when compared to the activations matrix shown in Figure 3.5.

Where are they coming from answers 'Where do visitors come from geographically'.

By using a matrix in this manner you start to rationalize all the questions and it is an important step to take to reduce the amount of work you need to do in order to develop good KPIs.

Once you have reduced the amount of questions down to key statements in the matrix you can now look at the next step of KPI creation.

KPI Creation

You are now at the stage where you have your business questions in the REAN matrix as a set of statements. You now need to put the statements into metrics that can then be set up in the web analytics tool you are using. To create the metrics you now need to get those business statements and apply relevant statistics to help answer your questions. There is a process you can follow which goes along the following lines:

1. Determine which counts or ratios are required to answer the question.

2. Determine external factors.

3. Determine reporting requirements.

4. Determine benchmarks.

Step 1: Determine Which Counts or Ratios are Required to Answer the Question

As already discussed most business questions will require that you know about unique visitors, visits and page views. These are the three fundamental factors being tracked by all tools. Depending on the tool you have at your disposal however, there are a myriad of other things you can use to help answer your business question. Consult with your vendor to find out what counts and ratios you can currently measure. Once you have done this you then simply apply the relevant metrics to the question. Some examples of how to do this with real statements will follow.

Step 2: Determine External Factors

External factors include but are not limited to costs that might not be reported directly from your tool, external data from a third party such as CRM data with identified visitors or other offline data which is to be compared to online figures. These are really specific to your business so once again we'll illustrate this with examples later.

Step 3: Determine Reporting Requirements

How quickly and frequently can you take action on your results? This is the one question you should be asking yourself before you start doing any reporting to anyone. The timeframe of a KPI is important because it will help you to determine your benchmarks.

Step 4: Determine Benchmarks.

External benchmarks of conversion rates can be found. Conversion Chronicles has compiled a list at – http://www.conversionchronicles.com/What_is_an_average_conversion_rate.html. You could also look at Hitwise at http://www.hitwise.com/ (a paid service) or Comscore at http://www.comscore.com/ to get Industry benchmarks

The best way to develop benchmarks is with your own data. External benchmarks such as published figures you might find from vendors aggregating a wide range of customers and industry conversion rates are available. However published statistics don't take into account the vast array of variables that apply to your business and it's difficult to accurately benchmark for instance a conversion rate. They are worth looking at to get a general idea but that is all they should be used for.

When it comes to improving your own KPIs you need a historical benchmark of (hopefully improving) numbers compared to your competition (see Chapter 7).

Using Standard Deviations to Determine Benchmarks

A standard deviation is the most common measure of a statistical dispersion, in other words measuring how widely spread the values in a data set are. If many data points are close to the average (or mean), then the standard deviation is small; if many data points are far from the mean, then the standard deviation is large. If all the data values are equal, then the standard deviation is zero.

The reason you could use standard deviations is to quickly spot deviations in data from normal levels. Sometimes trends are hard to spot, but with standard deviations they are easy to pick up. Look at the example in Figure 3.7 from Google Analytics. As you can see there is a circled peak, however that is not an obvious peak to an analyst looking at data every day. Over the course of this dataset, in this graph, it looks like a fairly smooth variation – a little more at the beginning of the month than the end but nothing drastic. The reason this was spotted was because the data deviated from the normal benchmarked figures and therefore prompted further investigation.

All traffic sources sent 96,126 visits via 1,272 sources and mediums

FIGURE 3.7 *Google Analytics traffic trend*

The practical value in web analytics of using standard deviations is basically to determine when the data tells you that something is moving away from the 'mean average'. It highlights things in your data that should be looked at. In the case above I drilled down over the time period to take a closer look and found that one particular site had driven more traffic from an awareness campaign that lasted approximately two weeks and then dropped off to normal levels.

The way to calculate the standard deviation is pretty easy. The longer the period of data you look at theoretically the more accurate your standard deviation should be. In the example above there were 30 days in the dataset, though to be safe you could take 3–12 months as your dataset.

You can benchmark visitors, visits and page views (or interactions) quite easily. You can also then work out ratio benchmarks such as conversion rates by working out the number of successful 'actions' with a standard deviation in the same manner (so once you have got a standard deviation for visits, then work out the standard deviation for actions and you have two average numbers which can then be used as your conversion ratio benchmark).

Day	#Visits
1	3180
2	3100
3	2950
4	2900
5	3050
6	3000
7	2900
	3250

Step 1: Firstly put all the data into Excel. You should format the data as days 1–30 and the visit numbers in a simple list as shown in Figure 3.8. NB: It's important you get the right number for every day in your list, so you have all the fluctuation in your data sample listed. If you're not interested in the maths behind the method go straight to step 4.

FIGURE 3.8 *Simply list of days and visit counts.*

Step 2: Find the mean of the numbers listed. In my Excel sheet this was done by using the following function =AVERAGE(B2:B31). My mean average was 3204.2 visits per day. I do this simply to verify what the numbers are telling me look about right.

Step 3: Find the standard deviation of the numbers. In Excel this is all worked out for you by simply using a function =STDEVA(B2:B31). Essentially what this function does is work out the data fluctuation from the mean. By doing this I had a standard deviation of 336.55. This means that on average my daily visits are 3204, my top limit is 3204 + 336.5 and my bottom limit is 3204.2 – 336.5. So if my numbers fall between roughly 2868 and 3540 based on the historical data for 30 days it's average behaviour. If the figure appears over or below that period it's showing abnormal behaviour and should be examined further.

Step 4: Use Excel to build a graph. Once you have the data it's very fast and very simple to display your deviation. Simply create a normal line graph of your data, days along the bottom visits as your data points. Once you have your chart click the 'layout tab' in Excel 2007 and then the 'error bars'. Then simply select 'Error bars with standard deviation'. What you should then see is a graph that looks a bit like Figure 3.9. As you can see the graph shows you the standard deviation shown by the black lines surrounding the data at roughly 3540 and 2868 across the 30-day sample. Because of this we can clearly see that there is a 'deviation from the norm' around the 8th until about the 15th of the month. This is the period you then want to examine more closely.

Standard deviations are very fast to set up in Excel and help you understand which trends you should be concentrating on. Here I've explained roughly

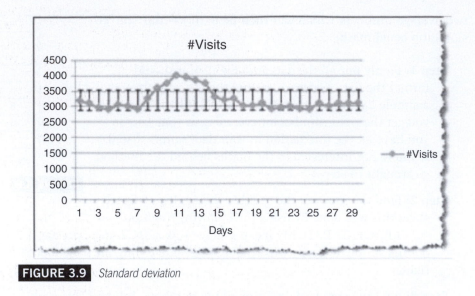

FIGURE 3.9 *Standard deviation*

the principles without going too deep into the math behind it. Suffice to say Excel works it all out for you. All you need to do is import your data, run a line graph and add error bars to 1 standard deviation (though you could add more) to see roughly what your benchmarks should be.

Examples of KPI Development

Taking a real example is the best way to illustrate KPI development. This company run a popular media website with primarily advertising as the main revenue source.

Firstly take the business questions from the Workshop itself:

1. What is the best reach source in terms of volume?

2. Where can we generate more visitors?
   a. Google isn't the answer anymore, what could be the other sources?

3. How do we activate visitors?

4. How do we get people to stay on our site longer?

5. How do we encourage visitors to buy more?

6. How do we encourage visitors to go deeper into content groups?
   a. Dynamics in the site → traffic flow analysis

7. Google's part is important for the sub-sites. How important search engines are in generating traffic to these

8. Email service:
   a. How to drive more people from this site to other sites?
   b. How to leverage users' preference information better?
   c. How to track promotions?

9. How do we get the TV-audience to our site?

10. How well does the navigation in site work (both horizontal and vertical navigation)?

11. How do people use the front page of the site?

12. How effective are different headlines in articles?

13. What kind of video content works best for people? Are there different video user segments in terms of usage behaviour?

14. Content navigation. Are people really reading content pages from top to the bottom?

15. How well do (external) banners work?

16. How well do internal banners work? How can we track paths from banner click to purchase?

17. How many leads do we get out of those who have seen television advertisements?

18. How can we increase sales? How to measure how shopping oriented the visitors are?

19. Are there differences in usage behaviour during the day?

20. Who are using different services in site? (Visitor profiles for different site sections.)

21. Which areas in the site have the greatest potential to leverage social media content in terms of activation? Should social media be used mainly in the sub-sites or somewhere else?

22. How does the free content do in promoting sales related items?

23. What percentage of the content can be chargeable? Where's the balance between free and chargeable content?

24. How many of the different operating system users have problems with the site? (Especially Mac users.)

25. How to increase visitor loyalty?

26. How far can we go with commercial material without irritating visitors too much? Does it have an effect on loyalty?

27. When do we change the content on the front page of our site? (Developers and content feeders need real time information about front page content performance.)

28. What does an individual visitor do during one visit?

29. Do visitors understand that they should scroll down the page in the front page?

30. How often do we need to make changes to the front page? (Relates to question 27.)

31. How many people have abandoned product carts during the shopping process?

32. Which products cross-sell the best? How do we find the content areas that generate the best sales/cross-sales?

33. How to track the lead generation process? (Path tracking.)

34. How can we add value to third party partners by tracking the leads?

Then we break this down into the REAN model as described previously.

In Figure 3.10 you see the four dimensions reach, engage activate and nurture and how we've consolidated the 34 questions into this model as well as defined the goals, listed the engagement and how the site would attempt to re-engage (nurture) the audience.

The reach dimension firstly shows the most important counts coming from the various referrers under the title 'Reach sources'. Of course there will be more referrers than listed but the company are particularly interested in those particular referrers because they may match their marketing spending patterns. Then we have the three questions we need to answer about reach and we will use ratios because we're combining cost information with traffic sources. The engage dimension has definitions based on average benchmarks taken from previous numbers and then has a list of engagement ratios we need to work out. There are also three major processes that need to be measured as abandonment rates. These are the shopping process, the lead generation process and the navigation processes. The

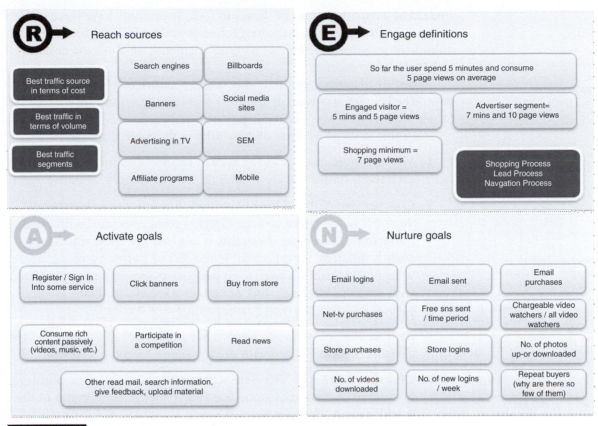

FIGURE 3.10 *The REAN KPI planning model*

segment definitions for engagement allow you to figure out which sources of traffic result in good advertising traffic, shopping traffic or simply the more engaged visitors (in terms of click depth and duration). Measuring the process funnel ratios mean you can measure drop-off points in a defined process such as a shopping cart or lead generation process and allows you to pinpoint certain areas. The activate and nurture stages are all simple ratios we need to create around each statement.

Reach KPIs

As we described earlier we're looking to break down the questions into common components. With the reach dimension for instance you might find that all reach KPIs can be designed with just three factors. Using cost, volume and geography as the core components of your reach KPIs means instead of having hundreds of things to look at you only have three or four metrics. You simply look at the best referrers and performers based on cost, volume or geography. Then add external elements, in this case costs need to be taken into account.

Reporting frequency for these KPIs is every month or is campaign dependent. The benchmarks were determined also from existing data sources but for obvious reasons won't be made public.

With this in mind we drew up four KPIs in the reach dimension.

1. Visitor volume ratio (VVR). This KPI requires counts of visitors from each reach source and the overall number of visitors.

2. Cost per visit (CPV). This KPI requires a count for the number of visits per reach source and the external costs associated with driving traffic from the referrer. Note this is not cost per click, which is slightly different. Cost per visit is the cost of a visitor arriving at your website and loading a page. Cost per click is simply a cost associated with someone clicking a link or banner you have paid for.

3. Cost per engaged visit (CPEV). This KPI requires a count for the number of visits per reach source that are defined as engaged and the external costs associated with driving traffic from the referrer.

4. Content visit ratio (CVR). This KPI requires a count of the number of visits to each content group from each referrer and a count of the overall visits to the each content group.

Of course these four KPIs are not the only ones that could be used. There are literally hundreds of counts and ratios you could come up with. You should start creating your KPIs based on your own business questions.

Once you have defined the counts required you should then record this and explain why you are using the KPI. What follows is a table of KPI definitions for the reach dimension.

KPI Name	Calculation	Explanation	Benchmark	Actions
Visitor volume ratio per referrer (V V R)	**Number of visitors per traffic source / Total number visitors**	Shows the best traffic sources in terms of volume (number of visitors) across all the methods to attract your visitors. Helps answer questions 1, 7, 9 and 15 from the KPI workshop on the 29/6	Historical – start with the first internal ratios and try to improve upon them. See also Chapter 7, scoring	Manage marketing campaigns to focus on higher volume traffic. Use in combination with engagement index and cost per visit to determine the highest ROI source of traffic

(*Continued*)

KPI Name	Calculation	Explanation	Benchmark	Actions
Cost per referred visit (CPRV)	**Total marketing cost per referring source / Total number of visits per referring source**	Shows the best traffic sources in terms of cost per visit. Helps answer questions 1 and 2 from the KPI workshop 29/6	Historical – start with the first prices per visit and try to improve upon them. See also Chapter 7, scoring	Manage marketing campaigns to focus on lower cost traffic. Use in combination with visitor volume ratio to determine the highest ROI source of traffic
Cost per engaged visit (CPEV) per referrer	**Total marketing cost per referring source / Total number of engaged visits**	Shows the best traffic sources in terms of engaged visits/cost ratio. Helps answer questions 2 and 4 from the KPI workshop on the 29/6	Historical – start with the first internal ratios and try to improve upon them See also Chapter 7, scoring	Manage marketing campaigns to focus on engaged traffic which costs the least. Drop high cost, low engagement campaigns and increase spend to highly engaged visitor sources
Content/visit ratio per referrer (CVR)	**Number of visits per traffic source / Number of visits per content group**	Shows the best traffic sources in terms of content consumed across all the top 25 methods to attract. Helps answer questions 2, 3 and 6 from the KPI workshop on the 29/6	Historical – start with the first internal ratios and try to improve upon them. See also Chapter 7, scoring	Manage marketing campaigns to focus on higher volume traffic to specific content groups. Use in combination with engagement index and cost per visit to determine the highest ROI source of traffic

Engage KPIs

When you use the REAN model and you talk about engagement, you should be looking at click depth and duration of stay as the engagement metrics. In this case we drew up nine metrics again based around a breakdown of the business questions that needed to be answered.

Once again what follows probably isn't all going to work for your business, again these were specific KPIs developed for a media company based on their business questions. You again use the same four-step method to determine the KPIs. Firstly we determine which counts are required, then look at which external source of information is required, then look at potential benchmarks (see also Chapter 7 for scoring and target setting) and finally determine the reporting period.

The KPIs that were developed to answer the business questions were:

1. Link click through rate (LCTR). This ratio requires a count of the links clicked and a count of the page views of the page where the link is.

2. Bounce rate (BR). This ratio requires a count of pages viewed (for each page examined) and a count of visits that only visited the page and didn't do anything upon arriving.

3. Video engagement rate (VER). This ratio requires a count of engaged visits and a count of page views to the video pages.

4. Shopping cart abandonment rate (SCAR). This ratio requires a count of visits to the shopping cart's first page and a count of visits to the last page is required.

5. Page time index (PTI). A count of the total time spent on each page.

6. Visit engagement index (VEI). This ratio requires a count of visits that are part of the engaged segment and a count of total visits.

7. Internal banner click through rate (IBCTR). This ratio requires a count of the banners clicked and a count of the page views of the page which the banner was shown.

8. System compatibility index (SCI). A count of visitors using systems which are not compatible with the content as a ratio of all visitors.

9. Content consumption index (CCI). This ratio requires a count of page views per content group and a count of total page views.

Again once this is defined you should record each KPI, state why you're using it and which business questions are answered by the metric.

KPI Name	Calculation	Explanation	Benchmark	Actions
Link click through rate (LCTR)	**Total page views / Link clicks**	Shows the performance of the link on the page it is active upon, this KPI helped answer questions 10,11,22,23,29 and 33 in the KPI workshop on 29/6	Historical – start with the first internal ratios and try to improve upon it. See also Chapter 7, scoring	Optimize link copy and positioning it if the ratio is too low
Bounce rate (BR)	**Page views / Number single page visits per page**	Shows the performance of the pages in relation to each other by the number of visitors who have taken no actions. This KPI helped answer questions 10,11,12,29 and 30 in the workshop of 29/6	Historical – start with the first ratio and try to improve upon it. Set three levels, short, medium and long term goals to improve the abandonment rate. See also Chapter 7, scoring	Optimize reach sources to be more relevant to the page, optimize keywords for relevance with the page in question, optimize headlines, increase the amount of relevant embedded links in the page
Video engagement rate (VER)	**Engaged visits to video content / Total number of visits to video page**	Shows the performance of the videos and allows you to compare which format engages visitors at a higher level. The KPI answered question 13 defined in the KPI workshop in the 29/6	Historical – start with the first ratio and try to improve upon it. Set three levels, short, medium and long term goals to improve the abandonment rate. See also Chapter 7, scoring	Least engaged video content should be removed or optimized

(Continued)

KPI Name	Calculation	Explanation	Benchmark	Actions
Shopping cart abandonment rate (SCAR)	**Number of successful purchases / Total number of visits to shopping cart**	Shows the performance of the shopping cart process . This KPI helped answer questions 3, 5, 18 and 31 in the workshop in the 29/6	Historical – start with the first ratio and try to improve upon it. Set three levels, short, medium and long term goals to improve the abandonment rate. See also Chapter 7, scoring	Measure this as a process funnel so that a continuous programme of improvement can be implemented. For instance you may see one area which causes a high abandonment point. Improving usability around that area may bring the overall SCAR % down whereupon you look at the next highest abandonment point
Page time index (PTI)	**Total time spent on page / Total number of visits**	Shows the most popular page in terms of page duration and helps answer the questions 14, 27 and 30	Historical – the ratios can be used to determine which pages are outperforming others, compared with bounce rates and gives an idea if people are reading enough of the content. See also Chapter 7, scoring	If a page you want to have read is not getting enough time spent then you need to optimize how it is viewed, optimize headlines and try to make it clear that content below the fold is clear and obvious to the reader
Visit engagement index (VEI)	**Engaged visits (as defined on definitions worksheet) / Total number of visits**	The engagement index should be used to determine which type of visits are the most engaged from an activation and reach perspective. This very useful KPI helped answer questions 4,25,26,27 and 33	Historical – the ratio's should have short, medium and long term targets, the objective being to engage more visits, thus driving more activation. See also Chapter 7, scoring	The least engaged visits should be encouraged by the use of effective linking and quality content to read more, download more and click through more pages. You should be careful however not to confuse good engagement with poor usability
Internal banner click through rate (IBCTR)	**Internal banner clicks / page views**	This will show the top performing (and the worst performing) banners internally linked on the site. This KPI helps towards answering questions 16, 30 and 33 from the workshop on the 29/6	Historical	The worst banners should be better placed and have content within them optimized
System compatibility index (SCI)	**Class A, B or C systems / All systems used to visit the site**	Class A = 100% compatibale systems, Class B = partially compatible systems and Class C is non-compatible. By using this ratio you can determine what percentage of the visits to your site can access all your content. This KPI helped answer question 24 from the 29/6 workshop	Historical	The ratio should be checked regularly in order to show which content to change if required due to incompatible systems, such as for instance mobile phones/MACS accessing your site or screens of too small size accessing your site on a regular basis

(Continued)

KPI Name	Calculation	Explanation	Benchmark	Actions
Content consumption index (CCI)	**#page views per content group / # page views**	Highest content consumption as a ratio of all the content consumed to give you a good idea of your best content. This KPI helped answer questions 6,11,21,30 and 32 from the workshop dated 29/6	Historical	The ratio should be checked regularly in order to show which content to change if the visitors are not reading the pages. It could also lead to a decision to drop a content section

Activate KPIs

The REAN model defines activations as meaning the visitor has taken an action on your website, preferably one that you had pre-defined and wanted them to take.

Once again you should follow the same four-step system and look at the statements you have already defined as activations.:

1. Determine which counts or ratios are required to answer the question.

2. Determine external factors.

3. Determine reporting requirements.

4. Determine benchmarks.

In this case we defined the following four metrics designed to be used:

1. Conversion rate (CR). We needed the counts 'visitors whom had taken a pre-defined action' and 'total visitors' so that we could create the conversion ratio. Note that there were many pre-defined actions (16 of them) but the KPI used is the same (conversion rate) for each action.

2. Engaged conversion rate (ECR). We needed the counts 'engaged visitors whom had taken a pre-defined action' and 'total visitors' so that we could create the engaged conversion ratio.

3. Content conversion rate (CCR). We needed the counts 'visitors whom had taken a pre-defined action whom had visited a pre-defined content group' and 'total visitors' so that we could create the content conversion ratio.

4. Cost per activation (or acquisition) (CPA). We needed the counts 'visitors whom had taken a pre-defined action' and the external factor of marketing cost so that we could calculate the cost per action.

Again once you have defined what you need you should record each KPI, state why you're using it and which business questions are answered by the metric.

KPI Name	Calculation	Explanation	Benchmark	Actions
Conversion rate (CR)	**Number of confirmed conversions (slide 16) / Total number of visits**	Conversion rate can be used for all the individual conversion points listed on slide 12. It shows the number of visits that took the action listed as a percentage of all engaged visits. This KPI helps answer the business questions, 5, 17, 18 and 33	Historical – The ratios should have short, medium and long term targets, the objective being to convert more visits. See also Chapter 7, scoring	The lowest conversion points can be tested in different ways, offered to different types of visitors or dropped altogether as an unsuccessful method of attracting activation. The highest conversion points should be generally encouraged and used to nurture other less activated visitors
Engaged conversion rate (ECR)	**Number of confirmed conversions (slide 16) / Total number of engaged visits**	Conversion rate can be used for all the individual conversion points listed on slide 12 as a ratio of the engaged visits listed on slide 11. It can be used to determine what the best level of engagement is to drive activation. This KPI helps answer the business questions 5, 17 and 18	Historical – Start with the first ratio and try to improve upon it. Set three levels, short, medium and long term goals to improve the abandonment rate. See also Chapter 7, scoring	ECR should be compared with reach sources and cost per engaged visit as well as cost per activation. The action should be to spend more on good sources of activation and engagement
Content conversion rate (CCR)	**Number of confirmed conversions (16) / Total number of visits to content group**	Conversion rate can be used for all the individual conversion points. This measurement differs from other conversion ratios in that it only measures visits to specific pre-defined content groups. This helps answer the business questions 5,17,18,21, 22,23,32 and 33.	Historical – The ratios should have short, medium and long term targets, the objective being to convert more visits. See also Chapter 7, scoring	CCR should be compared with reach sources, engagement indexes and costs to determine where spend needs to be allocated within each content group
Cost per activation (or acquisition) (CPA)	**Total cost of referring source / Number of confirmed conversions (16)**	Cost per activation (or more commonly cost per acquisition) shows the cost of delivering one conversion. This is useful in determining which is your most cost-effective source of traffic activation. This KPI helps answer questions 5, 17 and 18	Historical – Start with the first costs per activated visit and try to improve upon them. See also Chapter 7, scoring	CPA should be compared with reach sources and cost per engaged visit. The action should be to focus spend more on good sources of activation and engagement

Nurture KPIs

Nurture KPIs are designed in the same way. In the case being examined there is a website email service which is free to its users in a similar way that MSN works for instance. This is why the main nurture metrics took the form of email open rates. However the process for each KPI was the same.

1. Email open rate (EOR). The counts of registered visitors to the email service and emails opened was required.

2. Email click through rate (ECTR). A count of clicks to website services and a count of emails opened is required to calculate this KPI.

3. Repeat visitor index (RVI). The counts 'number of repeat visitors' and 'total number of visitors' were required to calculate this metric.

Again once you have defined what you need you should record each KPI, state why you're using it and which business questions are answered by the metric.

KPI Name	Calculation	Explanation	Benchmark	Actions
Email open rate (EOR)	**Total emails opened / Total visitors to email service**	This shows how many emails each person is reading (and how many exposures to ads they have). This KPI helped answer business question 8	Historical – Start with the first EOR and try and improve upon it	Improve the ways people can use the email services (personalization)
Email click through Rate (ECTR)	**Clicks to services / Emails opened**	This shows how effective offers and banners in the email service are. This KPI helped answer business question 8	Historical – Start with the first ECTR and try and improve upon it	Improve the incentives and offers, personalize the content. Continue the dialogue by sending newsletters and periodic sales calls
Repeat visitor Index (RVI)	**Number of repeat visitors / Number of visitors**	This shows how many visitors return to the site over a given timeframe. This helped answer business questions 25 and 26	Historical – Start with the first RVI and try to encourage more of the first-time visits to become repeats. Measure this monthly to get a good overall idea how many visitors come back	Improve the incentives to become a repeat visitor by adding fresh content for instance – also compare this with engagement and activation to determine if loyalty incentives work

There are many more KPIs we could have defined for nurture such as recency and frequency, however the company in question needed a starting point and therefore looked to these fairly simple KPIs in the beginning.

Mapping KPIs to Actors

The final part of the KPI process is to close the loop and infuse business logic into your KPIs, meaning that the part we start with, defining the people, is the part we end with, defining what the people do.

There is no reason doing the workshop and developing the metrics in the way described if you're not going to take actions on the metrics you've developed. In the hub and spoke process the way to do it is to pass all the metrics back to the hub if you as a spoke actor can't take direct daily action on the numbers you are looking at.

Back to the Hub and Spoke

You should have already defined at this stage who your hub and spoke actors are. The spokes should only receive the KPIs that they can directly act upon. The hub actors have the main responsibility to keep an eye on everything else and take the required actions when needed.

Going back to our MTV3 example, the editors are part of the spokes and they looked at only two KPIs for the first page bounce rate and page time index. They would only need to monitor two things and watch for when the amount of time goes down and the bounce rate goes up. When that happened they needed to change the page, the purpose being to get the KPIs back in line and keep the readers interested in clicking through the various content. They didn't need to see the other 20 KPIs developed, only those two.

The hub however would need to monitor all the KPIs and make sure that the steering group understood what (if any) business critical decisions needed to be made.

When mapping KPIs to spoke actors all you need is a simple answer to the question, 'Will using this KPI allow you to take an action that will immediately improve the KPIs performance?' If the answer to that question is yes then use it. If the answer to the question is no, or simply a nice to know KPI, then it is the hub who will take decisions themselves as to whether the spoke needs to know the results.

Examples of the KPI Process in Action (see Figure 3.11)

1. **Cost per acquisition** (CPA, cost per purchase) is one hypothetical example where a spoke actor might take an immediate decision:
   a. The hub analyst sends a list of CPA results to the spoke actor in charge of marketing spend for a particular campaign.
   b. The actor reviews the results and sees that search engine marketing is costing €1.50 per acquisition whilst some of her banner campaigns are costing €10 per acquisition.
   c. The actor immediately acts and tells her media buy company to stop spending money on banners and re-direct funding to search engine marketing.

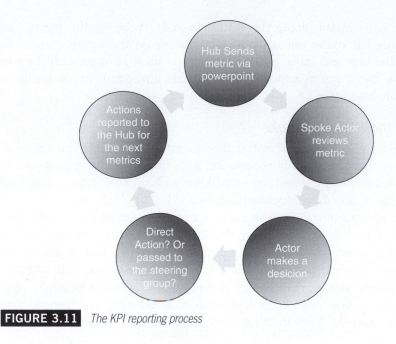

FIGURE 3.11 *The KPI reporting process*

    d. The hub is told of the changes and asked for new reports at the end of the week to see if the trend has continued and overall CPA has dropped as expected due to the changes made.

    e. Ends here.

2. **Shopping cart abandonment rate** is a hypothetical example where the hub analyst should take the lead in the organization:

    a. The hub analyst sends the abandonment ratio to the spoke actor in charge of marketing a particular campaign.

    b. The actor reviews the result (a 96% abandonment rate) and thinks it is shocking that 96 from every 100 visitors she drives to the shopping cart leave without buying. The benchmarks show that 94–98% is the norm for the cart over the last month and therefore it's unlikely that her campaign traffic is underperforming badly.

    c. The spoke raises a query to the hub asking the analysts to find out why the KPI is so bad (the only action the spoke can take).

    d. The hub does a heuristic analysis on the shopping cart (expert walk through in the customers' shoes) and conducts an exit survey of the visitors when they bail out of the process. They find out that there are both technical problems and usability issues that need to be fixed urgently. A feasibility study is then carried out to see what quick fixes can be done in house and what if anything needs to be outsourced. Two solutions to the problem are offered, both of which require funding and resources.

e. The hub raises the problem and the solutions to the spoke steering group. Because changing the shopping cart will affect the entire company the spoke director raises the problem to the executive steering group to take a long-term decision.

As you can see in the two examples above the information that the marketing manager needs is always given to her but she can only directly influence one of the KPIs. The hub has to do the rest and generally when big changes are required the steering group has to take the overall decision. It's why KPIs should be owned by the people who can act and improve the KPI in question.

Ask most people in an organization if they want to look at a massive set of reports with a lot of numbers detailing everything that happened around a campaign and they will answer 'Yes. I want it all'. And they will then only read part of it and nothing will happen.

The hub should offer the KPIs surrounding a campaign that the spokes can directly influence and try to answer the business questions they know are going to be raised in their reports to the spokes. They should use the numbers as part of their arguments and show the actors what they need to know and understand, rather than baffle them by showing them everything. The hub and spokes should work together to try to alleviate longer term and higher cost problems.

Monetization

To build culture and get people to take notice you need to monetize the results you find in the processes you measure. In the above examples you should be aware just how much the abandonment was costing every week and present that to the steering group. **Don't simply present a 96% abandonment ratio which while it sounds bad to an analyst, doesn't make as much an impact with a CFO sitting in the steering group as 'this is costing us €250K per week.'** (See Chapter 8 on simplified reporting and monetization.)

3.4 HOW OTHERS IN THE INDUSTRY USE KPIs

In 2007 Eric Peterson (http://www.webanalyticsdemystified) came up with the following formula that can be used in the context of REAN (see Chapter 2) as a visitor lifecycle score index. It could be used as a scoring mechanism to measure individual or the audience level of interest with your business based on their activity with your site.

Eric Peterson Engagement Index

The formula for this index looks complicated (Figure 3.12) but actually it isn't so difficult once you understand what each letter in the formula represents. Eric describes the formula and how to do the calculation below.

The individual session-based indices are defined as follows:

- **Click-depth index (Ci)** is the percent of sessions having more than 'n' page views divided by all sessions.

- **Recency index (Ri)** is the percent of sessions having more than 'n' page views *that occurred in the past 'n' weeks* divided by all sessions. The recency index captures recent sessions that were also deep enough to be measured in the click-depth index.

- **Duration index (Di)** is the percent of sessions longer than 'n' minutes divided by all sessions.

- **Brand index (Bi)** is the percent of sessions that *either* begin directly (i.e. have no referring URL) *or* are initiated by an external search for a 'branded' term divided by all sessions.

- **Feedback index (Fi)** is the percent of sessions where the visitor gave direct feedback via a Voice of Customer technology like ForeSee Results or OpinionLab divided by all sessions

- **Interaction index (Ii)** is the percent of sessions where the visitor completed one of any specific, tracked events divided by all sessions

In addition to the session-based indices, Eric has added two small, binary **weighting factors** based on visitor behaviour:

- **Loyalty index (Li)** is scored as '1' if the visitor has come to the site more than 'n' times during the timeframe under examination (and otherwise scored '0').

$$\sum_{\text{Visitor}} (C_i + R_i + D_i + L_i + B_i + F_i + I_i + S_i)$$

FIGURE 3.12 *Peterson's engagement index formula*

- **Subscription index (Si)** is scored as '1' if the visitor is a known content subscriber (i.e. subscribed to my blog) during the timeframe under examination (and otherwise scored '0').

You take the value of each of the component indices, sum them, and then divide by '8' (the total number of indices in my model) to get a very clean value between '0' and '1' that is easily converted to a percentage. Given sufficient robust technology, you can then segment against the calculated value, build super-useful KPIs like 'percent highly-engaged visitors' and add the engagement metric to the reports you're already running.

Eric designed this formula as an engagement index because he wanted to work out those prospects visiting his website that were the most likely to purchase consultancy. He needed a more complex KPI that measured the visitor lifecycle. This is what REAN is, a visitor lifecycle model which is designed to improve how we plan and measure visitors throughout their interaction with you.

Brand Awareness (Reach)

When Eric talks about brand index (Bi) it's part of the reach dimension in REAN.

Whenever a user arrives from a search engine where a branded term has been used to find you then you can call this a branded visit. Branded keyword terms might be someone searching for your company name or your product names. In many cases you can also say that when there is no referring domain that this is a branded visit, because the user has either typed in your website address (i.e. they knew your brand) or they had bookmarked it previously.

Click-depth (Engage)

When Eric discusses click index (Ci) and duration index (Di) they are engage activities from REAN.

This is simply the amount of times your visitors click when they move through your website. It may be flash events you measure or the amount of page impressions viewed to quote the web analytics terminology. Click depth is an engagement measure because it shows on average or individually how each visitor has 'engaged' with your creative.

Duration (Engage)

Duration is simply the length of time that the visitor stays on your website. I've used session time or time spent on site (as duration is also known as) to set-up segments as I discussed earlier with varying levels of success. When used in combination with activation or nurture data it can be very actionable and insightful.

Activation (Activate)

When Eric discusses interaction index (Ii), subscription index (Si) and feedback index (Fi) he is discussing Activations or pre-defined conversions in the REAN model context.

Activation is the most important of the four elements. Activation occurs when your visitor has 'acted in the manner you desired'. This is also called a conversion, a call to action, outcome or a success metric. Activation is typically what reach, engagement and nurture KPIs are measured against.

Loyalty/recency (Nurture)

When Eric discusses loyalty index (Li) and recency index (Ri) he is discussing methods of measuring how people return, or again in terms of the REAN model the nurture phase.

Nurture is the way you actively encourage your visitors to come back and consume more of your website content.

By using the method Eric describes you can use the formula to define and segment your audience into 'best chance of business visitors'. The action you might take is to offer these visitors incentives via marketing methods to encourage them to buy your services.

Neil Mason on Measurement Frameworks

Neil Mason (http://www.applied-insights.co.uk/) advocates the use of an online performance management framework to help focus an organization on its most important digital marketing KPIs or the 'measures that matter'.

While the terminology is different in Neil's model the method is almost identical to REAN. He is looking at comparing channels of different traffic sources (Reach), the efficiency of the traffic source (Engage) likelihood to become a lead or purchasing customer (Activate) and the outcomes after that (Nurture).

Shown in Figure 3.13 is an example of Neil's methodology for improving performance in different parts of the customer lifecycle from acquisition to retention.

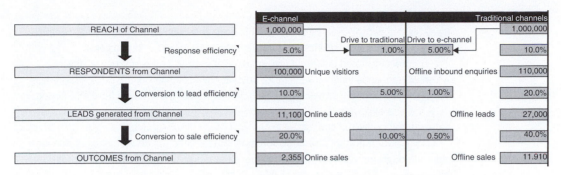

	E-channel				Traditional channels
REACH of Channel	1,000,000				1,000,000
Response efficiency	5.0%	Drive to traditional 1.00%	Drive to e-channel 5.00%		10.0%
RESPONDENTS from Channel	100,000 Unique visitiors		Offline inbound enquiries		110,000
Conversion to lead efficiency	10.0%	5.00%	1.00%		20.0%
LEADS generated from Channel	11,100 Online Leads		Offline leads		27,000
Conversion to sale efficiency	20.0%	10.00%	0.50%		40.0%
OUTCOMES from Channel	2,355 Online sales		Offline sales		11.910

Metric	Visitor acquisition	Conversion to Opportunity	Conversion to Sale	Customer Retention & Growth
Tracking metrics	Unique visitors New visitors	Opportunity volume	Sales volume	E-mail list quality E-mail response quality Transactions churn rate
Performance drivers (diagnostics)	Bounce rate Conversion rate: New visit to start quote;	Macro-conversion rate to opportunity and micro-conversion efficiency	Conversion rate to Sale E-mail conversion rate	Active customers % (site & e-mail active) Repeat conversion rate for different purchases
Customer Centric KPIs	Cost per Click and per Sale Brand awareness	Cost per Opportunity (lead) Customer satisfaction	Cost per Sale (CPA) Customer satisfaction Average order value (AOV)	Lifetime value Customer loyalty index Products per customer Advocacy (Net Promoter Score)
Business Value KPIs	Audience share	Order (n, £, % of total)	Online originated sales (n, £, % of total)	Retained sales growth and volume
Strategy	Online targeted reach strategy Offline targeted reach strategy	Lead generation strategy	Online sales generation strategy?? Offline sales impact strategy	Retention and customer growth strategy Advocacy
Tactics	Continuous communications mix Campaign communications mix Online value proposition	Usability Personalisation Inbound contact strategy (customer service)	Usability Personalisation Inbound contact strategy (customer service) Merchandising Triggered e-mails	Database / list quality = opt-out/churn rate?? Targeting Outbound contact strategy (e-mail) Personalisation

FIGURE 3.13 *Applied insights measurement framework*

Dave Chaffey describes Neil's process in his book *Internet Marketing: Strategy, implementation and practice* (Financial Times/Prentice Hall, Harlow, 4th edition).

The rows indicated different forms of tracking metrics and performance drivers which will influence higher-level metrics such as the customer-centric Key Performance Indicators (KPIs) and Business value KPIs. In the bottom two rows we have also added in typical strategies and tactics used to achieve objectives which shows the relationship between objectives and strategy.

Note though that this framework mainly creates a focus on efficiency of conversion, although there are some effectiveness measures also such as reach, profit and advocacy.

We have added strategies and tactics to show how these should be based on achieving goals set in measurement.

http://www.davechaffey.com/

The approach described by Neil and Dave is very close in essence to what we're trying to produce with the REAN method of designing KPIs:

Reach could replace what Neil calls **Visitor Acquisition.** It is in essence the same thing except that reach does not assume that you have acquired anything, visitor acquisition does. Reach allows you to plan for all forms of potential acquisition which gives you the opportunity to test out sources you may not have considered.

Engage could replace what Neil calls **Conversion to Opportunity.** The conversion to opportunity could be a variety of things but it means that in some way the visitor to your channel is interacting with you (or engaging with you) in some way.

Activate could replace what Neil calls **Conversion to Sale.** Again conversion to sale could be considered anything that is an activation such as conversion to a goal (meaning purchases, downloads, subscriptions) depending on what your business objective is. Activation is what we chose to use because it doesn't necessarily mean a sale.

Nurture could replace what Neil calls **Customer Retention and Growth.** By Nurturing your existing customers you encourage them to re-engage with you, purchase more and therefore grow your business.

3.5 KPIs BREEDING CULTURE

What you have read is a process to develop KPIs. It's a necessarily long process but it works and when the KPIs are applied you have a superb foundation to deliver on your business objectives.

You don't have to go down this route. Many books have been written about KPIs – *The Big Book of KPIs* is one that I already mentioned you could use to develop your own.

However this book is also about how to gradually change your company culture into an analytical one and in order to do that, you need to involve all the people critical to the success of your business. That's why the workshop process you've just read about was developed. When these workshops are well run they rarely fail to make an impression on all involved.

CHAPTER 4

Planning Quick Wins

*There are winners, there are losers and there are people
who have not yet learned how to win.*

Les Brown US author and speaker

CHAPTER CONTENTS

4.1 PROCESS TO PLAN THE QUICK WIN

One of the keys to changing the culture of your company to being more analytical is that of solidly proving that what you're doing works.

What you could do is hope that the changes you make work and that you can show successful results to your colleagues. Or you could plan the wins based on potential monetary gains brought about by successful analytics activities.

It's difficult to get anyone except an accountant excited about numbers and pie charts without putting it into context. So these simple planning steps and the method of communicating the information is designed to help you to develop wins when you need them (Figure 4.1).

The Pre-Study Phase

The pre-study phase is when you look to your hub analysts to find you some low hanging fruit in web analytics terms. Your skilled analyst should attempt to pinpoint some wins using the Insight model (see Chapter 7) to attempt to find potential areas of improvement.

Study Current Situation

If this is the first time the website has been analysed then there is a good chance you can improve an outcome. Start with conversion (activate) and work backwards.

In pre-study the analyst should look at:

1. **Reach.** Which ones are the best performers in terms of volume and cost? Why?

2. **Engage.** Which processes have high abandonment points? Which pages have too high bounce rates? Which keywords engage more visitors? Which pages have higher exit points than others? Which places on the website are not clicked very well when their main function is to attract click through? Where on the site is there poor time spent? Is this justified (link pages?) or is this content you want to have read which is being ignored?

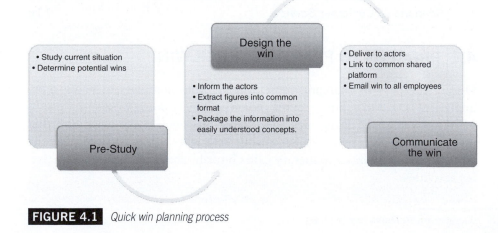

FIGURE 4.1 *Quick win planning process*

3. **Activate.** Which reach sources are the best at converting traffic? Which keywords generate the most conversions? How do your process funnels convert?

4. **Nurture.** For now you could look at things like email newsletter responses. You're looking for short-term gains, so simply by showing the lift in traffic (plus related activation and engagement) after sending a newsletter is proof enough.

Once your hub analysts have defined the opportunities you then define the potential win. This should be in terms of business objectives and related where possible to financial opportunities.

Determine Potential Wins

As the hub analyst you go out and try to determine things you can demonstrate have monetary value. Once you have identified a potential win it's then up to you to go out and take actions to improve things. You may need to run tests like A/B or MVT (see Chapter 7) to prove your case.

In short you hold back the win until you have proved it to yourself before you tell any of the spokes.

Design the Win

Once you have the information you then inform relevant actors of your findings and ask to show them more details. This is where you package it nicely into a good win everyone can understand (see Chapter 8 on the business dashboard).

Extract Data to a Common Platform

Then simply extract the figures you have already have in your web analytics system and pull it all into a commonly used tool. For instance Microsoft Office's Powerpoint, Word, Excel or Adobe PDF documents are good tools to use to package the information because everyone in your organization will understand how to use the tool.

Concept the Win

Easy to understand is the key to successfully conceptualizing your win. There is no point demonstrating that in January you got 300,000 unique visitors and in January due to reach activities you got 350,000 if you can't put it into context.

If you said that the extra 50,000 visitors reached earned the company 1 euro each on average resulting in €50K then you're talking the language your colleagues can understand.

If 300,000 visitors didn't buy what is the opportunity lost if they all did purchase your product? It's not accurate but I've seen some jaws drop when I said there was €100M potential earnings every month sitting on the table. Of course the first comment will be 'we'll never get everyone visiting the site to buy'. But that's where you answer; 'do you know the percentage of those people coming to our site who are prospects?' There will be an uncomfortable silence and that's when you say; 'Back this initiative and I'll find out the real figure for you.' See also Chapter 8 on monetization.

Communicate the Win

Once you have got your win and put it into a format everyone can read you now need to communicate it throughout your organization. This is the part where you show off your results to the stakeholders, actors and leaders you have already identified. You do it in accordance with your schedule where possible and over deliver if you can. Since you have already bought yourself time by planning the first win in a given timeframe your hub can do extra analysis to gain further insights. See Chapter 7 on the Insight model.

If you have a corporate Intranet put the win there and display it prominently with a strong headline: 'Using Web Analytics helped us earn €50K last month' is better than 'Conversion analysis PDF from Analytics Hub – January'.

Also don't forget your in-house email lists, send the intranet link to all staff celebrating the win, and call the business to action asking for them to follow up with their own questions that could be answered by web analytics. Maybe you could even show your staff the KPI workshop questions your team came up with.

What follows are some examples of some quick wins which can help your hub analysts find their own low hanging fruit.

4.2 QUICK WIN EXAMPLES

Scenario 1: Justifying Brand Awareness

Like the case I'm about to describe in this example, imagine you already run media campaigns with targeted online banners and search engines.

Your goal is brand awareness and your target is to get your brand seen by as many visitors as possible.

You already know the costs. However what you don't know is how to optimize your campaigns. You aren't selling anything, so your money best used on banners or SEM? How do you measure success of the campaign when there is no activation or conversion to look for at the end?

The Problem with this Scenario

The goal is typical of many media agency pitches. You might hear phrases from account managers that echo sentiments like:

> *"SEM is great for sales or lead generation but poor for branding and awareness", "Banners carry branding value that text ads don't", "We create brand experiences by using a media mix", "SEM is the best form of marketing currently available as it's cost per click" – Sound familiar?*

Ask for Proof

My opinion is that the media agency should prove their claims.

Firstly **you** have to define your KPIs.

It's not good enough to expect your media agency to handle this for you. If you let them they may select KPIs that help them like total number of ad impressions. This is potentially branding if the visitor to the media site sees the ad, but there is no proof of that and it's easy for the media agency to fulfill their end of the bargain by putting your ads on highly trafficked websites that get a lot of banner impressions.

If, however, your KPI defines that a branded visitor is someone who has been on the website for five minutes or more and been exposed to your product or service web pages then you have a different and much more powerful measurement.

Your target is clear. Optimize based around an engagement factor of five minutes. So if people stay less than five minutes from one campaign but stay longer in others, then you can allocate more spend to the highly engaging campaigns. This allows you to plan campaigns and wins.

With this kind of branding campaign there are three measures (KPIs) to take into account.

1. Impressions.
2. Clicks.
3. Engagement.

Impressions

When a page loads where your ad is presented upon someone typing a keyword (search engines) or on media websites where your banner appears, this is defined as an 'impression'. It doesn't mean that the visitor has seen your ad, but potentially he/she could have.

Clicks

Quite simply a click is registered when your ad is clicked. In this scenario someone either clicks your text or banner ad and your analytics software records the response.

Engagement

This is a measure you'll have to define. Segmenting your traffic into users that have arrived and stayed on your site for more than five minutes for instance could do this. We'll discuss more about segmentation in Chapter 5.

The Case

The tool we used was Omnitures' HBX. By setting up an active segment with HBX to filter out all those who have spent five minutes or more on the website we could compare how our campaigns fared against each other. So as a visitor you only became part of the engagement index KPI if you had spent five minutes on the site and had come from a campaign we had pre-defined.

The results were as follows:

	Google	Yahoo	Banners
Impressions	743,485	7,749,283	2,906,078
Clicks	16,958	4,351	2906
CTR	2.28%	0.06%	1%
Engaged visits	1547	113	503
Engagement index	9.12%	**2.6%**	**17.31**%

From Google there were 1547 visits that were engaged from a total of 16,958 paid clicks. That means 1547, stayed on the site for more than five minutes, meeting the success criteria and dropping into our index of 'engaged visits'.

On Yahoo, only 113 from 4351 visits were engaged. Couple that with the fact that Yahoo was getting a very low CTR (click through rate, from impression to click) it was judged that the Yahoo visitors were not as interested or as well targeted as the Google visitors.

The Yahoo campaigns were therefore dropped and the money was then re-directed to Google that was much the same price in terms of cost per click, but far more effective in reaching the goal. This turned out to be a huge success in terms of cost saving and improved engagement for my client.

What was even more interesting was that the banner campaigns placed on highly targeted sites were outperforming the search engines in this particular case.

It's interesting because banners often have a bad reputation of being overly expensive and have very low click through rates. In this case the data proved this partially wrong. Click through was very low at less than half that of Google and the media prices were much more expensive per click; however the engagement was considerably higher, nearly double that of Google campaigns.

By showing these results we could see immediately that the banners worked much more effectively (nearly twice as effectively) as the best SEM campaign in terms of engaging the visitor.

Because the banners were ten times more costly than SEM to place with the media sites, initially there was a lot of resistance by the marketing managers to keep the ads running, or indeed to allocate further funding there.

What the client now wanted to know was how we could improve the spending with the banner marketing to get a better return of engaged visitors to the website. This was done by drilling down into the campaigns and producing the same figures for each media website which displayed the company brand.

Description	Responses	Engaged Responses	Engagement Index
Media Site 1	4 311	708	16.42 %
Media Site 2	3 969	920	23.18 %
Media Site 3	2 461	516	20.97 %
Media Site 4	2 042	260	12.73 %
Media Site 5	1 885	379	20.11 %
Media Site 6	1 575	349	22.16 %
Media Site 7	697	199	28.55 %
Media Site 8	613	154	25.12 %

As can be clearly seen the weakest performers in the banner campaigns were Media Site 4 and Media Site 1. The other campaigns all had higher engagement than 20%. So the money spent on the banners could be re-directed to the campaigns which were the most effective like Media Sites 7 and 8 in this case.

By optimizing in this way the spending was dramatically improved and the branding became accountable and justifiable.

Of course questions arose like 'why did banners outperform search engines?', followed by why were the banners placed with Sites 1 and 4 less engaging than Sites 7 and 8? These are the kind of questions you long for as an analyst because it means people are starting to understand the value of analytics. To answer the questions you might have to use surveys or qualitative analysis (see Chapter 7, the Insight model) that might lead to more wins.

Scenario 1: Summary

1. **Identify your goal in terms of something that can be measured** – Branding is often called 'difficult to measure'. By setting KPIs however and branding objectives you can eliminate the argument and simply measure and attempt to hit your targets. The target here was to get users on the site for five minutes interacting with and experiencing your brand. It could have been many other success measures. It could have been visiting five pages, watching a flash application, downloading a PDF or software, reading the 'about us' section, whatever. Online most things can be measured, what's often more difficult is determining what to measure, which is the purpose of defining KPIs – see Chapter 3.

2. **Actionable** – When you see something displayed in your KPIs that you can improve, take action. In the above case by eliminating weaker campaigns and directing more funding to the stronger performing ones, the KPI, the engagement index improved drastically.

3. **It's a win which can be easily packaged and communicated** – The considerable money spent on both the banner campaigns and the search campaigns meant that the client saved approximately $2M in what would have been poorly spent money which didn't engage with the brand. This is very easy to show to the executive steering group and especially the spoke actors. Indeed the spoke that benefitted the most (the people carrying out the campaigns) are the ones who got the glory, because ultimately they acted on the business intelligence offered by the hub and made the win. As a member of the hub team you want that because it means more awareness in the spokes of the value of the hub.

4. **The hub can plan these kinds of wins** – By looking at previous or live campaigns and using well defined KPIs these kinds of wins can easily be manufactured.

5. **Communicating the win was easy** – When $2M is saved it becomes very simple to package and distribute the win to all concerned. This one saving brought a return on investment for the web analytics tool many times over. That kind of win is something that instantly justifies more investment in web analytics **people**.

Scenario 2: Improving Your Customers Sales Process via a Shopping Cart

This example is common in e-commerce. Imagine your business is spending money driving traffic to your website so that you may persuade consumers to purchase your products directly online.

The Problem with this Scenario ...

Average conversion rates are 2.2% according to research done by some of the vendors out there (for instance http://index.fireclick.com/), which means that 97.8% of your visitors leave your website at some point without purchasing your product.

While these kinds of benchmarks should be taken with a big pinch of salt the problem here is evident. If your website is anything like what Fireclick calls average your marketing budget may be being wasted due to your websites inefficiency. You have potentially a lot of money being wasted by poor shopping cart usability, poor product placement, poor copy and content and poor persuasion methods.

Measuring the way people complete a predefined process on your website is very easy with most tools available. The following example will help to explain how processes can be optimized.

Shopping Cart Abandonment

In this case optimizing the shopping cart process increased sales by quite quickly reducing the visitor abandonment from 98.8% to 50%. This means that abandonment (people leaving the process), from adding a product to the cart, through filling in credit card details, to a confirmed purchase, improved dramatically meaning far more customers for the same marketing cost. These improvements came about by making changes to the website based on the metrics reported by the analytics tool.

The first time we looked at the process the client (Jörgen Bödmar– CEO DesignOnline.se) used WebTrends and the log files that DesignOnline had already been gathering for some time.

As you can see in Figure 4.2 the first step in this process has a problem. The vast majority of visitors didn't continue from the 'add to cart page' (engagement with the shopping cart process, adding a product to the cart), to the second step, the CheckOut1 page. Indeed from the total visits that put a product in their cart, only 0.93% managed to find the CheckOut1 page.

This is the perfect quick win. It would be more difficult to make this worse than it currently is.

First do a Heuristic Analysis, take a walk in your customers shoes.

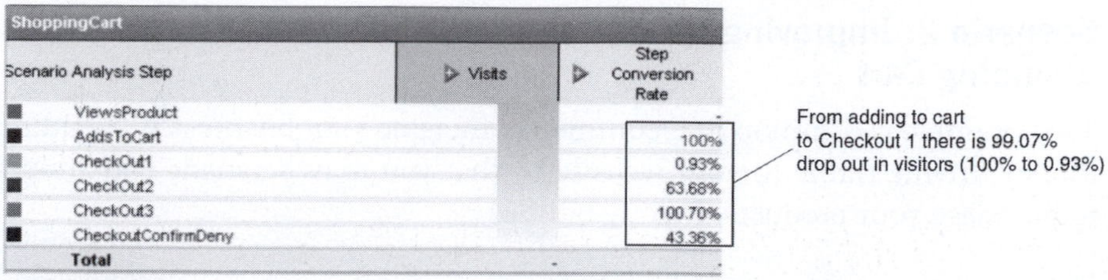

ShoppingCart		
Scenario Analysis Step	▷ Visits	▷ Step Conversion Rate
■ ViewsProduct		-
■ AddsToCart		100%
■ CheckOut1		0.93%
■ CheckOut2		63.68%
■ CheckOut3		100.70%
■ CheckoutConfirmDeny		43.36%
Total	-	

From adding to cart to Checkout 1 there is 99.07% drop out in visitors (100% to 0.93%)

FIGURE 4.2 *WebTrends scenario analysis*

Walking in Your Customers' Shoes

Before doing anything go back to the front page of your website. Decide on a product which is available and try to buy it as if you were completely new to the website. If you can get someone who has never seen your site to try to do the task and observe.

I personally did this for DesignOnline. At first I couldn't see anything obviously wrong. The site was clean, modern, professional and quick to load. It fitted all resolutions easily, was good on the eye and was clearly a store selling designer goods.

So I put myself in the shoes of a visitor who wanted to buy a rug. I settled on a product displayed on the home page, a rug that was decorated with pictures of an elk in fine Swedish style. When I got to the product page I pressed the 'add to cart' button and waited.

I was expecting a failure notice, a timeout or an error message because of the massive drop off rate at this page. However to my mind nothing at all happened.

I waited, 30 seconds and the page was still there. Nothing had changed.

Then I realized what the problem was and only because I was looking for a problem. Had I been a visitor really purchasing this product I might have tried to add again only to get the same result and then left.

Look at the page in Figure 4.3 and the potential problem becomes clear.

When a product was added to the cart (done by pressing an 'add to cart' button just below the central image, out of this screenshot) the page refreshed and then the circled area on the screen updated to say that one product had been added to the cart.

That was all, there was no other verification message, no physical page requesting that they complete the process or any obvious signal about what to do next. All that happened was that the number of items went from zero to one and the subtotal appeared.

It might be that the website visitors, like me, didn't see the updated box, thought there was a problem with the site, and left.

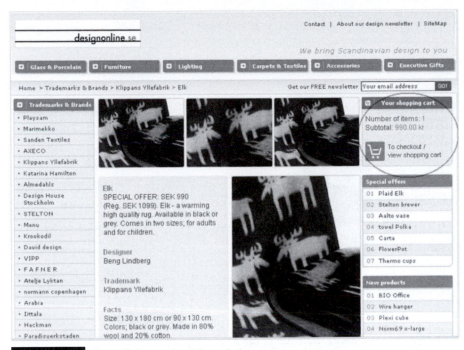

FIGURE 4.3   *DesignOnline pre-heuristic analysis*

After we pointed this out, DesignOnline decided that they needed to take action. This is of course the entire point!

It was quite an easy process programmatically to change to this page when a product was added to the cart.

In Figure 4.4 you can see a number of things have been added to help the visitor take the next step. The shopping cart was displayed allowing you to update the number of products. Clear calls to action were shown, 'To Checkout or Return to shopping' both obviously displayed and in the centre of the screen. The product in the cart was clearly summarized, shipping and handling processes were clearly positioned, satisfaction guarantees were displayed, even a link to privacy policies. All of these vital factors were missing from the previous page and this is why the second page was much more successful at directing people through the cart.

The first tests showed a 1500% improvement in people getting from the 'Adds to basket' page to the 'Address information' page, and then incremental improvements all the way down to the confirmation page (Figure 4.5).

The web analytics tools and bottom line results were telling DesignOnline that this page worked better than the previous way to add something to the

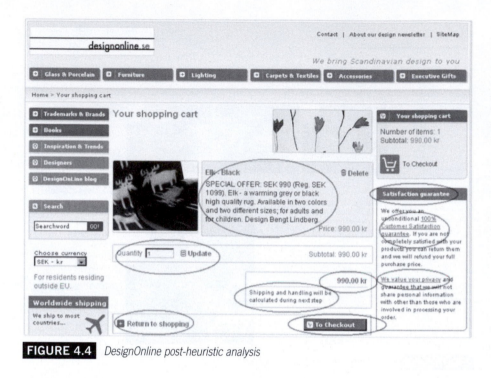

FIGURE 4.4 *DesignOnline post-heuristic analysis*

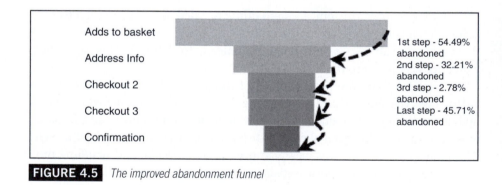

FIGURE 4.5 *The improved abandonment funnel*

cart. So they kept this system as their 'new control' and started testing around this version.

This meant that DesignOnline had a 'win' under their belt and led to the CEO/owner leading the charge to build a web analytics culture so that he could build on this first very significant success.

Scenario 2: Summary

Jörgen Bödmar, the CEO/owner of Scandinavian Design Online commented:

> After the successful start with Steve introducing us to web metrics and its potential we changed our focus from simply driving more traffic to our website to analyzing our visitors behavior on a permanent basis. Together with what Steve taught us, we use a number of KPIs based on Eric Petersons Book, *Web Analytics Demystified.* http://www.webanalyticsdemystified.com/about_wad.asp
>
> Every four weeks we sit down and analyze what to do to make further improvements. So far we have improved our shopping cart design from four steps to two steps and now down to one step with positive effects in all steps. We also have made changes in design of different buttons (colors and shapes) and we have experienced a 12% rise in the number of page views. The shopping cart abandonment rates after the changes are now down to well below 50%. Of course not all of our changes have been successful, however that is part of the game. We then change again, and again. I kind of feel that it is a never ending story as not all changes are correct and that the visitors' profile changes over the time. It is fun and very often rewarding work.
>
> Our change of focus has been very successful and I would highly recommend all merchants to follow our example using web metrics.

http://www.designonline.se

This case is an excellent example of how the hub and spoke process works.

1. **Led top down.** The CEO himself got involved.

2. **Urgency.** The CEO was directing things therefore everyone jumped, the urgency to follow this line was preached from top to bottom.

3. **Vision.** The CEO had seen that search engine optimization on his site worked very well, he had seen the potential of the Internet as a sales medium and he wanted to persue it as scientifically as possible.

4. **Communication.** The CEO arranged for his staff to undergo training in the tools that would allow him to stop hiring consultants and start doing it for himself. This communicated the intent of DesignOnline. They were investing in this course and therefore the staff would need to learn and take it seriously.

5. **Actionable.** The first scenario the company saw was easy to take action on. The onsite fixes were quickly made.

6. **Wins.** The first win was proven very quickly (within 2 months) and dramatically affected sales which encouraged further analysis and actions which led to more wins being demonstrated. As Jörgen commented the first win he saw, coupled with KPIs they had adopted, led to eventually improving the abandonment to more than 50%. This was fantastic news for his business and he kept communicating to everyone concerned.

7. **Organizational improvement.** The improvement in sales meant that roles were created, a team was formed (steering group) which looks at potential improvements monthly and analysts were employed to run the intelligence for the online channel.

8. **Routinely used.** Jörgen actually said: *'We then change again, and again. I kind of feel that it is **a never ending story**'*. DesignOnline have changed their entire focus to follow a web analytics process and now routinely use web analytics to help guide their decisions. A successful culture change.

In Jörgen's own words this approach was very successful and he would advise all merchants to follow their example. This was a company who were experts at selling quality furniture and interior design not at doing web analytics. The web was another channel that they have learned to use and by learning to use web analytics, they have improved their online business.

Scenario 3: Business to Business Lead Generation

You have already read about two scenarios that could improve lead generation techniques. The branding and marketing example in the first scenario could be applied to the amount of downloads, sign-up form completions or emails sent to your sales teams. The second scenario could also be applied to your lead generation process (if you had one). Say for instance you had a sequence of pages that pre-qualified your visitor as a lead, you could measure that linear process in the same way as you would a shopping cart.

Rather than running through the same techniques this example will demonstrate a scenario that takes a different approach to lead generation and allows your sales force to be pro-active.

You need information about potential prospects and partners that are coming to your website so that you can pass the information onto your sales team.

Prospect Gathering

This example focuses around a geographic location. The company in question (Satama) wanted to be able to see potential prospects in the greater London area for an event they were participating in there.

A number of web analytics tools will show the companies that look at websites based on the network used to find your website. This is something that Google Analytics and a local Finnish vendor Snoobi does very well.

There are a number of things you have to take into account.

1. Firstly you cannot identify the individual from the company. It's impossible to know unless the individual volunteers the information. It's also in most countries illegal to track personally identifiable information. However it's perfectly legal to look at which companies have visited your website.

2. The second thing you should know is that you will get a number of visitors that use a telecom, internet service provider (ISP) or broadband network provider to get to your site. The information you get about these networks is largely useless because the visitor could be from any company that uses for instance BT or NTL in the UK as their Internet service provider. The ones that are more interesting are the non-ISP network names, either company names or direct IP addresses.

Technique

In Google Analytics you enter your date range (in this case the last month), look for visitors, click on Map overlay and select the visitors that came from the City of London. Then you click on a feature called segment and drill down till you find network location.

The report Google returns to you is essentially a list of network names that have come from London to your site in the past month. This list needs filtering. You need to extract the results into Excel and delete all the network addresses that were obviously telecoms or ISPs.

Then you use the Google Search engine to look up the network location name to find the web addresses. The procedure took me about an hour. The following list was the result of my efforts.

On the left you have the list of non-ISP network locations.

Network Location name	WebSite	Potential	Search
design council	http://www.design-council.org.uk/	Partner	London Design Council
mckinsey & company inc.	http://www.mckinsey.com/locations/ukireland/index.aspx	Partner/Competitor	McKinsey & Company London
london school of economics and political science	http://www.lse.ac.uk/	Supplier	London School of economics and political science
microsoft corp	http://www.microsoft.com/uk/about/map-london.mspx	Partner	Microsoft London

(Continued)

Network Location Name	WebSite	Potential	Search
oxford_instruments	http://www.oxinst.com/	Prospect	Oxford Instruments London
Accenture	http://www.accenture.com/Countries/UK/default.htm	Competitor	Accenture London
bovis lend lease ltd	http://www.bovislendlease.com/	Prospect	bovis lend lease ltd London
haymarket publishing	http://www.haymarket.com/home.aspx	Partner/prospect	haymarket publishing london
jc legal ltd	http://www.jclgroup.co.uk/	Supplier	JC legal London
morgan stanley group inc.	http://www.morganstanley.com/about/offices/uk.html	Prospect	morgan stanley group london
terrapinn holdings ltd	http://www.terrapinn.com/	Supplier/Prospect	terrapinn holdings ltd London

The procedure was to take the network location name, add 'London' to the text string and then search in Google. In all cases I quickly found the desired website (listed above) and could quickly work out what the company's potential was in relation to Satama.

The right hand side are the queries I used in Google. The results as you can see are quite enlightening. There were three potential partners, six potential prospects, four potential suppliers and one competitor.

Because the Google Analytics report showed network locations that came from London adding 'London' to the search term in Google was smart because in many cases the companies were corporations that had an office in London.

This information is very useful if you can combine it with CRM data and determine who might be visiting your site. It's also very useful if you're in a small business and want to make a cold call to a business that might be a potential customer.

You might want to start using this information to write your content or develop personas (see Chapter 6). Your supplier will want to know different things than your prospect, and by catering for both you could make your website much more useful to your visitors. You could use the data to segment your audiences (more in Section 5.6 on segmentation) and try to see which prospect segments are your best targets.

You have just seen a demonstration of how to do this with Google Analytics along with your own research, a manual process but worth the effort. There are vendors that specialize in getting this kind of information.

Snoobi for instance is a vendor based in Finland specifically aiming at improving the Business to Business lead generation of its customers. Snoobi learns as you tell it which IP addresses are ISPs so that you can automatically filter these out, and ties into a CRM database suggesting people you know in the organization that you might want to contact. In usage they are just behind Google Analytics in Finland having over 3000 customers, so it just goes to show that this service alone is very useful to many small businesses for a variety of reasons.

Pekka Koskinen CTO of Snoobi

With lead generation, you have to know more than just that an organization has visited. Snoobi shows the full navigation path including search phrases so the user can instantly see what the visitor has looked for and flags people you might want to call.

http://www.snoobi.com/

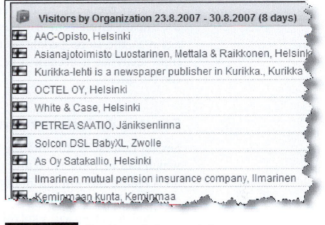

FIGURE 4.6 *Snoobi organization snapshot*

As you can see from Figure 4.6 a list of company names appears depending on which companies have visited your website. By determining what companies are looking for and what each company has done on your website you can flag actions in your CRM system so that sales people know what potential customers are looking for.

Scenario 3: Summary

By treating your website as a direct lead generation tool and finding out who your prospects are by using web analytics tools you can plan in various wins for your business.

This scenario illustrates how from analytics data you can find potential customers, customers you may have not even have thought of contacting. What's more by finding out which pages they were interested in, examining points of resolution you might need to improve, items they downloaded and items they didn't, you can begin to think about what your website requires in terms of content. It also indicates interest groups that you could segment (see Chapter 5) and follow specifically.

Follow the win planning process. Determine how many companies currently visit your website regularly and determine the potential wins to your business.

Inform the sales people or customer teams and package the information (based on your pre-study) as what you could potentially achieve.

Make it easy to understand. Fifty company names and their product/service interest by the end of the month is easy to understand. Once you have agreed then simply gather the data and communicate your win to the stakeholders, actors and leaders. Communicate with all the relevant spokes, put it on your intranet and send out newsletters reporting on the success.

If after the leads are delivered one of the sales people closes a deal with a company from your list then you should communicate the win all over again to the same people so that they know, not only did the lead come from analytics it became a deal, meaning that the tools have real value to the business.

Scenario 4: Customer Service

Saving money by automating customer service on a website is something which can be monetized and optimized very easily. What you're looking to do is reduce the amount of man hours spent in answering customer queries and complaints.

This scenario will explain a case study of how to begin that process, how to prove firstly whether your current systems are doing a good job and secondly if they could be doing better, what you have to do to improve things.

You have some work to do which has nothing to do with web analytics and more to do with investigating your internal costs. You should monetize everything at every opportunity but particularly with customer service costs. This will help give you an edge when talking to people who aren't interested in understanding web analytics but are interested in how to improve the business finances.

The next case study illustrates firstly finding the gain and secondly communicating this to the people that need to know.

The company in this illustration is a client which manufactures measurement instruments for a wide variety of industries, for instance, weather monitoring systems, laser machines to measure cloud density for airports around the world and oil temperature gauges for use in large engines like ships. Their website is primarily designed to be a business to business lead generation website but is also there to provide information to their business customers and be the first point of reference for support queries.

The Pre-Study

Before looking at the online numbers the company determined that on a weekly basis the costs of after sales queries was €100,000 a week.

By calculating the time that was used by staff answering the phone and multiplying that by the hourly rate we worked out the value. This monetized the cost situation.

Firstly they looked up how many customer service queries were requested from the website, and how many of these queries were actually completed. In proportion to the amount of total visitors to the site the number of visitors finding the pages there to help them was quite low. Unfortunately from all the visitors that arrived to the landing page only 0.5% of the visitors found the page designed to help answer their questions and put them through to aftersales.

It is a fair to assume that an average customer will seek assistance from the home page to find help, advice or information. Upon examining the website homepage there was very little mention of technical support (one tiny link in the bottom right hand corner). The site directed people to two major sections called Industrial Instruments and Weather Measurement, which are the two main places that information can be found about their products, the third section is Corporate Information.

When doing the heuristic test (walking in the shoes of this company's customer) with the task in mind of 'looking to get support' I'd be looking for a customer support centre. I couldn't find anything at first. This could be why the click through was so low because customers either didn't see the link then went to the contact points, clearly labelled in the menu, or they mistakenly went to the industrial instruments or weather measurement sections to seek further information.

On click through to technical support Figure 4.7 shows the page you were presented with;

This form had too much complexity for the average visitor who wanted to get help. It was long and it had lots of questions even the customer may or may not know the answer to. Not many people go to a website knowing their customer number, this form seemed to expect everything from serial numbers of the products purchased to the customer's invoice number.

The first finding from the analytics was the 0.5% click through to this form.

This second finding was that over 95% of those visitors were not happy with this support page including the form and either left immediately, went back to the homepage or sought answers elsewhere in the site.

At this point you have your potential 'win'. If you want to encourage people to use this support section and fill in this form it should be very easy to optimize firstly the click through to this page and secondly make the form less complex. The pre-study is now complete and you are nearly ready to go back to the stakeholders with your ideas about improving this part of the website and proving the win with web analytics.

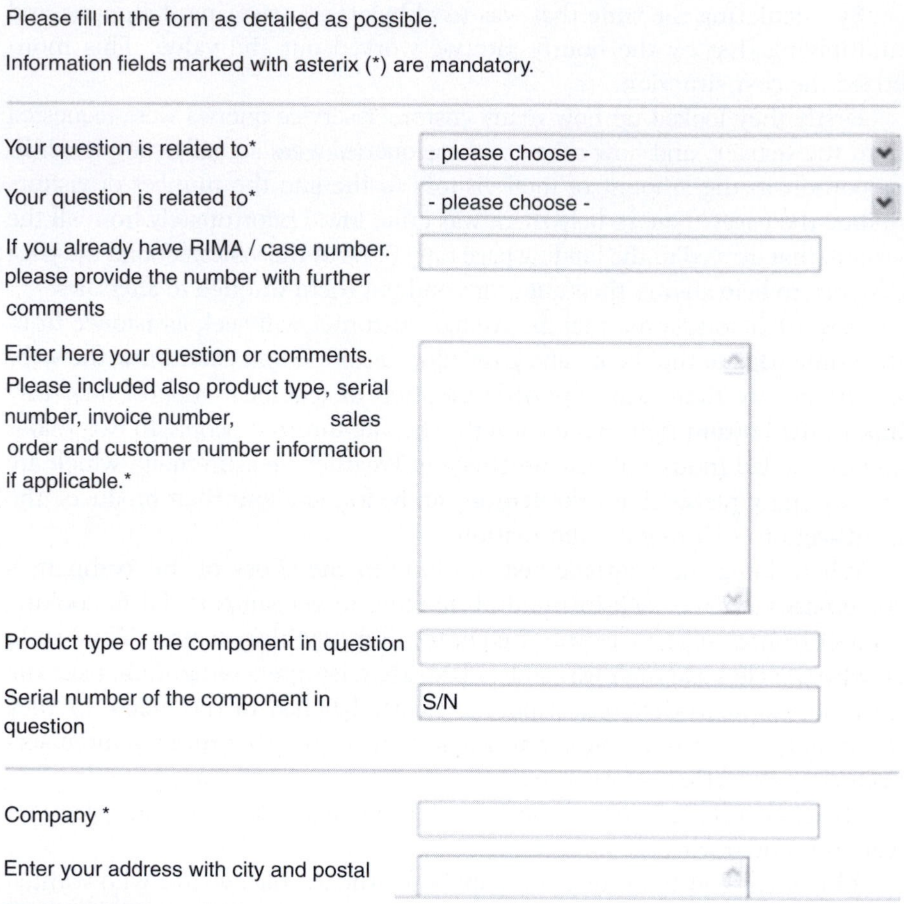

Please fill int the form as detailed as possible.

Information fields marked with asterix (*) are mandatory.

Your question is related to*   - please choose - ▾

Your question is related to*   - please choose - ▾

If you already have RIMA / case number.
please provide the number with further
comments

Enter here your question or comments.
Please included also product type, serial
number, invoice number,   sales
order and customer number information
if applicable.*

Product type of the component in question

Serial number of the component in
question   S/N

Company *

Enter your address with city and postal

FIGURE 4.7 *Complex form*

Design the Win

Pick the key stakeholders and say, 'we're only servicing 0.125% of our total visitors from our support section. Currently we're paying €100,000 a week to service our support requests. I think we can considerably reduce these figures by using the online channel as one of our key support centres.'

1. Urgency – It costs €100,000 a week.

2. Led top down – The key stakeholders might be the customer care spoke.

3. Vision – Create a win situation for the customer care spoke.

4. Communication – Cost saving per week can lead to huge savings per year (which can be easily communicated once they're realized).

5. Actionable – You've already looked at the figures and know they can be improved with better usability.

6. Win – The win is designed.

To actually follow this through a test should be carried out in phases. First test the help section clicks by making the customer support links much more prominent, perhaps with an accompanying support image such as an image of someone wearing an earpiece and mike typical of those seen in telesales. Does this raise from 0.5% of total clicks to the technical support section? Does the clearer message help you encourage more visitors to seek out advice (which is one of the site goals)?

The second phase would then to be to improve the online help form to something that didn't require human interaction but answers the customer's questions and as a last resort allow the visitor to get the online help required via perhaps an online chat feature. Again this is easily monetized into actual cost saving.

Communicate the Win

Once the tests show the results (which with those figures they can't really fail to) go back to the spoke and let them deliver the good news throughout the company. The hub will always be involved in the discovery but remember to always let the people running the business spoke take the credit. The people in the hub are often the ones that do a lot of the work in the beginning but in order for the culture to thrive everyone needs to see some insights and gain some understanding. In the early days the hub needs to provide a lot of wins like this to help the spokes get enthusiastic about analytics. Once each spoke has gained something and defined good KPIs many more questions will come from the spokes and that is what the hub should be looking for.

Scenario 4: Summary

Knowing how to optimize and what actions to make is really what KPIs are designed for. Taking action in this case was not a clear cut decision, it's easy to say change the front page of a website, but not easy to do. By testing and experimenting with the options **you learn what works and what needs to be improved.**

In order to develop quick wins you need someone who is qualified in using the tools. This is what the next chapter is all about.

CHAPTER 5

Tools of the Trade

I'd rather be a hammer than a nail, yes I would, if I only could, I surely would.
Simon and Garfunkel

CHAPTER CONTENTS

5.1 DATA

In this chapter you'll learn about the different types of data available, tools that process the data, how to select a tool that best fits your needs, learning how to establish a quality assurance process internally and last but perhaps most importantly how to segment your data to gain more insights.

In the introduction to this book you saw the process of factors involved in driving the cultural change required to make your company a data driven one (Figure 5.1).

FIGURE 5.1 *The cultural change process*

Data in this process is the underlying arrow driving change. If you don't have the data you don't have anything to show anyone. It may sound obvious to you reading this book having gone through the first four chapters, however without good quality consistent data you have no ammunition to change the thought processes of the people in the organization.

Good quality data is not 100% accurate. The data integrity should be 100% right but not the data accuracy. Striving for data accuracy is a waste of energy because there are so many variables that can affect your numbers.

5.2 THE INSIGHT MODELS DATA TYPES

The analytics hub has tools, people and process in its core and the objective is to get insights out to the people who need it in the business spokes. The most powerful insights come when all three datasets are used (Figure 5.2).

There are three types of data you should use in effective web analytics. Later in this book (see Chapter 7, the Insight model) you'll see how you can combine the three data types and develop an internal process to use the information you get to the maximum effect.

The first type is quantitative data measured automatically by analytics tools and is purely behavioural. This is often called **clickstream data**, outcomes data or visitor logs and is traditionally what web analytics has always been about.

Then there is data that comes directly from the **experiences** that the customer or prospect have about your offer, because of this it is also known as voice of customer data or attitudinal data.

The third data type is **competitive** data, where you rely on panel or ISPs to provide data about how well you're doing in comparison to your competition.

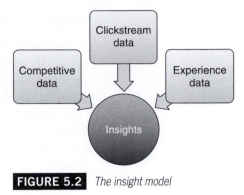

FIGURE 5.2   *The insight model*

The most powerful way of doing web analytics comes from combining these three data sources. Clickstream data will help you understand 'what' is going on in terms of visitor clicks, customer behaviour and task completion rates. Experience data will give insights into why your visitors have done things in the way they have which is also extremely valuable. Competitive data will give you an idea of where you stand and help you plan for the future.

Clickstream Data

Measuring quantitative clickstream data and trying to make sense out of it all is the challenge we face. This is why we have models like REAN (see Chapter 2) that can help considerably in planning mechanisms to capture data.

Clickstream data **in terms of reach** is finding out what the best source of traffic is by volume or cost. It's about the numbers of visits or visitors that find your site.

In terms of **engagement** it's how the visitors behave, what processes they complete, what processes they abandon, how they interact with your website, how long they stay with you.

But just having them arrive and interact with you is not the point. You want them to **activate**, convert, to do something (see Chapter 3, KPIs), so you measure the outcomes, the conversions of each reach source as well and start to make choices based on how the visitors behave.

In terms of seeing how you're **nurturing** your customers the clickstream data you're looking for is where your customers purchase a second and third time. It's about measuring how your audience consumes more of your products or services and predicting when you should *react* or be *proactive* in your contact with them.

Experience Data

As previously mentioned web analytics will tell you what people have done but it will never tell you **why they have done it**. One of the key differentiators between a very good analyst and an average analyst is the ability to find out why. When encountered with data that has deviated from normal levels a great analyst will investigate more deeply to try and find the route cause of the deviation. In many cases a great analyst can take actions based only on quantitative web analytics data and one type of experience data – heuristic testing.

> **Avinash Kaushik (http://www.kaushik.net/avinash/) on Qualitative Data**
>
> Combining the What (quantitative) with the Why (qualitative) will provide a company with a long-term strategic competitive advantage.

Experience Data – Heuristic Testing

Heuristic testing requires that you put yourself into the mind of the visitor who is on your website and take an objective look at how difficult it is to complete a given task. I've shown a couple of examples of heuristic testing already in Chapter 4. See also Chapter 6, defining a persona, for more information on getting into character. By looking at web analytics data you will be able to see where people are leaving the site, for instance the top exit points in process funnels, top exit rates on pages or high bounce rates.

Then by putting yourself into the mindset of the prospect or customer and following their click through process online (especially at the exit points) you may gain some insight into why they leave. Heuristic testing can give you excellent insight, especially if you have usability best practice knowledge and can combine that with what you've seen in your web analytics tool.

For example a typical heuristic test might be run on a shopping cart that had a high abandonment rate at a certain point. You go to the point where the visitor trend shows they have been having problems and do a heuristic test on a typical visitor's motivation around that point. It may be that by doing so you find a difficulty with the website that you previously did not know about, such as a problem with the checkout procedure for visitors using FireFox for example.

Experience Data – Survey Data

Another very valuable form of data is survey data. There are three forms of web survey data you can take advantage of.

Customer surveys (post-activation survey) – Typically a customer survey is carried out from customers who have bought one of your products or services. Surveys of this kind usually focus around the product or service, the level of satisfaction and the quality of the customers' experience. The information from this data can be used in product strategy and website design.

Visitor surveys (pre-activation survey) – Typically a survey is placed at strategic points on the website with an incentive for the visitor to complete a short questionnaire. Surveys of this kind usually focus on finding out how the visitor finds the site, how easy it is to complete tasks and what else the website could do to cater more effectively to the visitor.

Exit surveys (point of disengagement survey) – Similar to the visitor survey except that typically the survey is launched when the person leaves the website. Exit surveys are particularly useful to troubleshoot high abandonment points on the website. You're looking for trends that occur among the visitors who answer the questions to try and pinpoint root causes of abandonment.

A great free tool for visitor surveys is 4Q from iPerceptions (http://4q. iperceptions.com/).

Experience Data – Lab Usability Data

Often called usability studies this is where you have perfect conditions to observe what people do when they visit your website. For instance you can give participants a task to complete and ask them to go to a specially monitored PC where they try to complete the task at hand.

Their eye movements, hand movements, mouse movements, keystrokes and clicks are all recorded to be analysed later. This method can give you extremely valuable insights about how people do things on your website. Again you're looking for common trends from different participants so that you can pick up a common way that people generally look for things on the site you're studying.

In essence experience data is any data you gather which gives you ideas about why visitors or customers do things. Surveys, usability testing, eye tracking tests, heuristic analysis and interviews are all types of experience data.

Competitive Data

Neil Mason of Applied Insights (http://www.applied-insights.co.uk/) once said in his column on ClickZ (http://www.clickz.com):

Although growth is good, it isn't good enough. And that's the point. When markets are generally still growing organically, as they are in Europe, how do you know when good is good enough and that you're maximizing potential? By tracking what the market is doing and benchmarking against your competitors.

As Neil suggests growth alone is good, but alone not good enough. What happens if you grow at 15% but your competition grows at 25%? You'll soon find yourself being left behind.

You should also consider the data gathered by independent companies like Forrester, eMarketer, Marketing Sherpa and e-Consultancy who actually serve their customers by benchmarking best practices such as web analytics.

Forrester wave in Q3 2007(http://www.forrester.com/Research/Document/ Excerpt/0,7211,41242,00.html) compared eight products across 127 criteria using an excellent scoring method which was very well researched and fair across all the vendors. This kind of information is available for other industries too.

To look directly at your competition and compare yourself across different things you should concentrate on the five main types of competitive data you can find: search data, panel data, ASP data, ISP data and finally blog data.

Google Data (Google Analytics is also ASP Data)

Google Analytics has a free competitive benchmarking service if you opt in to their service. The benchmark will allow you to look at related industry websites with a similar amount of traffic and see if you're doing better or worse than they are.

Figure 5.3 shows the typical benchmark reports. The thin line slightly above the thicker line shows the average benchmark value for this statistic on sites of a similar size in a similar industry. The thicker line (which in Google Analytics' interface is blue) shows the actual number you achieved. You can get benchmark data for visits, page views, bounce rate, page views per visit, average time on site and percentage of new visits.

When using this data you must bear in mind that it's only opt-in data which does not give you an accurate picture and you can't view yourself head to head with your competition. Only those that have opted in to

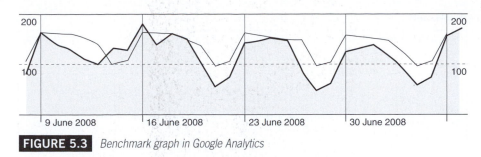

FIGURE 5.3 *Benchmark graph in Google Analytics*

receive the reports can get the benchmark view. Google readily admits any-where between hundreds and thousands of sites participate per category so it's certainly not the full story, but that is still a lot of visitors.

Google Trends (http://trends.google.com/trends)

Also from Google is the service Google Trends. Unlike Google Analytics this does allow you to see a bit more about your competitors. It shows how many people have used Google to get to the website that you type into the Google Search engine. For instance Nokia and Motorola are competitors in certain sectors of their vast markets. The data you see in Figure 5.4 and as in Figure 5.5 overleaf shows two search results from Google Trends and shows that Nokia is outperforming Motorola in the amount of visitors it is receiving by almost 2 to 1. It doesn't take a genius to figure out something happened around Nokia in mid 2007 where there was a notable peak. A quick search in trends revealed that Nokia had to recall 43 million faulty batteries and a lot of searches resulted in visits to Nokia.com in August 2007 – the date of the spike.

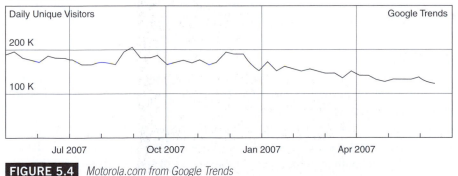

FIGURE 5.4 *Motorola.com from Google Trends*

Google Trends will also show you details about search terms you may want to know about. For instance in the case of the above two competi-tors it might be interesting to know how many searches for mobile phone have been made and what headlines effected the searches around those

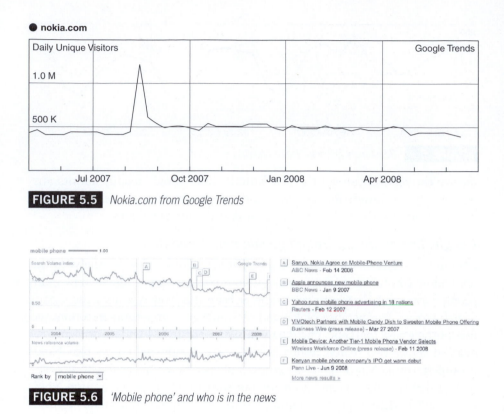

FIGURE 5.5 *Nokia.com from Google Trends*

FIGURE 5.6 *'Mobile phone' and who is in the news*

terms. The articles listed on the right in Figure 5.6 correspond with the flags you can see raised at the various peaks. It's bad news for both Nokia and Motorola here. Yahoo!, Sanyo and Apple are all mentioned but there is no mention of either Nokia or Motorola.

Panel Data

Panel data is collected from visitors who join a panel thus allowing vendors to track their movements across the Internet. This clickstream data is collected in a variety of ways (Figure 5.7).

Compete.com is a form of (largely) panel based data though they do use other ways to collect and compile their data as shown in Figure 5.7. Panels also consist of toolbars which people download to use on their browser software (Compete and Alexa for instance). Also shown in this figure is ASP (Application Service Provider) and ISP (Internet Service Provider). The ASP is typically a company that will ask a participating website to be part of its panel by inserting Javascript code on its pages. An ISP usually has an agreement with a partner (like Hitwise) to supply the vendor with anonymous aggregated data to track trends.

U.S. Clickstream Panel Comparision	Complete.com	Alexa	comScore Media Metrix 2.0	Hitwise	Nielsen//NetRatings
Active Monthly Sample*	2,000,000+	Undisclosed	120,000	Undisclosed	Undisclosed
U.S Distinguished from International Usage	Yes	No	Yes	Yes	Yes
Clickstream Data Sources	Compete Toolbar, Opt-in Panels, ISPS, ASPs	Alexa Toolbar	Opt-in Panels ASPs	ISPs	Opt-in Panels
Normalized	Yes	No	Yes	Yes	Yes
People Estimates	Yes	No	Yes	No	No

* Defined as the number of unique panelists who transmitted a clickstream event in the last calendar month

FIGURE 5.7 *Sample sizes and data sources (courtesy of compete.com)*

People Count

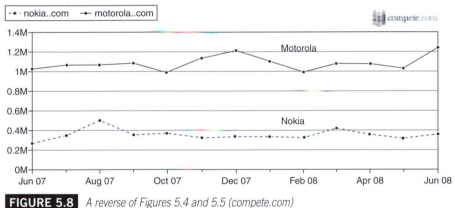

FIGURE 5.8 *A reverse of Figures 5.4 and 5.5 (compete.com)*

Compete (.com)

Compete allows you to compare yourself and your competition against each other in a similar way to Google. Running this test against the same sample as before (Nokia and Motorola) shows you a potential pitfall of relying on panel data (Figure 5.8).

As seen earlier (Figures 5.4 and 5.5), Google was suggesting that Nokia had close to 500,000 unique visitors per day and that Motorola had closer to 200,000 per day. This graph is showing that monthly Motorola have a much higher visitor count.

The question then is can the figures be believed?

What you have to remember is that compete.com is primarily a US centric tool and the Motorola brand is much more popular in the USA than it is in Europe. The figures at compete.com *probably* reflect that Motorola has a much stronger brand in the USA than Europe and therefore more of the 2 million strong panel visit Motorola rather than visit Nokia.

Competitive data like this is something I would classify as 'high risk data' which we'll talk about later in this chapter. It might be useful to know, but business decisions shouldn't be taken on it alone without acknowledgement that there is a risk the data will not be correct because it can't be validated (unless of course the vendor can guarantee the data quality).

This is still however valuable information for the marketing manager of Nokia trying to increase market awareness in the USA. Compete.com does offer paid services which are more globally focused, however all panels will have a tendency to reflect the popularity of the brands in the minds of their panelists.

Alexa (http://www.alexa.com)

Alexa is another largely US centric free panel based system offering a similar kind of service to compete.com. Alexa is an Amazon service so the panel is globally offered though there is a big US bias, especially on smaller sites nearer the bottom of the top 100,000 sites in the Alexa list.

Looking at the data as in Figure 5.9 overleaf though, the situation seems to suggest that Google's data was closer to the truth with Nokia having more than double the reach of Motorola.

Comscore

Comscore is another notable company in the panel space but offering a much more tailored service at a much higher premium. For instance our telecommunications giants (Nokia and Motorola) might be very interested in the following excerpt taken from the comscore website:

Telecommunication Solutions (http://www.comscore.com)

The Internet has quickly become an integral marketing, sales, and service channel for the telecommunications industry. comScore provides the data to help drive business decisions and optimize online and offline channel strategies in these critical areas:

- Online bill pay and customer service conversion
- Consumer segmentation and profiling
- Marketing tactics
- E-commerce strategies
- Competitive benchmarking

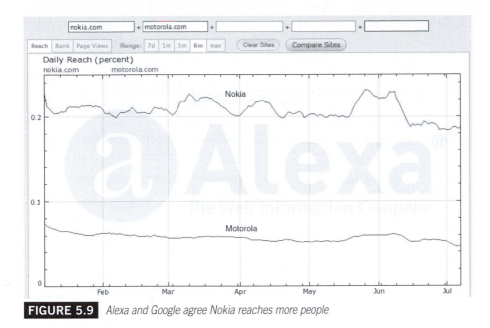

FIGURE 5.9 *Alexa and Google agree Nokia reaches more people*

ASP data

Application Service Providers are vendors which ask participating website owners to 'tag' their websites so that data can be collated and compared. Google Analytics benchmarking service is an ASP service using a panel of opt-in websites. In Finland TNS Metrix is one such service run by TNS Gallup.

TNS Gallup (http://www.gallupweb.com/tnsmetrix/)

This site is very popular in Finland with publishers and advertisers because it gives an unbiased and fair view of how many visitors each major media website in Finland gets. Just about every media player of note is on the TNS list meaning the site is very well visited by advertisers and often quoted and published by the media companies.

Figure 5.10 shows the top ten in Finland on week 27 (*viikko* is Finnish for week). The analysts among you will notice that all the figures are going down. There is a simple reason for this. In Finland that week signalled the beginning of July when the summer holiday period begins. Simply put Finland all but shuts down in July and the trend is reflected by the drop in numbers.

SUOMEN WEB-SIVUSTOJEN VIIKKOLUVUT
(WEEKLY SITE RANKINGS)

| Liity TNS Metrix-mittaukseen | | TNS Gallupin online-mittaus ja yksityisyyden suoja | | Vanha tulospalvelu |

Viikkoluvut

Viikko: 2008/27 ▼   Kategoria: –Kaikki–   ▼

		Site	Browsers	Browsers%	Sess	Sess%	PI	PI%	PI/Sess
1	±	Ilta-Sanomat	1233072	-5,2↓	6205530	-8,9↓	26793246	-4,7↓	5,0
2	±	Iltalehti	1215362	-8,3↓	6078672	-12,4↓	35008205	-10,4↓	5,0
3	±	MTV3	1128029	-2,9↓	5147589	-13,1↓	34325368	-4,0↓	4,6
4	±	Suomi24.fi	1053579	-7,8↓	4022922	-17,4↓	60915805	-6,0↓	3,8
5		MSN/Windows Live Messenger	939513	-2,3↓	5909680	-5,4↓	8042994	-7,0↓	6,3
6	±	Helsingin Sanomat	859400	-4,3↓	2934255	-8,8↓	12684924	-5,4↓	3,4
7		YLE	781036	-9,7↓	2783486	-15,7↓	18009777	-3,2↓	3,6
8		MSN.fi	772761	-1,4↓	3646000	-5,0↓	8332763	-4,9↓	4,7
9	±	IRC-Galleria	765369	-1,5↓	5260736	-11,1↓	292545339	1,0↑	6,9
10		Eniro.fi	537558	-7,5↓	1068893	-15,5↓	9006987	-9,0↓	2,0

FIGURE 5.10   *TNS Gallup weekly site rankings*

Fireclick®
A DIGITAL RIVER COMPANY

Top Line Growth | Fashion and Apparel | Electronics | Catalog | Specialty | Outdoor and Sports | Software

Fireclick, an industry leading provider of web analytics services, is proud to introduce the world's first publicly-available web analytics benchmark index. The Fireclick Index provides an objective comparison of key metrics across a variety of segments. Compare the performance of your online business to the many successful industry leading web sites using Fireclick today!

Top Line Growth

Business Metrics	This Week	Last Week	% Change
Conversion Rate: Global	2.10%	2.20%	-5% ▼
Conversion Rate: First Time Visitors	1.90%	1.90%	0%
Conversion Rate: Repeat Visitors	2.40%	2.60%	-8% ▼
Cart Abandonment Rate	74.50%	75.10%	-1% ▼

Global Conversion Rate
Last 7 Days

T F S S M T W
7d 30d 6mo 1yr

FIGURE 5.11   *Fireclick index*

Fireclick Index (http://index.fireclick.com)

FireClick is another ASP based solution (Figure 5.11). It's actually a web analytics tool that aggregates its data and publishes it publicly. Again not perfect because you're relying on a small sample size with the majority of the geographical distribution of visitors from the USA.

Quantcast

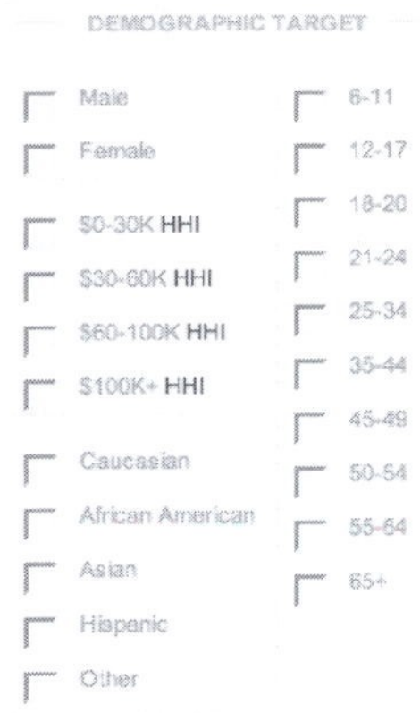

DEMOGRAPHIC TARGET

☐ Male   ☐ 6-11
☐ Female   ☐ 12-17
☐ $0-30K HHI   ☐ 18-20
☐ $30-60K HHI   ☐ 21-24
☐ $60-100K HHI   ☐ 25-34
☐ $100K+ HHI   ☐ 35-44
    ☐ 45-49
☐ Caucasian   ☐ 50-54
☐ African American   ☐ 55-64
☐ Asian   ☐ 65+
☐ Hispanic
☐ Other

FIGURE 5.12

Quantcast demographic filters

Adam Gerber CMO of Quantcast in an Interview with Shane Atchinson (Clickz) (http://www.clickz.com/showPage.html? page = 3630165)

We don't put ourselves in the web analytics space. Web analytics has been about understanding your own site traffic characteristics.

Notice I used the term 'traffic', which to me is about the 'what', not audience, which is much more about the 'who'.

Web analytics solutions are terrific because they give you a directly measured view of traffic flow, metrics tied to abandonment, content trends, merchandizing performance, etc. Analytics services up until now have been internal solutions. They are generally silo implementations that don't allow for Internet-wide models to be built (in aggregate form).

We are about audience measurement and activation.

Quantcast is a free service with data coming from mainly ASP sources but also part panel data (Figure 5.12). The interesting part about this solution is the amount of data it is gathering, with, according to Adam Gerber (CMO of Quantcast), over 10 million web properties now running adopting their technology.

With the user base that 10 million (and growing) web properties will attract this could soon be a very powerful free source of competitive data.

Hitwise – ISP Data

The best example of ISP data is HitWise which has deals with many of the worlds largest ISPs to process aggregate data from subscriber web browsing behaviour. The advantage is that HitWise can tie in demographic data and, like Comscore, bring far better tailored services to large enterprises. However, the big advantage is that because of the nature of ISPs the sample size is huge with a reputed 25 million users providing data (as of December 2006).

Going back to the Nokia/Motorola example look at Figure 5.13.

11 April, 2007 (http://weblogs.hitwise.com/to-go-uk/2007/04/ nokia_n95_leaves_competitors_i.html): Nokia N95 Leaves Competitors in Dust

According to Hitwise UK, the share of UK Internet searches for 'nokia n95' more than doubled in the four weeks to 7 April. Searches for the all-in-one handset were more than five times those for the next most popular handset online, 'samsung d900' last week.

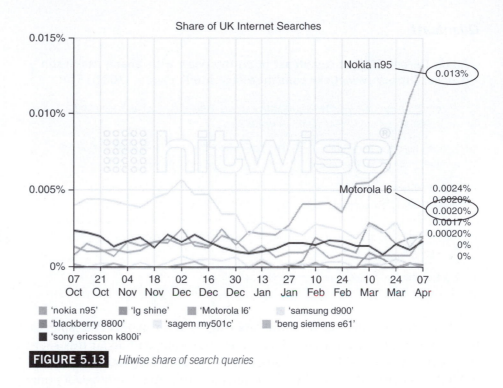

FIGURE 5.13 *Hitwise share of search queries*

Blog and Social Media Competitive Data

There are a number of free and paid blog tools which can gather competitive data for you.

BlogScope (http://blogscope.net/)

BlogScope is an analysis and visualization tool for blogosphere which is being developed as part of a research project at the University of Toronto. It is currently tracking over 28 million blogs with 396 million posts. BlogScope can assist the user in discovering interesting information from these millions of blogs via a set of numerous unique features including popularity curves, identification of information bursts, related terms and geographical search.

Going back to our Nokia/Motorola example refer to Figure 5.14.

BlogScope finds all the keywords used in blogs and trends them. As shown above you can also compare companies (and of course products/brands) against each other.

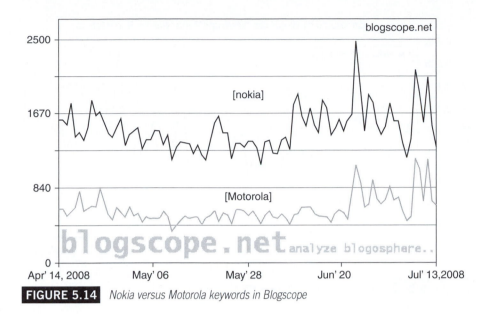

FIGURE 5.14 *Nokia versus Motorola keywords in Blogscope*

BlogPulse

BlogPulse is another tool with a similar function that shows a similar result.

> **BlogPulse (http://www.blogpulse.com/)**
>
> BlogPulse is an automated trend discovery system for blogs. Blogs, a term that is short for weblogs, represent the fastest-growing medium of personal publishing and the newest method of individual expression and opinion on the Internet. BlogPulse applies machine-learning and natural-language processing techniques to discover trends in the highly dynamic world of blogs. BlogPulse is brought to you by Nielsen BuzzMetrics.

As you can see competitive data is very valuable (Figure 5.15) and when multiple sources are used conclusions can be drawn. Everything we've seen here in the Nokia/Motorola example suggests that the Nokia brand is more successful than Motorola's brand. The only exception was Compete.com, a largely US panel based system (at the time of writing).

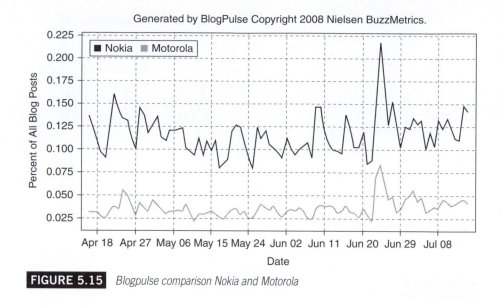

FIGURE 5.15　*Blogpulse comparison Nokia and Motorola*

The general data is maybe not so valuable as the specific information about products, services and brands, Nokia and Motorola were used to illustrate the point. How we go about combining the data sources to drive insights is shown in Chapter 7.

5.3 DATA COLLECTION METHODS

All web analytics tools have a method to track the visitor. It's important to understand the different types of data collection and understand the main differences between the collection methods.

Beacons

Beacons are usually invisible 1 × 1 pixels that are embedded into the pages you want to track. Email marketers often use them to track when an email has been opened and ad serving networks use them to track campaigns across multiple websites. The way the technology works is that when an email or web page is opened by the visitor the web server sending the page back to your visitors browser also sends a 'get request' to a third party server (the ad network vendor tracking the activity for instance). As the page loads it executes the request for the image. This then sends anony-mous data about the page view back to the vendor.

The disadvantage with using this kind of tracking is if the client soft-ware, i.e. the web browser or email program, has images turned off. If the image requests are turned off then you can't collect the data. Beacons also have to work with third party ad networks (or email providers) that can mean the third party cookie is used to identify the anonymous visit as a new or returning visit. Third party cookies are often blocked by spyware and adware software on the visitor's browser meaning the solution may not track all visits.

Tags/Javascript

Javascript tagging is one of the most popular ways to measure website traf-fic. The website being tracked has Javascript code inserted on every page. The Javascript (when loaded by the visitor) assigns each visitor a cookie and sends the information about the visitor and visitor session to a collection server. The technique does not record any personal data about the visitor, it just uses the cookie as an identifier so that if the visitor comes back they can be classed as a repeat visitor rather than a new visitor. If the visitor has cookies disabled then the tracking will only record the visit information in most cases (some systems also revert to visitor IP address and browser ver-sion if a cookie is not available – though this has questionable repeat visit accuracy).

The main disadvantage of tag based solutions is the fact that you have to tag every page you want to track. On an enterprise level when multiple implementation vendors are involved controlling the tagging quality can become challenging.

Logs

Site logs were the first method of tracking on-site behaviour and were origi-nally designed for technical reasons. Logs are records of all requests made to the web server. When a visitor visits a page the request is logged to the server. Unique visitors are typically identified by the IP address and header of the visitor but some more advanced versions like WebTrends also assign a cookie to the visitor for greater accuracy.

Unfortunately the log files also record all other requests to the server which can include search engine crawlers and email harvesters (programs crawling the web designed to gather email addresses), and because many solutions use the IP address to identify the visitor the number is consistently inflated. IP addresses are often dynamically changed by Internet service providers (sometimes even in the same session), meaning a repeat visitor to your site could be logged as two visitors (or three or ten depending on how often he/she logs out from the ISP and is assigned a new IP address).

For this reason the standard has shifted from log files to Javascript tagging despite the tagging issues.

Packet Sniffers

An alternative solution to tags and logs is the network sniffer. Hardware and software is installed on the web servers that capture all the network traffic. Traffic is identified by cookies and very light Javascript tagging is required to capture information such as which links are clicked in the browser or flash events. However the main bulk of the tracking is done at the network level. This is a good alternative for large enterprises as the tagging problem is less of a challenge.

The disadvantage is cost in terms of implementation and price. The network sniffing solution is typically more expensive than tagging both to purchase and implement, though savings in the longer term can be made by having less tag maintenance. You also need to be careful on privacy with packet sniffing. Configuration should mean that no personally identifiable information (PII) is passed or you could be breaking the law.

Best Practice

Generally speaking log files do not provide optimal accuracy without a lot of work and processes. Therefore I would avoid them unless there is a very good reason. Beacons have their uses for email and advertising purposes but still aren't ideal because of the image problem. The best practice at the moment is Javascript and cookies or the packet sniffing with light Javascript to track rich internet applications and overcome caching problems.

What the best practice is for your company brings to mind my favorite quote from Jim Sterne:

The Consultants favorite answer "It depends".

It does depend deeply on your business requirements.

Rather than go into the pros and cons of each paid vendor I decided to simply tell you what questions to ask and try to explain what you should look out for if you're going to select a tool.

5.4 ANALYTICS TOOL SELECTION

When selecting a web analytics tool business needs should be taken into account and it's why you should define what you want to measure before getting a system implemented.

Tool Awareness Recommendation

You might want to think about using free tools (such as Google Analytics, Google adwords optimizer, Microsoft Adcenter Analytics and IndexTools from Yahoo!) if there is the need to prove to your people the benefits of web analytics.

Using free tools means the analytics hub in the organization know what is possible and it gives them a benchmark for future selection. A tool selection phase should only happen when the business knows what it wants to measure and knows the free vendor offerings are not up to the task. I have purposely not listed the paid tools and tried to compare them. It is simply not feasible without knowing your business model.

For the record the paid vendors I would recommend looking at in Europe are, at the time of writing, in this order:

Omniture (http://www.omniture.com/)

Unica (http://www.unica.com/)

CoreMetrics (http://www.coremetrics.com/)

SAS (http://www.sas.com/)

WebTrends (http://www.webtrends.com/)

If you do speak to the vendors above then might help you to find out who you want to work with.

Tool Selection – Questions to Ask Your Vendor

Questions to ask your vendor are summarized in Figures 5.16–5.19.

Tool Selection - questions to ask your vendor

1) Data collection and storage	Questions to ask your vendor or consultant	The following considerations should be taken into account about how the product handles data sources	
Data collection sources	How many methods does the product use to collect clickstream data?	Data sources: - Web server log files - Web server plug-ins - Web Beacons - Page tags - Network sniffer - API to insert data directly - Other client-side approach - Other server-side approach	Generally the more ways the product has to handle data collection the better. It means the tool has the ability to be customized with other external data sources allowing you to combine offline data for instance. That means more of your business questions can be answered by the tool
Hybrid data collection	Can the product collect and merge data from multiple sources simultaneously?	No ability? Handled as a custom case? This might be important for websites which for instance need to combine site logs with data from tags in order to know when search engine spiders access a website for instance but the primary collection method is page tagging (which doesn't track spiders)	
Rich-client tracking	Can the product track Flash and other rich-client applications? How is this handled?	Data sources: - Flash events/clicks - Video streaming - Audio streaming	Important for sites with a lot of rich media applications because collecting and reporting the data is not standard
Data warehousing	Does the product offer an option to store everything in a data warehouse? How is this option priced (incremental percentage over base CPM rate, flat fee)?	Data warehousing is important for companies that require good segmentation, good historical data and strong filtering/data mining options. It's very important to find out what the vendors charges so that you don't get any nasty surprises after signing the contract. Many add a percentage to their overall prices or add to their cost per impression basis to have the ability to use a data warehouse. Some charge a one- off flat fee. Some don't charge and have it included as part of the base offering	
Custom variables	Can the product track custom variables?	Data sources: - Custom events/tracking	Usually this is useful for all companies and most vendors handle custom variables. Find out how and what kind of things custom variables track. Ask the vendor for an example relating to your business
Data storage/ownership: summarized data	How long does the vendor keep detailed and summarized data? Who owns the data?	Less than three months realtime data? Twelve months data? Unlimited? The data used to produce reports in the product is called summarized data. Often vendors will keep a certain amount of data instantly accessible and ready to work on but will require a few days to produce historical data. Also **does the vendor own the data in their databases** or do you as the client? Google Analytics will never let you delete data as they own it	
Data storage/ownership: raw data	How long does the vendor keep raw/ unprocessed data? Who owns the data?	Less than 15 months? Unlimited/term of customer agreement (or licensed software)? Retaining raw data is necessary for some analysis such as data mining	
Data import	How can data from exitsing systems (e.g., eCommerce, CRM systems) be imported to your tool to augment customer data?	No capability? Is it a manual process requiring the vendor to customize their product? Or is it automatic and inbuilt? Importing data allows you to compare other data sources to the web data. It may not be possible with some vendors or they may need custom set-ups. Some of them can do this automatically	
Data export	How does the product export data?	Data sources/programs Basic files (CSV, tab- delimited) Excel export Excel streaming Other options?	How are expovrts handled? Is there the ability to export directly into pre-formatted Excel sheets (for KPI processes) via streaming data directly into Excel or is the data exported manually? Can scheduled exports be sent automatically?

FIGURE 5.16 *Questions to ask your vendor – data collection (courtesy Trainers' House Analytics)*

2) Data integrity and security	Questions to ask your vendor or consultant	The following considerations should be taken into account about how the product handles data integrity
Validation – installation	How is data collection validated at product installation?	No formal validation procedures or tool? Are there Informal testing procedures? Or does the vendor have an extensive procedure? How is the vendor testing the quality of the data? Most free tools only have a limited process, for instance checking if the tag is on your site. Ask the vendor what differences they have to the free tools in this respect.
Content filtering	How does your product handle traffic filtering?	Filtering enables you to, for instance, filter out internal traffic so you don't get company employees included in the traffic reports. Can the system filter data retroactively to include/eliminate unwanted sources of activity like spiders, robots, or anything else you want to take away?
Cookie support	What form of cookies does the product support? (if applicable)	No first-party cookie support? First-party cookies support at extra cost? First-party support at no extra cost? First-party cookies are less likely to be deleted by visitors. Paid vendors almost always support this but costs may be incurred
Security	How does the product/service ensure the privacy of the site visitors whose data is being collected?	In Web Analytics the privacy of the visitor should be the holy grail. What measures are in place to protect the site visitors anonymity? How does the vendor allow control of access to the data?
3) Segmentation and profiles	Questions to ask your vendor or consultant	The following considerations should be taken into account about how the product handles data segmentation
Retrospective segments	Does the product allow creation of retrospective segments?	Is it possible to set-up segments on data that is already in the database? Can you go back and look at historical data based on a segment you set-up today? Very useful for campaign analysis for instance
External segmentation	Custom segmentation based on external data sources	Can you set-up segments based on data imported from external data sources. For instance could you set-up segments based on customer data and start segmenting known visitors from opted in sources?
Segmentation costs	How many segments can the user create at no extra charge?	Vendors almost always charge extra for the service. Find out how many segments each tool allows as standard, what extra costs are involved and whether for instance you need extra features to support segmentation (like data warehousing)
Customer profiles	Does the product support the ability to create, update and share customer profiles via database access or a profile API?	Customer profiles could be set-up for instance from CRM data sources. Does the vendor allow access to an API or database to upload customer profiles to the vendor? This might be useful in later stages for testing recency and frequency models of actual customers or customer profiles

FIGURE 5.17   *Questions to ask your vendor – data integrity and segmentation (courtesy Trainers' House Analytics)*

4) Reporting	Questions to ask your vendor or consultant	The following considerations should be taken into account about how the product handles reporting
Dimensions/ correlations	How advanced is the product's support for correlating data dimensions?	For instance is it possible to cross tabulate ordr ill down on different parameters like language, geography, campaign, keyword or referrer? Howmany correlations can bemade? Is the product limited in this respect to out of the box features or is it unlimited (i.e. can you easily create your own correlations?)
Scenario analysis	How many scenarios/funnels can the user track simultaneously?	Scenarios might be things like setting up a custom funnel analysis of a shopping cart or lead generation process. Are extra costs associated with scenarios? Are there limits on numbers of scenarios you can run at any one time?
Excel interface	Can Excel-based reports be refreshed automatically when the workbook is opened?	Does it work by generating a simple XLS file generation (a new file is generated every time you want new numbers?) Or is there an API through third-party tools or an API from within Excel to the Web analytics database? The latter two are better because it means you can get trended data much faster into Excel and generate KPIs based around automatically updated Excel data. The first means cut and pasting the data into your preformatted Excel sheets to get the same result which is time consuming
Calendars	Can clients base analyses on custom calendars relative to key events like the launch of products or media campaigns?	Most tools have this on a basic level (i.e. monthly, weekly, daily) so find out if there is support for reporting in variable time periods or advanced calendar reporting
Partner integration and APIs	Does the product provide APIs to enablepartner integration and access to data?	It might be important to your business for a CRM partner or datamining partner to be able to access your raw data
Ad-hoc query capabilities	Can you query a data warehouse for ad-hoc queriesor dataexploration without vendor intervention?	If not then what is the process involved? The data warehouse is very valuable source of information and if there is the requirement to get permission to access it then you need to Know how it's done and how long it will take
Path/scenario visualization	How advanced is the product's support for scenario/clickpath data visualization?	How good is the out of the box reporting of the funnel paths in a visual graph with incoming and outgoing traffic to/out of the path steps visualized
Report visualization	How advanced is the product's report visualization?	Important that the system is well visualized and easy to follow for hub analysts but also if any access is to be allowed then it needs to be easy for the average business user
Experimental design support	What native support (i.e. not through partnerships) does the product offer for conducting and analysing designed experiments (also called A/B or split-run tests)?	Most products have the ability to compare tests. The question is dose the vendor you're working with have more than simply the ability to compare datasets? Does it have any integrated testing technology allowing you to do on the fly A/B or multivariate testing? If not can external solutions be integrated into the vendor's product?

FIGURE 5.18 *Questions to ask your vendor – reporting (courtesy Trainers' House Analytics)*

4) Reporting (continued)	Questions to ask your vendor or consultant	The following considerations should be taken into account about how the product handles repa
Search reporting (internal site-based)	How advanced are the product's capabilities for reporting on site-based search results?	If you have an onsite search engine it's a superb source of qualitative data about what your potential customers are asking for. Nearly all vendors have a way of capturing this data. Ask what and how they do it and how it is displayed. The reporting quality varies greatly from vendor to vendor
Email campaign management	Does the product have features for email campaign analysis or interfaces to third-partyemail campaign management vendors?	Almost all prospects and customers are sent emails, whether it's newsletters, sales letters, thank yoy for your custom messages, or even simply answers to questions. How does the vendor integrate email and/or CRM. How does it report on email activity out of the box?
Campaign management	Does the product have features to automate search engine marketing campaigns, affiliates and/or banner ad placements	Undoubtedly at some stage you will run a campaign, be it a search marketing campaign, affiliate program or banner ad campaign. How does the vendor handle this? Is the cost of tracking this activity included in the package you're being sold and how well visualized is this?
Benchmarking	Does the vendor offer a benchmarking service across its client base? (e.g. retail conversion rates)?	Competitive data can help you to benchmark how well you're performing against the competition. Is this part of the vendors package. If so ask to see how it's reported

FIGURE 5.18   *(Continued)*

5) Service and support	Questions to ask your vendor or consultant	The following considerations should be taken into account about how the vendor supports and consults
Technical support availability	When is live (standard service) phone technical support available? Is backup (phone or email) available for off hours?	Usually this is business hours at least. However some vendors only offer email support. Make sure you know what technical support is available
Technical support locations	Does the vendor have more than one support location for in-market support?	Is the vendor in your country? It's possible they may have sales operations in your country but do they have a network of technical support analysts available? If not do they work with partners. If so who? What are their prices? You may need their services
Technical support service levels	How do reference clients rate the vendor's technical support responsiveness?	Call the reference clients and ask them for their best and worst experiences. Ask the vendor for names and drop them an email
Training curriculum richness	How do the vendor's training courses compare to competitors?	Do the training packages come as part of the cost? Is the training technical or analysis based? How long and how detailed are the courses? You will need to know this so you can allocate time for the hub analysts to train with the tool
Consulting/professional services	How robust is the vendor's professional services offering?	It may be that the vendor only has professional services in certain countries. If they don't consult around the tool do they work with agencies that do? Can they recommend any and what are their prices? You may need their services especially in the early stages

 FIGURE 5.19   *Questions to ask your vendor – service and support (courtesy Trainers' House Analytics)*

5.5 ANALYTICS TOOL SELECTION – IMPLEMENTATION

Implementation again depends greatly on your business. The more external agencies involved with the website design and campaign management aspects of your online marketing the more difficult it will be to control data integrity and quality. Where possible centralize any page tagging with a process that goes through the hub. Whenever the website content is updated a control version of the website should be created with the old tags and old version as a form of quality control. Using a version of CVS control will help this process.

If you have to use a number of agencies use one agency to project manage the whole exercise as part of your hub team. It should be made clear to them the importance of analytics and the tagging requirements you have.

Implementation Planning

The best way to implement is to let the vendor specifically implement the solution basing their implementation around a pre-defined set of measurements important to your business (KPIs).

What's important is that your hub is involved intimately with this process and is taught the technical requirements to make day to day changes themselves, or that a vendor/client agreement is in place so that the vendor deals with all future requests within a certain timeframe.

Data Quality Control

The rest of your implementation planning process should be focused around data quality.

In Figure 5.20 the first four entries in part 1 of the data quality checklist show suggested ideas for the hub to implement in order to help verify and control data quality. Again these ideas will depend greatly on your tool of choice but some form of testing along these lines can be carried out with any tool. The last three sections in part 2 of the checklist are important to understand from the enterprise process perspective.

Data Ownership

It is important that a senior person in the hub is responsible for enterprise-wide data ownership and data quality. He or she should be responsible for setting up and ensuring processes are followed and audits carried out. I would suggest your platforms manager (see Figure 1.3) working closely with senior analytics specialists are responsible for data ownership and quality.

Data quality checklist (Part 1)	Quality control test to undertake	The following considerations should be taken into account in order to ensure data quality and integrity
Validate data	**Data validation test** – monthly spot check and site upgrade testing after any new content uploaded.	Is the data being recorded in exactly the manner it should? Is it being recorded in the right analytics profile or account? Finally and most importantly is there an effective plan in place to upgrade websites with new information while retaining data quality? Is there a good system of version control in place? i.e. CVS? Validation version should also be recorded in any audits.
Data types	**Data classification** – Certify the data type based on the difficulty of maintenance	1. Clientside data – flash applications, rich media 2. Count data – tagging required on specific actions and specialist requirements such as campaigns 3. Automated data – syndicated or dynamic content that is automatically tracked upon going live
Define terms	**Terms definition document** – Internal terms glossary	Make sure when you're discussing a count that everyone knows what a count is. The Web Analytics Association has defined standard terms: http://www.webanalyticsassociation.org/
Count accuracy	**The big 3 test** - quarterly quality testing	Do a page views, visits and visitors (the so called big 3) quarterly deviation check. Use standard deviations to measure overall count trends. If they deviate from the normal levels investigate further
Data quality checklist (Part 2)	**Quality control test to undertake**	**The following considerations should be taken into account in order to ensure data quality and integrity**
Data ownership	**Hub quality manager** – overall responsibility for data quality	Name and contact details of the person responsible for overall data quality and names of hub specialists responsible for each spokes data quality. If this is handled by vendors or consultants list them and share the information across the organization
Audit trail	**Paperwork or data quality record** – any report containing data without an audit trail is classed as high risk data	1) High risk data – non-audited 2) Standard data – data validation test carried out 3) Low risk data – data validation test carried out for specific report or analysis
Staff training and process	**Quality process** – how will the process be communicated and implemented?	All staff should be made aware of the audit trail and understand that they cannot rely on high risk data being accurate. They should have the hub responsible personnel carry out a test and make sure the data is valid

FIGURE 5.20 *Data quality checklist (courtesy Trainers' House Analytics)*

Audit Trail

The audit trail should be documented and clearly defined. Any reporting, analysis or data extracted from a web analytics system should be classified as 'high risk' data unless the person doing the analysis has had the data validated by someone qualified.

If reports and analysis are submitted to decision makers with high risk (in other words data that was not checked for its validity due to time/resource constraint for instance), then the high risk should be transparent. This should then help build good practices. No responsible manager is going to rely on high risk data to take major decisions and will ask for validation to be carried out.

In reality a spoke may request data that is high risk due to urgency (early results on hastily set-up campaigns for instance) and that in itself is not an ideal situation. However at least the spoke manager knows the data is not validated and decisions he/she takes could be based on erroneous data. **Transparency is better** than hoping the numbers are right.

Staff Training and Processes

Best practice here is to make sure everyone understands and follows the audit trail. How the hub sets this up depends entirely again on the business in question but where possible integrate your data quality process with other existing processes. This again helps you to build things that are followed by the rest of the organization.

> **Best Practice**
>
> The first thing anyone receiving reports or analysis should ask is 'has the data been validated?' If not it should be classed as high risk data and not be relied on for major decision making until the data has been validated. In short in the hub and spoke method of doing things it is the hub's responsibility to ensure data is validated and the hub should live by the mantra that '*Transparency is better than hoping that the numbers are right.*'

5.6 SEGMENTATION

As you may have seen earlier in this book segmentation has been mention many times. Marketers have always grouped their target audiences into different types of people based on various criteria. It might be that they group people based on their age, gender or geographic location for instance. This is so that they can begin to figure out the best type of person to market their product to. For example, a young woman living in Paris will buy cosmetics more frequently than an 80-year-old man living on a farm. Your job as a marketer is to figure out the differences between the people you're marketing to and position your product accordingly.

Web Analytics can help this process by allowing you to segment or filter visitors that come to your website based on certain criteria but in a different way to the way marketers do it with demographic or psychographic data.

For instance you can set up your web analytics tool to view how visitors from a certain country, or city act on your website as compared everyone else and see if there are any differences. You can also (by using registration data) determine if the audiences are male or female, if they are interested in a certain type of product or service and actually record behavioural differences between different types of audience.

In our cosmetic example for instance, if our Parisian lady had logged into her favourite cosmetics website and given them all the data that she had been asked for (name, address, age, interests, survey information, etc.), you as the website owner could aggregate the data across all your registered visitors and use your web analytics tools to segment them into groups. You could then present offers to the right people. Our lady might be interested in a certain type of perfume along with thousands of other registered users to your website. It means you could send a tailored email to them because your web analytics tools have told you that these particular groups of users buy a lot of this kind of perfume.

Registrations require that the visitor opts in and gives you the information at some point in time and it's often difficult to attain. It's why companies like Amazon are very successful because they know so much about every customer or registered user that goes to their website and can present products matching the interests of their visitors.

There are some practical things you can do with your web analytics systems that will give you much more insight by using segmentation. By doing this you might be able to start and see some quick wins (see Chapter 4) which will give you much more credibility when you ask for larger investments around analytics and online marketing.

Practical Segmentation Tips

1. Segment by Paid Traffic Sources (Reach)

If you have a paid banner or search engine marketing campaign filter the visitors arriving from the campaign source. By comparing how each campaign works and how the visitors behave on your website you can easily see where to spend your money. If for instance you find that the €10,000 a month you're spending on banners has a 1% conversion rate with very low user interaction (low page views per visit and high bounce rates) as compared to the 3% conversion rate from search marketing, it makes sense to spend more on search marketing than banner ads. It's a quick win because it saves you spending money on poor campaigns and allows you to spend bigger on more successful ones.

2. Segment by Un-paid Traffic Sources (Reach)

You should look to find which your best partners and referring websites are. Is there a website which is driving high quality traffic that converts highly? If so it may be worth offering incentives to get better exposure on that website.

On the other hand if you're getting a lot of traffic from a partner and the traffic is converting at low level then it might be worth changing your message for that traffic depending on what they are coming to your website for. Again by segmenting by the reach source you're able to show the difference between different audiences.

3. Segment by Location (Reach)

Many of the tools can actually see where the visitor comes from by looking at the visitor's IP address and referencing it to see which city the IP address comes from. It's not 100% accurate (web analytics tools very rarely are) but it will help you to see for instance if Paris is a better area to concentrate your efforts on than Nice.

4. Segment by Search Phrase or Keyword (Reach)

Search engines are very important. Knowing how people use them and more importantly which keyword groups perform better than others is very insightful. Is Google better than Yahoo at converting the visitor on a selected set of keywords? This will allow you to gauge where to spend your search marketing money and bring more evidence that segmentation works to drive insights.

5. Segment by on Site Behaviour (Engage)

Many visits to your website may be 'useless' visits in that they arrive at one page, find that they have found the wrong place and go back to a search engine. It is worth filtering these out in many cases to see if your useful visits are finding what they need. It might also be useful to segment visits by the areas of your website. Are the visits to your shopping cart performing better than other areas?

6. Segment by System Variables (Engage)

This might sound like a weird thing to do, but we've found huge differences in onsite behaviour in someone who has a low screen resolution in comparison to someone who has a high resolution. Similarly look at operating systems and connection types. Your audience may have low technology and you have a high tech website which they find very difficult to use. Are you catering for them well enough?

7. Segment by Successful Conversions (Activate)

Another obvious thing to do is segment out the visitors who convert to the goal and compare them to those that don't. Are there any trends that you can see that differ from the visitors that don't convert? Are the conversions coming from similar reach sources? Do they have similar onsite behaviour? If anything stands out what actions can you take such as improvements on marketing spend or onsite improvements?

8. Segment by Loyalty (Nurture)

You can also segment by repeat visits, recency and frequency. Do your more loyal visitors convert more easily? Do loyal visitors have any common reach sources so that you could focus efforts? These and many other questions can be answered by segmenting out the loyal visits that come time and time again to your website. You can also segment by the amount of visits. I visit some of my favourite websites thousands of times a year. My behaviour is more likely to be much more effective and useful to the marketer than someone who visits once or twice. The marketer wishes everyone was like me. By learning about my behaviour (and the behaviour of others like me) he/she can figure out what we like and promote it more on his/her site if it's relevant.

When selecting segments you should always closely follow your business goals and objectives, in other words your KPIs. When the spokes in your business are happy and understand why you're segmenting then you are on your way to building an analytics driven organization. This is why you always have to go back to the hub and spoke, the KPIs and the REAN model when explaining why you're segmenting.

Planning Segmentation with REAN

There is a simple process involved for planning segmentation. In Chapter 2 you learned about the REAN planning process. In order to visualize which data you might want to look at as a segment you can use the REAN model here too. Figure 5.21 shows how we use REAN to show segmentation plans.

The dark grey boxes in the online reach section show how to plan the segmentation of the reach sources filtered out as 'paid traffic' with the idea being that you can track how only the paid traffic engages and activates. You should also combine this information with campaign tracking, for instance to get a very good overview of what your campaign traffic does differently to the rest of your traffic. Once you have told the hub (see Chapter 1) to set up this segmentation you will see differences in the data.

As you can see here because you're not focusing on everything at once you can begin to learn what works and what doesn't.

Better still by focusing on traffic that only activates you might notice something really insightful as shown in Figure 5.22. By segmenting only the conversion, in this case 'Spares sold', you can see which traffic drives those conversions. You might see something like Figure 5.22 that shows partner sites have driven traffic through the engagement process – the Spare cart process and ended up converting at Spares sold. It's very valuable to segment like this. You can quickly see which reach source to focus on. For instance in the above case you might want to start rewarding your partner's efforts by offering them a higher reward in order to drive more quality traffic your way.

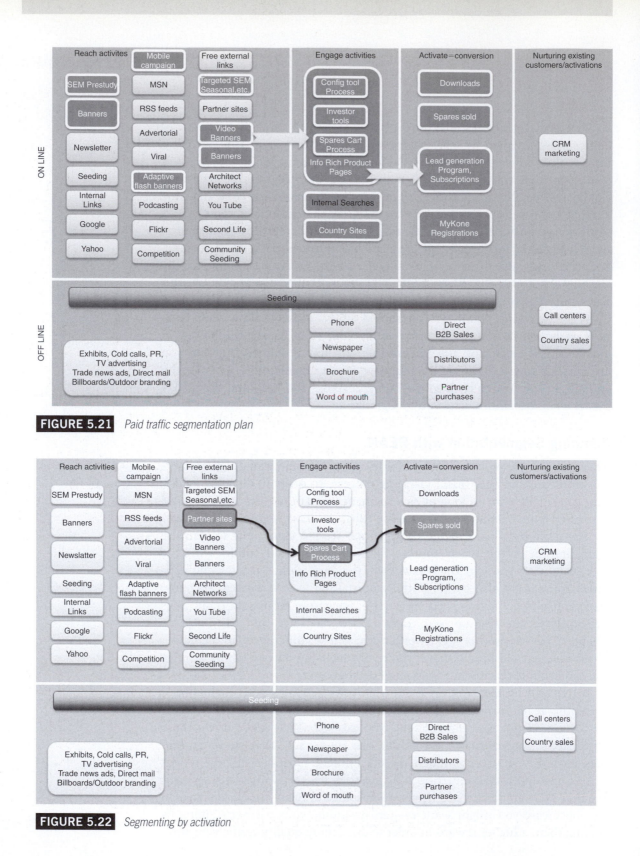

FIGURE 5.21   Paid traffic segmentation plan

FIGURE 5.22   Segmenting by activation

REAN Helps Build Culture

Because it's easier to show everyone in your business a REAN plan in a one slider than explain difficult web analytics segmentation concepts, this is a perfect way to help you build analytics culture. Once people know that the above scenario is easily measurable via web analytics tools they will start asking more questions of the analytics hub. This is what you want.

Segmentation that Helped Find a $1million Dollar Hole

The following case describes a situation where I helped one of my clients find a leak worth $1million per year by using segmentation to help analyse their website. The case describes how we used a key performance indicator (KPI) to flag the problem and then goes on to describe how we then found out what the issue was on the client's website. The client was an e-commerce operation selling catalogue items in bulk to businesses.

The KPIs

In Chapter 3 you learned how to define your KPIs in your own organization. Some KPIs are tightly tied in with monetary business objectives and some of them are more behavioural. Figure 5.23 shows the KPIs that this business was using.

Visits
% Add to cart
Conversion Rate (Visit to purchase)
Marketing Cost
Cost Per Visit (CPV)
Cost Per Add to Cart
Customers
Average cart value
Cost Per Customer
Sales
Profit
Profit Per Website Visitor

FIGURE 5.23   *KPI table – segmentation*

Visits and the percentage of those that added to the cart were KPIs important to help the marketing spoke to understand which visits to focus their efforts on.

They also used 'cost per visit', 'cost per add to cart' and average cart value to determine what they had to spend to keep their conversion rate constant. While they had confidence in their conversion rates they had confidence in their cost per customer and finally the ultimate goal profit per website visitor. What they wanted to do was improve the overall profit firstly by improving conversion of existing traffic.

They were a smart company and knew that if they spent more money on traffic when they had a higher conversion rate the profitability would go through the roof.

Adding Behavioural KPIs

What they didn't have however were any behavioural flags. So we added 'page views per visit' and 'time spent on site' as engage KPIs to see if there were potentially any problems or issues.

One way you can set behavioural flags is to find out how many pages it takes to complete a desired action. In this case the desired action (a purchase) took a minimum of seven pages. Then consider what a good browsing experience might be from your businesses point of view. In this case we decided if the visitor viewed between five and seven pages and then completed a purchase (another seven pages) it would be a good visit from the businesses point of view. While it's always a little subjective it might mean that the visitor finds out that more is on offer than simply the product they were looking for and have a pretty good experience with the site. Then we added another seven pages on top of this to flag a too many pages warning.

So we have a bottom limit of seven pages, a happy medium of 14 pages and a top limit of 21 pages. We then calculated the time spent in the same way and came up with less than five minutes, between five and ten minutes is OK and over ten is the higher warning.

There was a good reason for setting the top limit flag of 14–21 pages. In the case in Figure 5.24 when an average visit to the website was more than 14 pages in our view it meant one of two things. Either the visitor was extremely happy with the website and was browsing around enjoying the experience which was good or the visitor was extremely frustrated and couldn'tt find what they wanted.

A good experience from any visitor's point of view on a **catalogue based e-commerce website** is that they find what they want very quickly, and in this case we figured that should mean browsing less than 21 pages on average.

What we found shows why this metric is important. The KPI went off the scale showing that on average a visitor viewed 22 pages per visit (Figure 5.25).

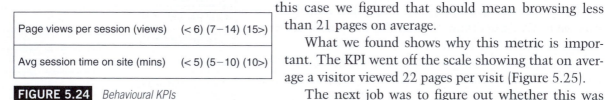

Page views per session (views)	(< 6) (7–14) (15>)
Avg session time on site (mins)	(< 5) (5–10) (10>)

FIGURE 5.24 *Behavioural KPIs*

Page Views/Visits

09/01/05 - 09/30/05

7   14

0

FIGURE 5.25 *Omniture HBX goal monitor*

The next job was to figure out whether this was a good thing or a bad thing. If an average visit took 22 pages it meant that either the average visitor was happily browsing around and our client should be very happy, or it meant that there was a problem. We also found that most visitors were spending over ten minutes on the website. Another reason to be slightly concerned.

Behavioural Segmentation

As discussed it's possible to segment the visitors into groups of people that follow the same behaviour patterns. We wanted to know if the visitors were flicking through pages very quickly (a sign that they were unhappy) or if indeed they were traversing a great many pages each and spending a normal amount of time on the site (a sign that they were happy).

Therefore we segmented the visitors into only those that spent less than 2 minutes on the site and those spent over ten minutes on the site. This would enable us to see if the page views per visit of those visitors only on the site for a short period of time were racking up lots of page views or whether it was those that were there longer that had trouble finding what they wanted.

Figure 5.26 shows the difference between the traffic segments. Visitors on the site for less than two minutes showed normal behaviour. The people that spent less than two minutes on the website generally browsed two or three pages per visit. The people that spent ten minutes or more on the site again went off the scale but this time it was even more problematic.

The average page views per session was **57 pages**. These were the people who were having problems.

Since we'd found the segment of visitors who had the problem we now needed to know what they were doing. We checked the path analysis of individuals to see if we could locate trends in those whom had browsed 57 pages or more.

One visitor had traversed 97 pages. We looked through the visit path and noticed that the path kept referring to one page – *a search results error page*. We checked other individual visits and noticed the same key trend – *the search results error page*.

This lead us to check the failed searches on the website. When we totalled them up there were over 2000 failed keyword searches and the vast majority were product codes.

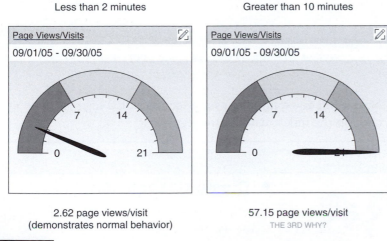

2.62 page views/visit
(demonstrates normal behavior)

57.15 page views/visit
THE 3RD WHY?

FIGURE 5.26   *The difference between segments (Omniture HBX)*

Onsite testing revealed that the site's **internal search engine simply couldn't read a letter and number combination**. Most of the codes coming from the printed catalogue, the **product codes, consisted of numbers and letters**. We'd found an issue. We deduced that people were visiting the site with catalogue in hand and trying to enter the product code but couldn't find what they were looking for due to a faulty internal search engine. Once we had tested this theory we recommended that the search engine be fixed.

Going back to Figure 5.4 we knew that the KPI *average cart value* was $99 (from figures supplied by the client). Because we knew that around 1000 visitors per month were abandoning the carts after hitting the search error results page we knew that they could save just under **$1.2 million dollars per year**.

This particular case has been used as a classic quick win (see Chapter 4) with my clients since 2005. The monetization alone shows the value of segmentation.

How to Do Segmentation

Since segmentation is so important I decided to show how to set this up in the free tools available. At the time of writing there are two such tools out of beta, Google Analytics and Yahoo! Web Analytics (formerly IndexTools). Please note that this data, the names and the layouts are correct at the time of writing but may be subject to change by the respective vendors.

IndexTools (http://www.indextools.com/)

1. Login and click on settings as shown above.

2. Next scroll down until you see a section called segmentation and click on the link 'create visitor segments'.

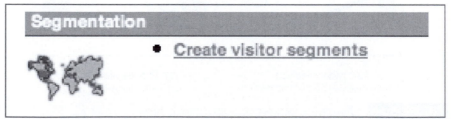

3. Click on the form button 'Open the Segmentation Wizard.'

You will be presented with a large popup window looking like this.

On the left hand side you can see the different ways that you can segment audiences and on the right hand side you can see a dynamic screen that allows you to drag the groups together to create the traffic segment. For instance you can segment by visitor demographics, visitor activity, how people navigate, the source of traffic people come from or by custom metrics you have hard coded into your site.

If for instance you wanted to separate your traffic into those that have visited more than five times to work out a KPI that you had previously defined called Heavy Visitor Share you would do the following in IndexTools to start filtering the visitors.

1. First you open the drop down menu Activity and then select number of visits.

2. Once you have selected the number of visits you drag it over onto the right hand side whereupon you will be presented with a number of options depending on which group selection you have chosen.

3. Once you have dragged the number of visits into the dynamic field you will see another drop down menu selection as shown below.

4. Because you're trying to see visitors that have visited five or more than five times you should select 'is greater than or equal to' and then add 5 to the form field to the right of the drop down menu. This then means that your segment starts to take shape and looks like a sentence reading, 'Number of visits is greater than or equal to 5'.

5. It is then simply a case of naming your segment 'Heavy Visitor Share' and giving your segment a simple description. You should have something like the screenshot below. To save the segment press 'Save segment' circled in the top left corner.

6. Once the segment is saved you can start using it from your normal reports. Shown below is the area you select from the normal report set. By default the selection is set to 'Show all data'. Once you have segments designed you will be able to open a drop down menu that will show the segment you have just created – Heavy Visitor Share.

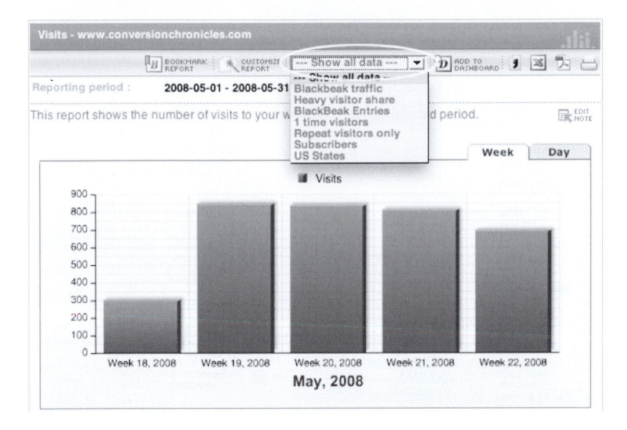

7. By Selecting Heavy Visitor Share from the drop down list available in your ordinary reports you would see the amount of visits who were 'heavy visitors' as per your definition and be able to make your KPI calculation as required.

8. Heavy visitor share can now be seen as shown below

Week	Visits		%	
	ALL	Heavy visitor share	ALL	Heavy visitor share
Week 18, 2008	303	1	8.66%	1.14%
Week 19, 2008	848	37	24.25%	42.05%
Week 20, 2008	839	17	23.99%	19.32%
Week 21, 2008	813	20	23.25%	22.73%
Week 22, 2008	694	13	19.85%	14.77%
Total	3,497	88	100.00%	100.00%

9. In addition you could apply the segment to any report and get the result of it. Here are the latest three visitors who were part of my 'heavy visitor share' segment.

1.	**Date:** 2008-05-31 22:39:40	**System:** Windows XP
	IP/Host: 60.234.209.56 (orcon.net.nz)	**Browser:** Firefox 2.0.0.
	Country: New Zealand	**Language:** English (United States)
	No. of visits: 19 visits	**Javascript:** Enabled [1.5]
	Entry page: The Power of Wh...sion Chronicles	**Monitor color:** 16 bit
	Visit path: VIEW VISIT PATH - 1 page view	**Resolution:** 1024x768
	Referrer: Direct access or bookmark	**Cookies:** Disabled
	Search phrase: n / a	

2.	**Date:** 2008-05-30 22:16:47	**System:** Windows XP
	IP/Host: 60.234.209.56 (orcon.net.nz)	**Browser:** Firefox 2.0.0.
	Country: New Zealand	**Language:** English (United States)
	No. of visits: 18 visits	**Javascript:** Enabled [1.5]
	Entry page: The Power of Wh...sion Chronicles	**Monitor color:** 16 bit
	Visit path: VIEW VISIT PATH - 1 page view	**Resolution:** 1024x768
	Referrer: Direct access or bookmark	**Cookies:** Enabled
	Search phrase: n / a	

3.	**Date:** 2008-05-30 21:51:45	**System:** Windows XP
	IP/Host: 99.226.159.30 (rogers.com)	**Browser:** MSIE 7.0
	Country: Canada	**Language:** English (United States)
	No. of visits: 5 visits	**Javascript:** Enabled [1.5]
	Entry page: Conversion Chro...nvert with copy	**Monitor color:** 32 bit
	Visit path: VIEW VISIT PATH - 9 page views - 15m 13s	**Resolution:** 1280x800
	Referrer: http://www.google.com/search?s...	**Cookies:** Enabled
	Search phrase: difference between web content and web copy	

As you can see all the visits in this segment have returned a number of times. Visit number 1 has come from New Zealand and visited 19 times. Visit number 2 is the same person from the previous day and visit number 3 is someone from Canada who also subscribed to the website as shown by the exclamation mark defining that an action was taken.

Yahoo! Web Analytics

Dennis Mortensen is the Director of Data Insights at Yahoo! Web Analytics and is writing a book on the subject. Information can be found here: http://visualrevenue.com/blog/yahoo-analytics-book

Dennis' gave me a sneak preview and I'd highly recommend this if you want to learn more about Yahoo! Web Analytics.

Google Analytics (http://www.google.com/analytics/)

There are three ways to see segmented traffic in Google Analytics.

1. Using Filters in Profiles

It's also possible to use profiles to filter out traffic into different segments based on the behaviour you find important assuming you know the behaviour or content groups you want to segment before you design the profile.

Lets say for example we want to filter out the visitors that came from the USA and UK. First we create a new profile to collect just the filtered data.

> It's best to create a new profile for the filter segment rather than try to filter the raw data. Any filter you apply to any profile will affect all data for that profile, therefore create a new profile copy tracking all your data and then filter it as needed.

Website Profiles							Visits ▼		+ Add new profile
Name↑	Reports	Status	Visits	Avg. Time on Site	Bounce Rate	Completed Goals	% Change		Actions
http://www.conversionchronicles.com UA-58419-1									
Articles	View report	✓	247	00:03:26	55.06%	0	○ -7.49%		Edit | Delete
☆ Blackbeak Total	View report	✓	858	00:01:41	69.70%	0	○ -1.61%		Edit | Delete
Chronicles - Finnish Visitors only	View report	✓	223	00:03:02	59.19%	0	○ 14.36%		Edit | Delete
☆ Conversion Chronicles - All data	View report	✓	8,444	00:00:47	87.66%	6	○ 49.74%		Edit | Delete
Find profile:						Show rows: 10 ▼	Page 1 of 1 ◄ ►		

Add Website Profile»
A profile allows you to track a website and/or create different views of the reporting data using filters. Learn more

User Manager»
Number of Users: 4
Add or edit Users. Learn more

Filter Manager»
Number of Filters: 15
Filters can be used to customize the way data is displayed in your reports. Learn more

Select the circled area labelled 'Add a Profile for an existing domain'.

Name your profile and then click finish. This will save a new profile based on your existing domain name traffic called (in this case) US and UK visits. The result should be that you have two profiles. One called US and UK visits and the other your base data set.

Next you need to edit the filters on the new profile.

On the login screen of UK and USA visitors only click 'Edit' under settings.

Create New Website Profile

Choose Website Profile Type

Please decide if you would like to create an additional profile for an existing domain or create a profile to track a new domain.

○ Add a Profile for a **new** domain   OR   ● Add a Profile for an **existing** domain

Add a Profile for an existing domain

Select Domain: http://www.psychotactics.com ▼

Profile Name: US and UK visits

Time zone country or territory: New Zealand ▼

Time Zone: (GMT+12:00) Auckland

Cancel   Finish

---

1. Select add new filter for profile.
2. Name the filter (UK and US traffic only).
3. Click include (to include traffic from these countries).
4. The filter field drop down shows all the possible filters you can apply. In this case select Visitor Country.
5. Underneath that you should then add filter patterns which are found in the Google support section. In the case the filter is United Kingdom|United States.
6. Finally click save changes.

Analytics Settings > Profile Settings > **Create New Filter**

Create New Filter

Choose method to apply filter to Website Profile

Please decide if you would like to create a new filter or apply an existing filter to the Profile.

● Add new Filter for Profile   OR   ○ Apply **existing** Filter to Profile

Enter Filter Information

Filter Name: UK, US traffic only

Filter Type: Custom filter ▼

○ Exclude
● Include
○ Lowercase
○ Uppercase
○ Search and Replace
○ Lookup Table
○ Advanced

Filter Field   Visitor Country ▼

Filter Pattern   United Kingdom|United States   What kind of special characters can I use?

Case Sensitive   ○ Yes ● No

Save Changes   Cancel

You will be presented with a screen called profile settings. Scroll down until you see a box which says 'Filters applied to profile' and click on 'add filter'. This will bring up the following.

You now should be able to go into Google Analytics and see two profiles. One is your traffic profile with no filters applied (global traffic) and the other is your UK and US traffic profile.

You can now view all reports in Google analytics for just the UK and US traffic by selecting the profile from the drop down list.

2. Out of the Box

There are many pre-defined segments that come out of the box in Google that allow you to cross segment with another metric in the reporting system. So if for example you had visits open and you wanted to view visits that came from adwords you could click the segment button and select from the drop down list shown.

The traffic can be matched with various filters already determined by Google Analytics as important, such as how many of your visitors are repeat visitors for instance.

The difference between looking at a country/territory out of the box and with the previous filtered profile is that you can only see the single report segment – visitors from a certain country from your global traffic for instance. In the previous profiled method you could see all reports across the entire suite for only the visitors coming from the US or the UK.

3. Advanced Segmentation

The third and most powerful way to segment in Google Analytics is by clicking on the advanced segmentation link seen in on the left hand side navigation after you've logged into a profile. After doing so click on *create new segment*. You will be presented with all the elements on the left that you can use as your behaviour filters (such as pages, time on site, etc.). In the same manner drag and drop the segments as you require and add parameters.

The image below shows a segment of visitors that have visited three times and spent 60 seconds on the site.

Google don't have an official manual for Google Analytics but the best book on the subject is one written by the ex EMEA director of Google Dr Brian Clifton. The book can be found here: http://www.advanced-web-metrics.com/blog/2008/04/07/book-launch-advanced-web-metrics-with-google-analytics

Segmentation Summary

Of all the uses of web analytics tools segmentation is the most insightful in terms of what you can learn from the clickstream data. In most business websites you hawve a large amount of visitors coming from a wide variety of different sources all of whom have different agendas and goals based on their own motivations, not necessarily your reasons for having them there.

Segmentation can help split that traffic up so you can understand those motivations.

CHAPTER 6

Developing and Measuring Motivational and Behavioural Personas

When dealing with people, remember you are not dealing with creatures of logic, but with creatures of emotion, creatures bristling with prejudice, and motivated by pride and vanity.
Dale Carnegie

6.1 AN INTRODUCTION TO PERSONAS

Since Forrester (http://www.forrester.com) published the best practices in 2005 I've seen many websites designed with persona-based models at their core. Most user-centered design (UCD) philosophy has been preaching the use of persona models for well over a decade. While I applaud Forrester and the design industry for having the right idea I believe that the 'primary persona' as defined in UCD circles is flawed for the purpose of designing persuasive and measurable websites.

I know there is a better way to design because I've measured the results and seen for myself.

I've long been a student of the excellent work done by Bryan Eisenberg and his colleagues at FutureNow Inc. as well as Martijn Van Welie from Phillips Design around personas. Over the years I have found myself experimenting with personas in order to learn how to measure and improve the websites I've worked with. I've shamelessly adopted both methodologies because they both work in different ways depending on the situation and they can be easily combined.

One method is based on the FutureNow work around the Keirsey personality model. Part of FutureNows' Persuasion Architecture®, it is the best approach for designing measurable persuasive websites. Because the method is based on how people tend to behave rather than a one fits all primary persona it means you can segment your audience into behavioural groups based on the type of behaviour they demonstrate. That's very different to UCD persona design. Segmenting the audiences means you can measure which persona type is not being as well catered for on your website and take action accordingly.

The other method is a template based approach. Alone this can be used for assessments (see section 7.3) and was developed by Martijn Van Welie of Phillips Design. He usually used four or five of these motivationally driven personas in his design work for websites.

I've had a lot of success with this method when using it in combination with the Insight model for e-commerce or lead generation operations when testing a single user motivation or goal. If you've never used personas before it might be a good idea starting with the Persona Template method (see section 6.2), and moving onto the Persuasion Architecture® method when you have some wins under your belt. Personally for full website design I would combine the two techniques.

6.2 THE PERSONA TEMPLATE METHOD

The template method is used to design a persona based around the web visitors' motivations. If for instance you go online with the intention of buying something it's rare that you know exactly where to go to get the best deal. Every decision you make is based on your previous knowledge and experience. If you feel something is risky, you're less likely to do it.

The template helps you define what the risks might be and the questions that need answering in the mind of the visitor before they will take action. When you have defined the questions you can compare how well your website answers those questions.

It can help you learn a lot about rights, wrongs and how your competitors compare with you. The advantage is you get a lot of insight around a specific motivation. The disadvantage is that your website might have 20 different reasons for attracting visitors in which case there will be 20 different personas and you can't design a single site for all of them (This is where the Persuasion Architecture® method comes in handy). However for measuring a single motivational process like lead generation or e-commerce it's very good. This is why I'd advise you use this kind of method to develop quick win, reach, engagement or conversion assessments (Figure 6.1).

Research Stage

> **Bryan Eisenberg (Click Z) http://www.clickz.com/showPage.html? page = 3430871**
>
> The principle value of a persona-based message campaign is understanding each type of customer's approach to initiating relationships, gathering information, and approaching decision-making. Learn what type of language resonates with customers, what builds their confidence, how they prefer to obtain agreement and closure, and so on.

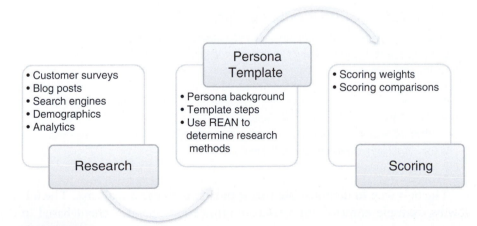

FIGURE 6.1 *Persona template process*

When designing your persona you should look at a number of different sources of data to define how you get to your role model. These are:

1. **Demographic data** – age, gender, geography (data acquired from customer surveys, CRM data or other sources like Hitwise/Comscore).

2. **Customer psychographics** – what the customer does in the pre-purchase phase found by looking at a number of different sources in addition to the demographic data, for instance:
   a. Web analytics keyword data.
   b. Blog post phrases angled at user motivations.
   c. Top search engine phrases (Google trends).

3. **Market data** such as how the branding and market place effects the decisions of the persona:
   a. Who else sells your product/service (competitor analysis)?
   b. Which competing websites do your visitors engage with (Google Trends)?
   c. What other things are your customers looking at (Google Trends/Keyword tool)?

The Persona creation template (Figure 6.2) is an adapted version of a persona template created by Martijn Van Welie who works for Philips Design in Amsterdam as a senior design consultant and was my colleague at Satama Netherlands prior to that.

Persona Template

Martijn Van Welie (Philips Design) http://www.welie.com

The persona template aims to capture and understand the users' goals and tasks in a particular context. It is important for any designer to know what considerations will influence the users' tasks so that a fitting design solution can be created. The considerations and pain points help to understand the decision making process of the user and how to achieve a positive effect, i.e. 'conversion'. The same information can therefore also be used for analytic purposes since it has a direct relation on search keywords and the click paths that will lead to a conversion. The paths are basically the reflections of the tasks and the conversion is the achievement of the goal.

The best way to demonstrate this approach is to use a real case. The following example comes from a telecommunication operator client based in

Persona template

Goals – Determine your personas key motivation or reason for visiting you website. Note that it's the personas goal not necessarily your business goal. This data about key motivations comes from the research stage.

Scenario – Describe the person as typical scenario and reasoning for visiting your site.
- What would be the typical way that the persona would know about your product or service?
- How would they find out about the product or service?
- What specific methods are involved in reaching you (REAN – chapter 2)?
- How would the person do his/her research?

Tasks prior to taking action – Determine all the tasks the persona will need to accomplish before being in a position to take the action you want them to take.
- What does he/she need to find out?
- What is his/her first major concern about the product or service?
- What are the next 4 factors that need to be understood out in order to have a better idea of all the risks involved?

Considerations and questions – From the scenario and the task list determine what questions your persona may have about your product or service. It should be relatively easy at this point to come up with around 10 key questions that the persona would want answered before deciding to purchase.

Pain points – Will be different for each persona and very personal.
- What makes the persona cry out in frustration?
- If he/she is potentially defecting from one product or service to yours, what pains him about the current situation?
- If not what are the needs that really pain him/her the most?

Trigger terms – Based on the pain points and considerations
- Trigger terms are words people look for or use to try and solve their problems.
- Used in search engines, on blog posts, in emails.
- Determine 5 terms that will be used to search on Search engines that relate to the pain points and problem the person has. It's good to do prior research around these keywords on Google trends/Google Keyword tool.

FIGURE 6.2 *Persona creation template*

Finland. The persona was created to see how someone typically might go about making a decision to sign up for broadband in Finland.

Tapio persona – research definition stage

The demographics are taken from CRM systems to build Tapio's personality. The psychographics used that helped define pain points came from web analytics keyword data and customer surveys.

The market (competitive landscape) mapped Tapio's research procedure. He knows all the major brands by URL, he has got this information from TV, newspaper, public transport and billboard ads all around Helsinki.

He will use search engines to see if there are any deals, to get information about broadband and to quicken his search. He's Finnish so he uses Finnish terms as shown though I've put the English terms in parentheses to show the relation to his pain points.

As an advertiser running a campaign you may be interested in mapping all the potential points that might persuade Tapio to go to your website to find out more.

The reach sources that you're using can all affect Tapios' research strategy, which again goes back to good planning and the REAN model as shown in Chapter 2.

Tapio Persona – Template Stage

As shown in Figure 6.2 there are a number of things you need to do to flesh out the persona. Go through each step until you've defined all the points listed in the template (Figure 6.3). The more detail orientated you are the better the persona will be.

Scoring

After creating your persona and defining Tapios needs, his pain points and his trigger terms you're now ready to score how you're doing based on his needs.

The scoring method is really designed to help simplify things which helps build your analytics culture. Scorecards can level the playing field in large organizations and help build understanding:

1. Zero is bad.
2. Five is good.
3. Everyone can understand this.

The hub and spoke (see Chapter 1), REAN (see Chapter 2), KPIs (see Chapter 3) the Insight model (see Chapters 4 and 7), the persona template, the persona method (this chapter) the tools and all the other things you have read about to get to this point don't need to be understood by everyone in the company.

You need analysts that can do it in order to succeed, but no matter how data driven you become not everyone will understand how web analytics works or what the point is until you show them a scale that they understand. When zero is bad and five is good most people get it. Chapter 7 shows examples of how to use a scorecard to answer the needs of the persona.

Personal details -Tapio is a 36-year-old Finnish entrepreneur living in Töölö a region of Helsinki. Often working on the road, in the office or from home, Tapio has a variety of different needs from his broadband service provider. Primarily to be able to check email, store contacts and easily upload and download files through secure networks.

His wife also needs a good home internet connection for her own home/office lifestyle having even more needs for the ability to upload and download large files.

Goals	Purchase broadband connection for home use
Scenario	Tapio has decided he needs to get a broadband connection for his own personal home use. He has just moved apartment and needs a new service. He and his wife both know through word of mouth that they are in a buyer's market and will use the Internet to find the best deal they can. Also through word of mouth Tapio heard technical details that 100MB was a fast broadband connection. Tapio knows all the major brands via offline branding campaigns such as TV, billboards and stickers on the sides of public transport vehicles
Tasks prior to purchase	Check brand websites directly Compare brand prices (Google) Compare full service offers (Google) Figure out if 100MB is what he needs to run a good connection from home Learn how to install the system

Considerations and questions	The area variety of broadband deals in Finland so it is important to find out what the brands offer: • What is the price per month? • How many service/price (speed to MB ratio) options are there and are they understandable? • Does the cost vary based on usage? If so how? If not is the price fixed or could there be hidden surprises? • Tapios wife doesn't to use cables to connect to the Internet. Is the broadband connection wireless? Does this cost more? • Do any free accessories (i.e. wireless modem) come with the service? • Are there any free offers in Finland around broadband? • If so are the free offers comparable in terms of features? • Tapio heard that a full system contract including digital TV could be purchased with broadband access to the Internet? Is this possible in his location? • Does the system come home fitted? Is it manual installation? If so is it easy? • Are there service guarantees? Money back options or trial periods?
Pain points	Neither tapio or his wife have any idea how to install broadband and don't know anything about the technology. Tapio heard he needed a 100MB connection because it's fast but doesn't know how much benefit he will get for the extra money.
Trigger terms	Finnish terms (same in English): Laajakaista (broadband) Laajakaista Yhteys (broadband connection) Laajakaista Nopeus (broadband fast/speed) Laajakaista Hinnat (broadband prices)

FIGURE 6.3 *Sample persona Tapio – Finnish male entrepreneur*

6.3 THE PERSUASION ARCHITECTURE® (PA) METHOD

This method of creating personas was developed by FutureNow Inc., and is based on the Myers/Briggs behavioural studies adapted by David Keirsey in the 1950s. Where the prior template approach is a good starting point that will help you to start using personas scientifically, the PA method should be the foundation of your website copy and content strategy. It goes into much more depth and closely follows Keirsey's observations about how people act.

Keirsey spent decades studying how people behave. He observed personality traits, such as habits of communication, patterns of action, and sets of characteristic attitudes, values and talents. He also examined personal needs, the kinds of contributions that individuals make in the workplace and the roles they play in society.

He discovered that in essence people have four personality types that dictate how they are likely to act. FutureNow adapted this approach to how people behave on the Internet and started developing personas based around behaviour. Because we're dealing with measuring behaviour in the clickstream using web analytics tools it's a natural progression to start measuring behavioural personas.

You start to deal with the reality of how people act and not try to determine who they are.

It's **not who comes to your website** that is important it is **how they behave** when they get there that is key to your success. I know personas work because I can measure how effective they are with web analytics tools. Your visitors **behave in a predictable way** based upon their temperament.

There were four primary temperaments defined by Keirsey:

- Sensing/Judging (SJ).
- Sensing/Perceiving (SP).
- Intuitive/Feeling (NF).
- Intuitive/Thinking (NT).

Keirsey argued that the four primary temperaments are basically hard wired into human beings. We all act like one of these temperaments primarily and depending on the situation will change to be more like one of the other temperaments when our attention is engaged on something else.

My own temperament falls into the Intuitive/Thinking temperament. I am the kind of person who'll use the best possible way to get information. I'll use a search engine on an individual site, or examine web pages scanning for keywords and links before flicking to the next page if I don't find what I'm looking for. I spend most of my day online and haven't got much time on my hands to browse around.

On the other hand if I am browsing around a subject that I'm emotionally tied to like football (specifically SAFC.com or ReadyToGo.net message boards) I can easily spend hours looking at everything and absorbing all the information – behaviour that is closer to the Sensing/Judging temperament. I can also get very emotional and spontaneous (SP). This doesn't mean I'm some sort of Jekyll and Hyde, it just indicates that my normal behaviour changes when I am dealing with something I'm more personally invested in. But the point is that I fall into one of the 'types' regardless. Either I am an NT or in the case of football I'm an SP or SJ.

This is why designing for the four kinds of temperaments is more effective from a design perspective than trying to figure out the primary persona visiting your site. Design for all four types and then measure which type you succeed with the most. This gives you a starting point to develop a roadmap for improvement.

FutureNow Inc. (FUTR: http://www.futurenowinc.com/) is the pioneer in using Keirsey's methodologies in order to design personas. As a company and as individuals they have nothing but my respect for the way they have shared their knowledge in white papers and e-books over the years.

The Keirsey temperaments were renamed by FutureNow to be more intuitive and relevant for today's audience.

- Methodical (SJ).
- Spontaneous (SP).
- Humanistic (NF).
- Competitive (NT).

I think it's a better description to describe me as competitive, or when I'm looking through SAFC.com and ReadyToGo.net as methodical or spontaneous. It's easier to understand.

FutureNow have translated Keirsey's work into modern day buying modes adding fast, slow, logic and emotion to the mix which simplistically shows emerging behaviour patterns (Figure 6.4).

Emerging Behavioural Patterns

Competitive people (like me) take logical decisions quickly and strategically based on what they see. Methodical people are also logical but slower paced and more deliberate. Spontaneous people are quick, fast paced people who do things on the spur of the moment based on how they feel. Humanistic folks want to feel like they are doing the right thing and want evidence that other people have also enjoyed doing the same thing.

It's possible that in any given situation you can see yourself represented in the above behavioural patterns.

I know my primary type is a competitive personality because I have taken the tests and saw the same result – NT. Actually my exact personality type was what Keirsey calls 'The Field Marshall – ENTJ'. I can recommend two very good books if you want to learn more about temperaments, Keirsey's *Please Understand Me II* and for lighter much easier reading Stephen Montgomery's *People Patterns*. If you want to take the test yourself it's on the Keirsey website: http://www.keirsey.com/sorter/register.aspx

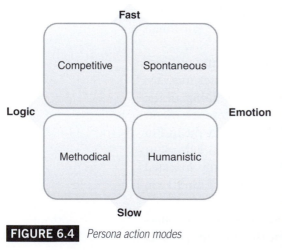

FIGURE 6.4   *Persona action modes*

The point here is to show that while my primary personality is competitive, fast paced and logical it doesn't mean that I will act that way all of the time. This means that knowing your audience type won't tell you which mode they will be in when they buy from you.

If SAFC.com relied on my primary personality type of competitive, fast paced and logical they would only succeed in irritating me immensely. I am emotionally tied to them, I want to connect with the club, I want to read in-depth articles, watch video highlights and can easily spend hours with the subject of football and Sunderland. I act irrationally when normally I'm rational. It's the curse of being a Sunderland football fan.

Luckily for SAFC.com they have Sunderland fans in charge of writing and developing the website, so most of the time they get it right. This is one reason why traditional UCD (user centric design) based on traditional research is not always relevant when building websites.

To take another example, grouping me as a tech leader based on a Nokia survey I took gives them useful information for fleshing out a persona, but useless information for designing their website. Nokia might know from a survey that I'm male, 36, in Helsinki, writing on a wirelessly connected MacBook Air, have an N810 (which is better than an iPhone by far in my opinion), use an E71 daily, but knowing that doesn't mean that Nokia's website will serve me any better. They don't need me to tell them that it would be unwise to design a website for 36-year-old males with an N810 in Helsinki. There are too many people who also took that survey that don't match my profile.

By knowing how I'm likely to behave when I visit their websites Nokia could improve how their website satisfies my needs. By satisfying my needs they have more chance of making me a returning customer.

6.4 HOW TO DEVELOP PERSONAS BASED ON THE PA METHOD

What follows is my interpretation of how to use personas the way FutureNow do. It may not be the exact method they use but I know that this method works due to the testing I've done using web analytics to measure the relative success or failure.

Competitive Persona

- **Attitude:** Businesslike, power orientated.
- **Time:** Disciplined, strategic/fast paced.

- **Typical question:** What can your solution do for me?

- **Approach:** Provide options, probabilities and challenges.

- Competitives need you to clearly define what the benefits of your product are. They want to know why they should choose you over their other options. They are looking to keep a competitive edge and have products/services that will make them feel and look better than others. There should be an introductory paragraph that explains who you are, what you do and what benefits you offer the visitor. You have guarantees in the active window listed as bullet points.

Humanistic Persona

- **Attitude:** Personal, relationship orientated.

- **Time:** Undisciplined, slow paced.

- **Typical question:** Who has used your solution to solve my problem? Who are you and why do you care about me?

- **Approach:** Offer testimonials and incentives

- Humanistics need more information about who the founder of the company is and who the people in the organization are. They want to see pictures of the people who work there. They want to see testimonials on how purchasing your products has worked out for other customers, as well as testimonials that indicate you offer incredible customer service.

Methodical Persona

- **Attitude:** Businesslike, detail orientated.

- **Time:** Disciplined, methodically/slow paced.

- **Typical question:** How can your solution solve my problem?

- **Approach:** Provide hard evidence and superior service.

- Methodicals want to make sure they know everything before they move forward. They do not mind reading through to the bottom of a page to find out what they need. They are concerned with how you operate and need to know that you're competent. You should provide them with all the details so they don't go elsewhere to find what they're looking for.

Spontaneous Persona

- **Attitude:** Personal, activity orientated.

- **Time:** Undisciplined, fast paced.

- **Typical question:** Why is your solution best for my needs?

- **Approach:** Quickly address values and provide assurances, credible opinions rather than options. Offer immediate gratification where appropriate. Your homepage should speak to this personality type, begin to build rapport, raise confidence and propel them toward immediate gratification. They will not spend a lot of time reading content; rather, they are skimming for interesting and captivating information within the most obvious sections of each page.

With this basic information you can now run a quick workshop to figure out how the personas visiting your website will behave (Figure 6.5).

Research and Team Selection

In this phase you need to select the best team and gather as much information as you can in order to design good personas. The team should be from the spokes (see Chapter 1) with diverse backgrounds that are responsible for the product or service. You should always include a hands on spoke member, someone who is dealing with customers on a daily basis such as an account manager or a face to face sales person. The people in your team should all have a strong understanding of the benefits of the product or service to the customer.

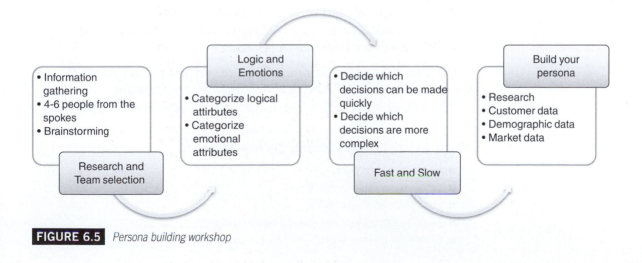

FIGURE 6.5   *Persona building workshop*

Upon selecting your team you should collect all the data you can gather about your customers. This information can be gathered from the following sources:

1. **Demographic data** – age, gender, geography (data acquired from customer surveys, CRM data or other sources like Hitwise/Comscore).

2. **Customer psychographics** – what the customer does in the pre-purchase phase found by looking at a number of different sources in addition to the demographic data, for instance:
   a. Web analytics keyword data.
   b. Blog post phrases angled at user motivations (BlogScope).
   c. Top search engine phrases (Google trends).

3. **Market data** such as how the branding and market place affects the decisions of the persona:
   a. Who else sells your product/service (competitor analysis)?
   b. Which competing websites do your visitors engage with (Google Trends)?
   c. What other things are your customers looking at (Google Trends/ Keyword tool)?

The workshop facilitator should present this information to the team to kick off the workshop and then move into the brainstorming.

The brainstorm should focus on listing the benefits and unique selling points of the product or service. Ask the team:

1. What is the best benefit of this product/service from the customers' point of view?
2. How is this product/service completely unique?
3. Why would a customer buy from us and not the competition?
4. When will the customer be better off buying from someone else?

I've found that these four questions are very good to get people focused. You should end up with a list of key benefits on a whiteboard.

The following list comes from a customer for demonstration purposes.

Case Example – Broadband Service Benefits

- Highly respected brand
- Comes home fitted on request
- Full service level agreement
- Flexible pricing (any speed/service can be bought)
- One bill for communications (mobile and broadband service in one billing method)

Once the benefits are listed you're ready to move to the second phase of the workshop.

Post-it Method: Logic and Emotions

Once you have all the product/service attributes that everyone agrees on and is clear about you should determine whether each benefit appeals to logical or emotional decision making on the part of the customer. I personally ask everyone to write this on a post-it note and suggest why they feel it is one or the other. Then stick the post-it notes next to each attribute on the white board and discuss until the attribute is agreed upon as either one or the other.

The customer I worked with had the following attributes listed as either logical or emotional.

Logical:
- Comes home fitted on request.
- Full service level agreement.
- Flexible pricing (any speed/service can be bought).
- One bill for communications (mobile and broadband service in one billing method).

Emotional:
- Highly respected brand.

The only emotional connection out of the five attributes is the branding. Emotion happens when a feeling is caused usually without thinking. The brand has an emotional effect. The other four attributes are purely logical. A home fitted product doesn't appeal to your deeper emotions and make you feel good inside but it might make a difference to someone who doesn't know how to fit it. Similarly pricing, billing and service agreements are purely logical decisions, not emotional ones.

Post-it Method: Fast or Slow

Fast:
- Comes home fitted on request.
- One bill for communications (mobile and broadband service in one billing method).
- Highly respected brand.

Slow:
- Full service level agreement.
- Flexible pricing (any speed/service can be bought).

Next you need to decide what is fast and quick to explain and what takes more time. How hard is it to understand each attribute? If it's immediately obvious it goes into the Fast section. If it's going to take some careful reading it goes into the Slow section. Again, in your team use the post-it notes.

As you can see from the example, three of the attributes are quick to explain – it doesn't take five minutes to say 'It comes home fitted', it is clear as you read the words. The branding is either known or it isn't, there is no middle ground. Think BT or NTL in the UK. Do you know them as a respected broadband service provider or not? It's that fast. The one bill for communications is again something that can easily and quickly be transmitted to the reader in one sentence.

It does take longer however to explain the full service levels. It also takes a while to build up a connection speed tailored to individual customers and also depends on the location the customer lives in (demographics), so these attributes fall into the slow side of the whiteboard.

Build Your Personas

Now map the attributes back to a persona whiteboard.

- Competitive personalities are strategic/fast paced and look for logical attributes.
- Spontaneous personalities are fast paced but undisciplined and emotional.
- Methodical personalities are slow, deliberate people also focused on the logical attributes.
- Humanistic personalities are slow paced, deliberate and focus heavily on emotional attributes.

As can be clearly seen in Figure 6.6, the personas you need to persuade are the competitive and methodical personalities. This isn't to say that you only design two personas catering for the two personas. The case shows that the service provider needs to become more emotional in their sales approach. However you would now have a clear starting point to design your website based on the strengths of your service. You would also know what your weaknesses are in terms of how you're communicating.

The two personas would need to be fleshed out (based on research) answering their needs.

Competitive Persona

- **Attitude:** Businesslike, power orientated.
- **Time:** Disciplined, strategic/fast paced.

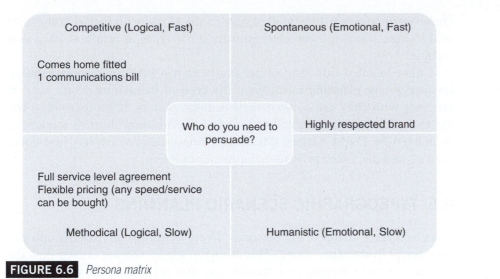

Competitive (Logical, Fast)

Comes home fitted
1 communications bill

Spontaneous (Emotional, Fast)

Who do you need to persuade?

Highly respected brand

Full service level agreement
Flexible pricing (any speed/service
can be bought)

Methodical (Logical, Slow)

Humanistic (Emotional, Slow)

FIGURE 6.6   *Persona matrix*

- **Typical question:** *'What can your solution do for me?'*
- **Approach:** Provide options, probabilities and challenges.
- What are the benefits of the broadband service? Why are you as a provider better than the rest of the broadband service providers? I know your brand but it doesn't impress me, I need to understand why you're stronger than the other brands I know. Are you the fastest provider out there? Are you the best service? Do you provide home delivery and installation? Provide images and options that signal your service options immediately and obviously. There should be an introductory paragraph that explains why you're better, what you offer and give quick answers. You have guarantees in the active window listed as bullet points.

Methodical Persona

- **Attitude:** Businesslike, detail orientated.
- **Time:** Disciplined, methodically/slow paced.
- **Typical question:** *'How can your solution solve my problem?'*
- **Approach:** Provide hard evidence and superior service.
- Methodicals want to make sure they **know everything** before they move forward. They do not mind reading through to the bottom of a page to find out what they need. They are concerned with **how you operate** and need to know that **you're competent**. You should provide them with **all the details** so they don't go elsewhere to find what they're looking for.

Once you've uncovered the USP of your products and who they're going to be sold to then you can move onto measuring the types of people visiting your website.

I have labelled this kind of persona scenario planning '**typeographics**' because you're planning to measure the **type of behaviour** people tend to take **not who they are** or what their demographic is. It's a method of trying to predict what people will do based on their natural human tendencies as defined by David Kiersey, Myers and Briggs before him but first documented and discussed by Plato from Ancient Greece.

6.5 TYPEOGRAPHIC SCENARIO PLANNING

Once you have mapped the personas' likely behavioural patterns you can now begin to measure them. This is again where scoring comes into the equation. Firstly though you should plan the behaviours of the personas into the REAN model.

Scenario planning based on the REAN model (see Chapter 2) should allow you to map all the points of acquisition, the points of engagement and points of conversion. This framework is a good planning procedure for your persona measurement. Once the scenarios are mapped you can then define behavioural segments based on the actions the visitors in each typographic scenario take.

For instance looking at the REAN map dimensions, which of its component parts are more likely to be used by competitive people? Which by more methodical? Humanistic? Spontaneous?

Reach

By identifying trigger words used by different personas to find your website you can segment your audience by keyword groups.

Engage

By identifying pages of content, images, links, linear processes or offline touch points in your engagement model you can segment by visitor or session behaviour.

Activate

By identifying conversion points you can segment by actions taken.

Nurture

By identifying how people repeat their actions (or don't) you can segment based on likelihood to re-convert.

Identifying segments that represent a persona type is very useful. If you can identify by way of a persona segment which part of your audience is taking the actions you want them to take and which ones are the most likely to re-convert, you can design your online sales pitch more scientifically.

In order to illustrate this in action we need to go back to the competitive broadband persona example.

Competitive Personas REAN Segmentation

Reach

You now know that competitive people, for example, are likely to be influenced by the terms 'comes home fitted' in relation to the broadband connection. They might also therefore be influenced by similar terms (found in Google's Keyword Tool: https://adwords.google.com/select/KeywordTool) such as home networking wireless, home fitted wireless network, how to set-up a wireless network. Adding folks who enter the site with these key phrases from a search engine is the first part of the filter/segment you can set up.

The second focus on keyword entries is '1 communications bill'. If your personas are looking for this they might (according to Google) be looking for terms like: communications billing, single billing, simple broadband billing. Again by adding any visit that arrives from these keywords to your segment you may be attracting competitive personalities.

Engage

What competitive personalities do on your website should also be mapped. So what is the likely scenario these people are likely to take? One linear scenario might be searching on your internal search engine for words around the trigger phrases. By segmenting internal search queries in the same manner as external search queries you can add additional filters to your Engage competitive segment.

You may also want to track the competitive behaviour in a wireframe designed for the competitive personality and segment by accessed content. If links 'a' and 'b' were identified with competitive personality elements in mind and were linked to each other, then if the visit has consisted of page 'a' AND then page 'b' there is more likelihood your visitor is a competitive personality.

Activate

Certain conversion scenarios may be mapped specifically for the competitive types. For instance in this case a download could be offered to a competitive personality that discusses one bill for communications and how it comes home fitted. This could then be segmented because as we have already determined competitive personalities are more likely to want to know about this kind of information.

Nurture

Re-conversion scenarios could be mapped. For instance customers that have broadband but no mobile phone could also be sold a mobile contract at an attractive rate based around the one billing idea, again based on the assumption that your competitive personalities will see this as an advantage. Once the re-purchase is made then those visitors could also be segmented.

Methodical Personas REAN Segmentation

Reach

You know that methodical people are likely to influenced by terms around 'full service agreements' and 'flexible pricing' in relation to the broadband connection. Again they will be influenced by similar terms such as terms and conditions, broadband price plans, plan your own connection, flexible pricing and such like. Adding folks who enter the site with these key phrases from a search engine is the first part of the filter/segment you can set-up. They may also come from comparison websites that means specific referrers you can use as a filter for a segment.

Engage

What methodical personalities do on your website should also be mapped and planned. So what is the likely scenario these people are likely to take? Scenarios might include looking at a number of pages and long periods of time spent reading pages. Targeting this kind of persona in your segmentation might mean tracking people with higher than usual engagement with your website.

You may also want to track the methodical behaviour by identifying links in a similar way to competitive types.

Activate

Similarly conversion scenarios may be mapped specifically for the methodical types. For instance in this case a download could discuss terms and conditions in an easily printed out form from a link explaining how flexible the terms are. Again these personalities may convert more than the average visitor. They may subscribe to receive more information.

Nurture

Re-conversion scenarios should be mapped. These customers are more likely to convert to lower risk conversions like downloads, signing up for newsletters and being sent a brochure to a home address than buying the broadband contract immediately on the first visit, so measuring repeat conversions is vital.

Spontaneous Personas REAN Segmentation

Reach

So far the only thing that signals a potentially spontaneous persona is the branding. It's possible that people from direct sources of traffic or coming in on brand name keywords will be spontaneous. However it's a dangerous assumption alone. All personas might know the brand but not be emotionally attached to it. Therefore you need to look at trigger words that at least show a level of knowledge on behalf of the visitor, such as a brand name keyword and broadband as a phrase.

Engage

This scenario doesn't have enough unique selling points to appeal to an emotional type of person and this might be a problem. It's therefore worth testing by adding spontaneous attributes to the website, especially if you aren't converting enough visitors from the competitive segment you created. If you don't have something which appeals to this large user group you may miss out on a lot of deals. What about your offer can appeal to this kind of character? Is it possible you can quickly address values and provide assurances with credible opinions rather than options? Can you use third party testimony? Your homepage should speak to this personality type because many direct/bookmarked visits will come from this group of people. You should offer them ways of quickly getting information rather than making it hard for them.

Activate

Spontaneous people might buy something if they have enough information from you and have the budget. By offering fast ways to get that information on the website you might help convince them, so your copy should focus on getting the benefits quickly summarized at the top of a page. Track all links to conversions from within these summaries with specific link IDs to help identify spontaneous behavior. This will allow you to segment spontaneous behaviour.

Nurture

Re-conversion scenarios should be created for these types. An email with a powerful emotional reason to go back and re-purchase could be a good trigger.

Humanistic Personas REAN Segmentation

Reach

So far nothing signals any reason for the humanistic persona to find your broadband website. Branding might be a reason if the visitor has an emotional tie to the brand, but in the case of broadband (a commodity) it's unlikely to influence the visitor. However you may find that this persona has come from forums discussing broadband and heard from other people that your service is good, something which you could use as a filter for a segment.

Engage

Again this scenario doesn't have enough unique selling points to appeal to an emotional type of person and this is likely to be a problem. It's therefore worth testing by adding humanistic traits to the website, like great support, online live chat (where you can connect with a person in realtime), testimonials, case studies, blogs and anything that the visitor can interact with. It's the difference between selling your service as a commodity or offering friendly, helpful advice and support from real people. By offering this kind of service you show that you care about your customers (live chat). That you care about my opinion (blogs), that I'm not the guinea pig for your service (others have tried and love your service). All these little triggers will help the humanistic persona to feel like they are in the right place.

Using link IDs or content pages designed for these personas can be your segment.

Activate

Humanistic people buy when they have enough confidence in you as service provider. Tracking logins to chat applications, blog posts, blog comments and similar interactive methods of engagement can be used as filters for segmentation. Similarly downloading case studies and reading testimonials are also ways in which you can spot these folks.

Nurture

Re-conversion scenarios should be created for these types. Emailed blog response is a perfect way to get the visitor to re-connect and build up a community feel about your service. Once you have their loyalty it's worth introducing methods such as tell a friend and incentives to do so because these people are potentially your strongest evangelists.

Typographic Segments

Once you have defined the actions in each typographic scenario and segmented each type of persona in your analytics tool you can then attempt to score them based on the differences between the segments and the average traffic. Average traffic is scored first to give you a benchmark.

Then you want to see if the various segments are acting better compared to your KPIs. If for instance bounce rate (an engagement KPI to measure landing page relevance) is being measured then you want to know if your persona reach segment is better or worse than average.

If it is better than average you're doing something right – your trigger terms are working to show that the typeographic keywords are outperforming other keywords and therefore more relevant than average.

If the bounce rate is worse than average either your landing page needs optimizing to improve the relevance to a particular personality type or you need to re-think trigger terms and how you're reaching your audience.

Your segments can be filters designed to look at the behaviour of each type of persona or can be scored purely on the content accessed by your visitors. It depends on your websites goal and really boils down to the one that is the easiest to measure.

There is more about the scoring method in Chapter 7.

Using the Insight Model to Improve Conversion

Most people use statistics the way a drunk uses a lamp post,
more for support than enlightenment.

Mark Twain

CHAPTER CONTENTS

7.1 THE INSIGHT MODEL

In Chapter 1 (discussing how the Internet has changed your world) you saw a situation described that affects most businesses trying to do analytics today. The number one problem faced by most businesses today is not

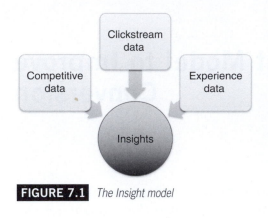

FIGURE 7.1 *The Insight model*

the lack of information, it's data abundance! Too much information and not enough action! The problem is deciphering the data can be overwhelming for those who don't have an analytics background.

Many vendors are earning their living by supplying tracking tools that deliver the thousands of reports. The trick is to know what to look at which is why in Chapter 2 we have already discussed REAN and in Chapter 3 we have already discussed KPIs.

What you now need to know is how to learn what data is valuable and what data isn't and stop wasting your time on the stuff that doesn't help you. This is why I have produced a simplified relationship diagram (Figure 7.1) that shows 'The Insight model'.

Holistic Benchmarks

The Insight model works because it takes a holistic approach to analysing the problem you may have. You may have a KPI like conversion rate that is 3% and bounce rate that is 40% but how do you know if those figures are good or bad?

You could take an approach that says 'lets develop internal benchmarks which we try to improve' which is not a bad approach at all, but it would be better if you had competitive data so that you knew how they were doing in comparison.

Competitive Data

As discussed in Chapter 5, it's great if you improve by 10% but what if the rest of the market is improving by 20% every month? It then means you're growing more slowly than the competition. Competitive data and analysis can help you understand the marketplace you're in and help you to take action accordingly.

Experience Data

If you also have data that describes your visitors' experience, you have data that can help answer why competitive and clickstream data indicates there is a problem (or not as the case may be).

Clickstream Data

Finally do the 10–20 KPIs that your hub and spokes deem important all result in you taking actions every time you get a report, or do the KPIs simply sit in their Powerpoint presentation after a routine read every month?

This is a vital question that you have to ask yourself when developing your analytics culture. There is a rule of thumb which you might want to follow:

> If a KPI, a report, an assessment or an analysis does not allow you to take specific actions that improves the situation or doesn't otherwise give you insights then stop and do something more useful instead.

> Beware that you don't simply use KPIs as a support mechanism that will quickly lose value and the confidence of your staff.

7.2 PUTTING THE INSIGHT MODEL TO WORK (SCORING)

In this chapter you'll learn how to combine the data types to help you to understand how to improve your conversion rate in an analysis called an Insight Assessment.

This will help you to develop the quick wins (see Chapter 4) you will need in order to continue to build your analytics culture. Before you get into the analysis however you need to understand how it is scored. The scoring mechanism you adopt, whether it be a balanced scorecard method or a variation like the one included in this chapter, is one of the most important things that will drive you away from passive reporting into taking action in your business.

Scoring

The scoring method is really a process of simplifying the data you have (Figure 7.2). Anything that makes your data easy to understand helps build your analytics culture.

Zero is really bad and 5 is really good. Everyone can understand this.

There is no way to define in a book what the right scoring method for you is as it's all based around the KPIs you have designed. However there are some guidelines you can follow when setting up a scoring method that works across all businesses.

The REAN Cycle

REAN is the strategy that underlies all the other work that you do. You design your REAN map in the planning phases before developing your KPIs (see Chapter 2).

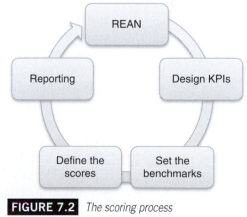

FIGURE 7.2 *The scoring process*

Once your KPIs are designed (see Chapter 3) you set benchmarks based on historical or competitive data.

Scoring should be aligned with benchmarks to help you work toward your goals.

You should tie the scores into your business objectives. Let's say for example your process abandonment is 80% meaning a conversion rate of 20% resulting in 1000 sales. In order to get 2000 sales you would need to either drive twice the visits or improve your cart conversion by another 20% to 40% thus meaning your abandonment was 60%. If your goal is to double sales then scoring a 3 for a 60% abandonment rate is good (you hit target). Exceeding your target would score a '4' 'or '5'.

This is a simplistic example but it illustrates the way the scores help pinpoint problem areas. Once you have determined what your benchmarks are you then move onto developing the scoring system around those benchmarks. This chapter will cover how to do that (see setting the scoring scale based on KPIs).

REAN Dashboard

Then finally you can report the results – how and what to report is covered in Chapter 8 but you should also average your score for reach, engage, activate and nurture and map each spoke's main score back to a master REAN dashboard. This allows you to benchmark your spokes (hub and spoke – Chapter 1) against each other regardless of the business objectives and KPIs of each spoke.

This is why the relationship has the underlying arrow in Figure 7.2 that starts and ends at REAN. Comparing spokes directly to each other might sound impossible. A common question is 'how can you compare our e-commerce unit to support services?'

Actually you're not comparing sales numbers to support queries. What you're doing is comparing spoke effectiveness at doing it's job and it's fully comparable when done right. If the KPIs of both business units tie into business objectives they all have to reach an audience, engage with them, activate them and nurture the relationships with their customers. They are probably both using different methods to attract audiences in their reach strategies, but when each reach attribute is scored on a 0–5 scale you can then average this to get an overall reach score. Similarly you can do this with engage, activate and nurture.

Once you have REAN at 0–5 you can then compare different units (spokes) directly allowing you to say, e-commerce is less effective than support at meeting its business objectives or vice versa depending on who scored higher. This is key to introducing performance based pay schemes and other proliferation techniques (see Chapter 9).

Setting the Scoring Scale Based on KPIs

There are two types of data you can use to set benchmarks historic internal data and market data.

Market Data

Outside of your REAN model is the whole world. The amount of people in any given country determine the size of your market and this needs to be examined before you can decide to do any reach strategies. If you're doing Internet marketing in any given country or part of the world the first thing you should ask is if the market is big enough to warrant the investment. How you answer that might depend on the level of Internet penetration the market has in the area.

You can get this information quickly from sources like internetworld-stats.com, but for more in-depth information the CIA Library (https://www.cia.gov/library/publications/the-world-factbook/) has extensive data on every country in the world.

Then you would need to understand the competitive landscape, how big is the competition in a part of the world? Google Trends across your top competitors' websites is good for this. Comscore or Hitwise would also be a good investment.

Market data really should be used to formulate your business case and set business objectives. If you know that there are 105 million Internet users in Europe and your competitors are reaching 1 million of them a month it at least lets you see the level of possibilities and the level of spending you might have to make.

From a scoring perspective the market data should affect what the numbers are in comparison to the market size and the reach of your current competition.

Historic Data

Historical data is commonly used to develop benchmarks. It's easy to say for instance that the target is 25% growth and rely on clickstream data to design an internal benchmark. However as discussed in Chapter 5 it has to be taken into context. If you grow at 25% and the competition grows at 50% you're still being left behind.

It's not possible in all cases to use competitive market data but if you can historical data used in combination with market data is the best way to

FIGURE 7.4 *The scoring parameters*

FIGURE 7.3 *Set the scoring scale*

develop a good benchmark and therefore be able to develop a good scoring mechanism.

Scoring Scales

Going back to some KPI examples from Chapter 3 is the best way to illustrate how to set the scoring scale (Figure 7.3).

Scoring might be designed in the manner shown in Figure 7.4.

Of course 4 and 2 should be added as well in most cases but the idea is clear. 4–5 is what the business is aiming for, 3 is acceptable and shows the business is on course, 1–2 is designed to pinpoint areas of improvement and 0 is unacceptable and shows a failure which needs addressing.

Scoring Reach KPIs

Cost per referred visit (CPRV)	**Total marketing cost per referring source / Total number of visits per referring source**	Shows the best traffic sources in terms of cost per visit. Helps answer questions 1 and 2 from the KPI workshop 29/6	Historical – start with the first prices per visit and try to improve upon them	Manage marketing campaigns to focus on lower cost traffic. Use in combination with visitor volume ratio to determine the highest ROI source of traffic

The above KPI is an example from Chapter 3. In order to set the score follow the process shown in Figure 7.3.

1. Get an aggregate number (€0.10 – see below).

2. Define your target based on historical (clickstream) data and competitive data (25% cut in costs).

3. Develop your scale (0 is failure, 3 is 25% decrease in cost, 5 is better than 25% decrease in cost).

Cost per referred visit as a reach KPI is listed as 'per source' but in order to score we should aggregate first to get the total cost of marketing and divide it by the total number of visits.

For arguments sake let's say the aggregate cost per visit is €0.10 (100,000 visits at an expense of €10K). Your competitors have twice the amount of traffic that you have. The market indicates that you and all your competitors combined are only reaching 10% of the total market. Your target therefore is to cut cost per visit by 25% and grow the amount of visitors by 200% in one year. This should mean you start outgrowing your competitors and increase your market share.

That means the scoring for the cost per referred visit might look like so:

Score 5 = 50% + improvement over benchmark 0.10 euro (€0.05 or less CPV)

Score 4 = 41–50% improvement over benchmark 0.10 euro (€0.06 to €0.05 CPV)

Score 3 = 25–40% improvement over benchmark 0.10 euro (€0.075 to €0.06 CPV)

Score 2 = 10–24% improvement over benchmark 0.10 euro (€0.09 to €0.075 CPV)

Score 1 = 0–10% improvement over benchmark 0.10 euro (€0.09 to €0.10 CPV)

Score 0 = no improvement or worse than €0.10 CPV

This would then be scored across all sources of traffic. For instance if the reach sources were:

SEO = 3 cents (editorial costs)	Score 5
SEM = 8 cents	Score 2
Banners = 30 cents	Score 0
Radio = 10 cents	Score 0
TV = 200 cents	Score 0
Offline seminars = 7 cents	Score 3
Direct branding = no cost	Score 5
Own traffic = no cost	Score 5

As can be seen from this list there are immediate areas of improvement for this KPI. A target of €0.075 means SEM requires work to bring it down so that it hits target.

Banners and TV are very expensive and would probably never hit the target – a decision needs to be made whether to continue with these traffic sources. Radio could work – testing and targeting might be tried here. Seminars are already on target, next time a seminar is launched the same process should be tried with perhaps even better speakers and event hosting whereas SEO, branding and own traffic sources are very cost efficient.

If the above scores are all 3 or higher at the end of the year then the cost per click is effectively less than 7.5 cents which hits the target 25% improvement goal set by the spoke business manager. The easiest approach would be to remove banners and TV while working on radio and SEM to improve the cost per click.

However the targets were to double volume and reduce costs at the same time. This is where the second KPI from Chapter 3, visitor volume ratio, comes into the picture.

| Visitor volume ratio per referrer (V V R) | **Number of visitors per traffic source / Total number visitors** | Shows the best traffic sources in terms of volume (number of visitors) across all the methods to attract your visitors. Helps answer questions 1, 7, 9 and 15 from the KPI workshop on the 29/6 | Historical – start with the first internal ratios and try to improve upon them | Manage marketing campaigns to focus on higher volume traffic. Use in combination with engagement index and cost per visit to determine the highest ROI source of traffic |

Again this KPI is measuring the volume per referrer but in order to set a score we need to first get the aggregate numbers and then work our scoring method into it. We know already that we're getting 100,000 visitors but in order to reach our target we need 200,000 per month. It is again quite easy to score this, in order to double the traffic we need to either increase the amount of traffic from each source or add new sources of traffic to the equation.

Because there are unlimited numbers of referrers we need to break them down into common dimensions. In the case of referrers we use:

1. Own traffic – Traffic that arrives from your own company such as specific country traffic or partner websites that are part of your own network.

2. Earned traffic – Traffic that links to your site freely such as PR, articles, SEO, blog posts, feed links, social media links and direct traffic.

3. Bought traffic – Traffic you have specifically paid for in targeted campaigns (such as SEM and banners)

4. Unknown – Unknown traffic sources.

The scoring might look like this:

5 = Contributes 50% or more of the target level (100,000 per month)

4 = Contributes 26–49% of the target level

3 = Contributes 25% of target level (50,000 per month)

2 = Contributes 12.5–24% of the target level

1 = Contributes 1–12.5% of the target level

0 = Contributes less than 1% of the target level. (Less than 2000 per month)

The traffic breakdown at the moment looks like this:

SEO (earned) = 25,000

SEM (bought) = 20,000

Banners (bought) = 4000

Radio (bought) = 1000

TV (bought) = 500

Offline seminars (bought) = 200

Direct access (earned) = 29,300

Own traffic = 20,000

Earned total – 54,300	Score 3	Weight 33%
Bought total – 25,700	Score 2	Weight 33%
Own traffic – 20,000	Score 1	Weight 33%
Unknown – 0	Score 0	Weight 1%

This means the only traffic on target at the moment is the earned traffic meaning that in order to get 200,000 visitors per month the site is going to have to drive much more traffic from it's own network if possible or buy much more in by using campaigns.

One important point to note is that the scoring method has to have the ability to adapt to the variables surrounding it without being changed. So if for instance we suddenly get ten new sources of traffic then while the number of referrers being measured increases the scale isn't affected because of the dimensions you invent (own, earned, bought and unknown).

You'll notice I used TV and radio in the example. These mediums would be scored 0 in the current scorecard. This doesn't however take into effect the awareness generated by those mediums. You should refer to your business case in this instance. How big is your target audience? How do you make them aware? TV and radio could be dropped from Bought sources if you decide measuring them in this way is unfair, but it could remain a critical part of your overall marketing strategy.

Additionally you could decide to set up a layer outside of reach called awareness (AREAN) and focus on awareness measurements such as panel data or measure control groups.

Weighting the Scores

Using scores means you should understand weighting. The weight is important to classify which is more important to your business strategy. If for instance you think that your 'bought' traffic is the most important you could assign a weight of 50% to bought traffic meaning that 50% of your score would be based on the score from bought media.

The weighting works by adding a simple calculation to an Excel spreadsheet. The idea is that whatever you weigh as a percentage represents the importance of the variable being scored.

In this case own, earned and bought media is very important while unknown traffic is a problem. I would always score unknown traffic very low (i.e. 1%) because you have to work hard to find out where the traffic is coming from and therefore scoring 5 for loads of unknown traffic should not be great.

If your scores are therefore like this:

Own	0	33%
Bought	0	33%
Earned	0	33%
Unknown	5	1%
Overall score	0.05	

If you score 5 in a system that assigns 1% to unknown as shown above the overall value still shows a very big problem. In the above scenario you would only score 0.05 out of 5 overall.

If however you had not weighted the score based on importance and had just given each score 25% of the overall value it becomes less of a problem to your overall score:

Own	0	25%
Bought	0	25%
Earned	0	25%
Unknown	5	25%
Overall score	1.25	

Scoring Engage KPIs

Bounce rate (BR)	Page views / Number single page visits per page	Shows the performance of the pages in relation to each other by the number of visitors who have taken no actions. This KPI helped answer questions 10,11,12,29 and 30 in the workshop of 29/6	Historical – start with the first ratio and try to improve upon it. Set three levels, short, medium and long term goals to improve the abandonment rate	Optimize reach sources to be more relevant to the page, optimize keywords for relevance with the page in question, optimize headlines, increase the amount of relevant embedded links in the page

1. Get the overall site bounce rate aggregate figure: **total number of single page visits/total visits.**

2. Set targets against this benchmark. 20% improvement across site average in 1 year.

3. Set the scale.

In this case if the bounce rate is site average of 50% and the target is 20% improvement overall the target scale is 40%.

Set the scale at 3 if 40% is reached, more if it's better than 40% and less if it's worse than 40%.

Score 5 = 50%+ better than average (≤25% bounce rate)

Score 4 = 35–49% better than average (32–26% bounce rate)

Score 3 = 20–34% better than average (40–33% bounce rate)

Score 2 = 10–19% better than average (45–41% bounce rate)

Score 1 = 1–9% better than average (49–46% bounce rate)

Score 0 = no better or worse than average.

This means that regardless of which page you're looking at you're always comparing to the aggregate figure and seeing if it's better or worse than average and scoring accordingly. The individual page bounce rates are worked out as before and compared on page or content group level. If for instance the page bounce rates looked like so:

Page	Bounce	Score	Weight
Contact page	56%	0	25%
Home page	33%	3	25%
Services page	65%	0	25%
About us page	46%	1	25%
Overall score		1	

This scenario clearly shows that the site has big problems on the contact, services and about us page with only the home page hitting the target. Optimization processes listed in the KPI actions would begin on the other three pages.

Visit Engagement Index

| Visit engagement index (VEI) | **Engaged visits (pre-defined) / Total number of visits** | The engagement index should be used to determine which type of visits are the most engaged from an activation and reach perspective. This very useful KPI helped answer questions 4,25,26,27 and 33 | Historical – The ratio's should have short medium and long term targets, the objective being to engage more visits, thus driving more activation | The least engaged visits should be encouraged by the use of effective linking and quality content to read more, download more and click through more pages. You should be careful however not to confuse good engagement with poor usability |

The engagement index requires that we get the number of engaged visits as we've defined them and divide that by total visits to get an overall site engagement index.

The same method as previously defined is used to set the scoring:

1. Get the overall site visit engagement index (current 10% engaged): **total number of engaged visits/total visits.**

2. Set targets against this benchmark. 100% improvement (20% engagement) in site engaged visits in 1 year.

3. Set the scale.

Score 5 = 200% better than index ($\leq$30% engagement index)

Score 4 = 151–199% better than index (25–29% engagement index)

Score 3 = 100–150% better than index (20–25% engagement index)

Score 2 = 50–99% better than index (15–19% engagement index)

Score 1 = 10–49% better than index (10–15% engagement index)

Score 0 = less than 10% better or worse than index.

The scores can then be compared to any traffic source, keywords and used to identify the pages that are the least effective at keeping engaged visits on the site. These would be your starting points of optimization.

Scoring Activation KPIs

Conversion rate is perhaps the most important KPI of them all and should be scored across reach sources, engagement methods and nurture sources. For instance you should measure which initial reach source converts at the highest level, which source engages best before the conversion and which conversion results in the most retained customers. You should also score costs (like cost per conversion/activation) so that you can immediately see the most valuable reach sources to target conversions from.

| Conversion rate (CR) | **Number of confirmed conversions (slide 16) / Total number of visits** | Conversion rate can be used for all the individual conversion points listed on slide 12. It shows the number of visits that took the action listed as a percentage of all engaged visits. This KPI helps answer the business questions, 5, 17, 18 and 33 | Historical – The ratio's should have short medium and long term targets, the objective being to convert more visits | The lowest conversion points can be tested in different ways, offered to different types of visitors or dropped altogether as an unsuccessful method of attracting activation. The highest conversion points should be generally encouraged and used to nurture other less activated visitors |

Looking at the conversion source you again follow the three steps:

1. Get the aggregate conversion rate of all sources (**total number of conversions/total visits**). This is your average conversion rate and your benchmark. (For arguments sake lets say 1%.)

2. Next look at your targets. Business target requires a 2% conversion rate overall by the end of the year. This means double or a 100% conversion rate improvement is required just to hit target.

3. Set your scale. 100% improvement is a score of 3 (hit target) so lets scale realistic efforts around that.

Your scale might look like so across each reach source:

Score 5 = 300%+ better than average conversion rate (>3% actual conversion)

Score 4 = 250–300% better than average conversion rate (2.5–3% actual conversion)

Score 3 = 200–250% better than average conversion rate (2–2.5% actual conversion – the target level)

Score 2 = 150–200% better than average conversion rate (1.5–2% actual conversion)

Score 1 = 100–150% better than average conversion rate (1.0–1.5% actual conversion)

Score 0 = less than benchmark (<1%).

This then means that you score higher conversion sources at a higher level and find your points of optimization from the lower scores.

Cost Per Activation (CPA)

| Cost per activation (or acquisition) (CPA) | **Total cost of referring source / Number of confirmed conversions (16)** | Cost per activation (or more commonly cost per acquisition) shows the cost of delivering one conversion. This is useful in determining which is your most cost effective source of traffic activation. This KPI helps answer questions 5, 17 and 18 | Historical – start with the first costs per activated visit and try to improve upon them | CPA should be compared with reach sources and cost per engaged visit. The action should be to focus spend more on good sources of activation and engagement |

The cost per acquisition is similar to cost per referred visit except you replace visits with converting visits in your calculation. You follow exactly the same process:

Cost per conversion as a KPI is listed above as 'per source' but in order to score we should aggregate first to get the total cost of marketing and divide it by the total number of conversions.

1. Aggregate: For arguments sake lets say the aggregate cost per conversion is €10 (**1000 conversions at an expense of €10K**).

2. Your target is to cut cost per conversion by 25%, this means the target cost per conversion is €7.50.

3. Set the scale with 25% improvement being a score of 3.

That means the scoring for the cost acquisition might look like so:

Score 5 = 50%+ improvement over benchmark 10 euro (€5 or less CPA)

Score 4 = 41–50% improvement over benchmark 10 euro (€6 to €5 CPA)

Score 3 = 25–40% improvement over benchmark 10 euro (€7.5 to €6 CPA)

Score 2 = 10–24% improvement over benchmark 10 euro (€9.0 to €7.5 CPA)

Score 1 = 0–10% improvement over benchmark 10 euro (€9 to €10 CPA)

Score 0 = no improvement or worse than €10 CPA

Scoring in this manner allows you to quickly pinpoint high costing conversion sources and reduce spend to them or optimize content. Scoring 3 or higher shows which sources are hitting the businesses target.

Scoring Nurture KPIs

Nurture KPIs can be scored in exactly the same manner.

Email open rate (EOR)	**Total emails opened / Total visitors to email service**	This shows how many emails each person is reading (and how many exposures to ads they have). This KPI helped answer business question 8	Historical – start with the first EOR and try and improve upon it	Improve the ways people can use the email services (personalization)

The email open rate is the rate that we first need to aggregate. Then we need to look at all individual sources of email traffic in comparison to the benchmark to score each campaign against the average.

1. Aggregate the numbers (**total emails opened over given time period/ total emails sent over a given time period**). The total emails sent and opened would include all the different campaigns.

2. Set the target based on open targets. If the open rate was 20% and it was found that these people were the most likely to re-purchase the target might be set at a 25% improvement (25% open rate).

3. Set the scale. A 25% improvement scores 3.

Score 5 = 50%+ better than average (30% or better open rate)

Score 4 = 35–49% better than average

Score 3 = 25–34% better than average (minimum target)

Score 2 = 10–24% better than average

Score 1 = 1–9% better than average

Score 0 = no better or worse than average. (current level)

Doing this quickly allows you to pinpoint campaigns that were opened by the email recipients at a higher rate and optimize the poorer ones accordingly.

Scoring REAN

In a large organization you may have a number of different business units each with it's own budget. These 'spokes' are often acting independently of each other and regardless of how good your hub is at combining information from different spokes a method is needed to compare the different units.

Each spoke should have it's own KPIs and each KPI should fall into either reach, engage, activate or nurture (or perhaps two or three of the dimensions). These KPIs are by their very nature business critical. Scoring an overall REAN score for each spoke then allows you to compare how each spoke is doing based on each unit's business critical goals. Once you have normalized the REAN score for each spoke then it is simple to compare across business units and this allows you to see how you're doing in comparison to each business unit. More importantly if the scorecard method is implemented business wide then you're designing a method of in-house competition as well as laying the groundwork for incentive based bonuses. If you score each reach source 0–5 you can then average your overall score to be your 'Reach Score'. Once you have your overall reach score you then have something you can use to compare departments (or spokes).

For instance the last example had seven KPIs, cost per referred visit (CPRV), visit volume ratio (VVR), bounce rate (BR), visit engagement index (VEI), conversion rate (CR), cost per action (CPA) and open rate (OR).

1. If both business units have the same KPIs for different reasons then these are comparable.

2. If business units had different KPIs in each dimension (such as reach) then they can still be averaged and compared to give a reach score.

3. If a business unit doesn't need to reach anyone then it could still be measured across engage, activate and nurture.

4. If a business unit has different measures of engagement it doesn't matter as long as you can define the business critical requirement in the KPIs for each spoke. For instance if one spoke had an engagement index criteria that said three page click depth and one minute on site there is a reason for that. It could be that it takes at least that long to get required information for instance. If another spoke had ten pages and three minutes as an engagement index then the point is mute about how long it takes, the point is that the information is passed to the visitor. So engagement can be compared.

5. All businesses have costs even if that cost is free. So all cost metrics can be compared. If there is a reason one business spoke gets lots of free traffic then perhaps other business spokes can learn from that. If the cost metrics are free for an unfair reason then the weight of the scores should be adjusted to suit this.

It could mean that across your business spokes you have some kind of comparison table that looks like the table in Figure 7.5 for upper management. The

Spoke	Reach	Engage	Activate	Nurture	REAN score
Sales/E-commerce (20%)	3	2	1	0	1.50
Product support (20%)	4	2	2	3	2.75
Corporate/Finance (10%)	2	1	0	0	0.75
PR & Media (10%)	2	1	1	1	1.25
Supporting software (20%)	2	4	3	3	3.00
Community marketing (20%)	1	4	4	3	3.00
Overall Score					2.25 (weighted average of all spokes)

FIGURE 7.5 *Spoke scoring sample with REAN*

business shown in this figure has six spokes each weighted as shown on the left in terms of the investment capital put into each spoke by the management.

The only businesses that are on target are the Community marketing and the Supporting software spokes. Both of these spokes can be improved by improving their reach elements that are below target. This is because the product support and e-commerce/sales functions get priority on the companies' main website in terms of the teasers on the home page. So a lot of the 'own traffic' is directed there rather than supporting software and community marketing. Because the rest of their results are on target or better they have a good case to fight for more teasers from the home page.

The worst cases are PR and media and Corporate/finance. They underperform across all their KPIs and therefore need improvements across the board. Combined they are only considered to be worth 20% of the overall investment strategy. However by improving their numbers the staff in these spokes should be awarded the same levels of bonuses.

Lower investment importance means less staff per spoke and less overall investment, but the staff that are there should not be penalized because their contribution to the business is as vital as any other spoke. Without them the business will fail which is why the investment happens in the first place. They will however need to improve across engagement, activation and nurturing relations with their target markets as well as find new ways to reach them.

A big priority for the e-commerce unit is to improve engagement and activation. They have to do this before they can even think about nurturing existing customers.

The upper management can set targets based on the numbers they receive and can make decisions about what they need to do in each spoke. It could be that a steering group from corporate comes and asks for money to improve their part of the website showing substandard results as proof that the money is required. They would have a strong argument especially if they backed it up with a plan showing how they would improve things.

Developing spoke REAN scores provides top management with a tool to see where they need to improve and breed in-house competition across your spokes.

Regardless of your KPIs you can set scores accordingly and make a scale that quickly shows anyone in the business what the optimization opportunities are. It is better as a business that you have similar base KPIs across things like costs and then have individual spoke specific measures that the hub can look at.

Optimization Opportunities

The Insight model uses scoring methods throughout to normalize the KPIs, to help spread understanding but most of all to drive business insights for your spokes. Insights that help to optimize your marketing and online business are what you can use throughout your organization to help drum home the analytics message. This brings us to the next stage of this chapter. Doing an assessment of your business activities using the Insight model.

7.3 USING THE INSIGHT MODEL TO IMPROVE CONVERSION

The Persona Definition and Research Stages

Both of these stages have already been shown in Chapter 6. In this example we're going to take Tapio's persona and motivation as the basis for explaining how to do the analysis.

Analysis Stage

As shown in Figure 7.6 the analysis stage contains a competitive assessment, an experience assessment and a clickstream assessment. The reasons for this are that when the persona (Tapio) does his research he is going to be looking at competitive websites therefore we need a competitive analysis, he is going to be helped or hindered by your website's usability and how it relates to him (a study of his experience is needed) and generally he is likely to have the same major issues (if there are any) as everyone else which is why the clickstream assessment is needed.

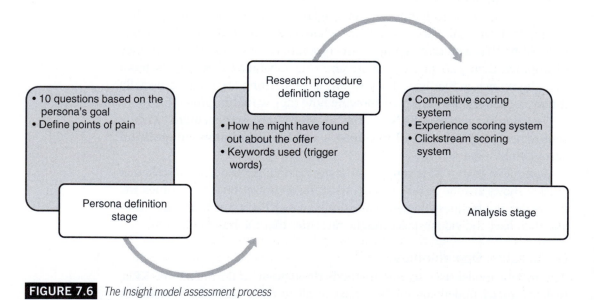

FIGURE 7.6 *The Insight model assessment process*

Combining the three data sources and pinpointing the weakest areas is what the conversion assessment shows. Then you need to do some testing designed to see if improving the weakest points improves the conversion rate.

Competitive Analysis

After creating your persona and defining Tapio's needs, his pain points and his trigger terms you're now ready to score each question across the market and see how your site fares. It may be good to assign the role of Tapio to someone not familiar with your website, or assign/hire someone who can take an objective view.

The questions, tasks and considerations that Tapio has now need to be assessed. Which site has the best fit for Tapio's needs?

The questions defined as the persona was created were:

- What is the price per month?

- How many service/price (speed to MB ratio) options are there and are they clearly differentiated?

- Does the cost vary based on usage? If so how? If not is the price fixed or could there be hidden surprises?

- Tapio's wife doesn't want to use cables to connect to the Internet. Is the broadband connection wireless? Does this cost more?

- Do any free accessories (i.e. wireless modem) come with the service?

- Are there any free offers in Finland around broadband?

- If so are the free offers comparable in terms of features?

- Tapio heard that a full system contract including digital TV could be purchased with broadband access to the Internet? Is this possible in his location?

- Does the system come home fitted? Is it manual installation? If so is it easy?

- Are there service guarantees? Money back options or trial periods?

These ten questions will all help Tapio make a decision if they are answered well. Upon doing a Google search for 'laajakaista' (broadband), one of Tapio's key trigger terms, we see a number of companies appear both in organic and paid search results. Where possible I would suggest at least the top three preferably the top four competitors across all trigger phrases would be selected as study cases.

We then keep it as simple as possible and playing the role of Tapio go to each website and ask how well each company answers each question. The questions are then scored with the following criteria:

Persona question	What is the price per month?	Is the question asked by the persona answered on the study website? If it is not answered at all score zero. If it is answered on the website is it answered better than the four competing websites? Score the five sites 1–5 for the questions.	5 = Answers the question better than all competitors 4 = Answers the question better than three of the competitors 3 = Answers the question better than two of the competitors 2 = Answers the question better than one of the competitors 1 = Answered no better or worse than any of the competitors 0 = Worse than all the competitors or not answered at all

This process is repeated for the ten questions until you have scores for each website. In Tapio's case it resulted in five websites scoring as shown in Figure 7.7 (website names replaced with 1–5).

Competitive Analysis – Answering the Needs of the Persona

Figure 7.7 shows a table of scores that are averaged across the ten questions. You'll notice that the scores are weighted averages (this is a calculation method in Excel). The weighted average means that the higher the weight the more critical it is to answer this question well. It is based on the pre-determined pain points of the persona. If you look at Tapio's template you'll see that his main pain points were installation issues and speed (questions 2 and 9 which total 30% of the whole weight of 10 questions).

If anyone answers these two questions well they are 30% of the way there to impressing Tapio. Price point is also important. Tapio doesn't want to be ripped off. Amazingly however this study shows that while all the websites focus on free offers it is very difficult to actually discern what the price per month is which is Tapio's main issue. Tapio understands that free comes with conditions usually (like long contracts) so he isn't so interested (only 10% of the total weight is based around free offers). Free accessories (like hardware) might have helped sway him and two out of five websites mentioned that. All in all many of the sites scored poorly and even the best site (number 5) got less than 2/5.

Number 1 the worst (and coincidentally this study was done for site number 1) showed that in 7/10 cases, their competition (sites 2–5) were answering the questions better than they were.

Website	Weight	1	2	3	4	5
Competitive analysis		1.80	2.30	2.73	2.15	2.58
Answering the needs of the persona		0.85	1.35	1.70	1.05	1.90
1 What is the price per month?	15%	2.00	0.00	1.00	0.00	2.00
2 How many service/price options (speed to MB ratio) are there and are they clearly differentiated?	15%	2.00	0.00	3.00	2.00	3.00
3 Does the cost vary based on usage? If so how? If not is the price fixed or could there be hidden surprises?	5%	1.00	1.00	1.00	1.00	1.00
4 Tapio's wife doesn't want to use cables to connect to the Internet. Is the broadband connection wireless? Does this cost more?	5%	0.00	5.00	5.00	0.00	2.00
5 Do any free accessories (i.e. wireless modem) come with the service?	10%	0.00	5.00	5.00	0.00	0.00
6 Are there any free offers in Finland around broadband?	5%	3.00	4.00	3.00	5.00	0.00
7 If so are the free offers comparable in terms of features?	5%	1.00	4.00	3.00	5.00	0.00
8 Tapio heard that a full system contract including digital TV could be purchased with broadband access to the Internet? Is this possible in his location?	5%	0.00	3.00	0.00	4.00	5.00
9 Does it come home fitted? Is it manual installation? If so is it easy?	15%	0.00	0.00	0.00	0.00	5.00
10 Are there service guarantees? Money back options or trial periods?	10%	0.00	0.00	0.00	0.00	0.00

FIGURE 7.7 *Competitive analysis, answering the needs of the personas*

This is a HUGE opportunity. Not only have they identified why they might be losing business to their competition they have also identified that their competition is very poor as well overall so they can quickly gain a competitive advantage.

You might ask 'what constitutes answering the questions "better" than the competition?' Answering the question better is simply satisfying the needs of Tapio. Any subjectivity on the part of the analyst should really be cut down to a minimum by answering ten questions.

The second part of the competitive analysis comes from comparing how each site displays trigger words.

Competitive Analysis – Trigger Word Analysis

Trigger word	Laajakaista	Does the persona have a relevant experience when clicking the link from his/her search result? Score one point for each item below (max five)	Score 1 point for each criteria (max 5 minimum zero)
		1. Keyword used is visible on the landing page	
		2. Keyword subject is discussed at length on the landing page (more than 250 words)	
		3. Links to more direct information regarding the keyword subject exist	
		4. Links to related topics exist	
		5. Graphics/images used relate directly to the keyword	
		6. Customer testimonials discussing the subject exist	
		7. Analyst finds out something new from the landing page related to the topic	

The trigger words are all compared to the landing pages after searching for them in the search engine. You then ask does Tapio have a relevant experience when clicking the link from his/her search result. One point is given for each of the criteria mentioned above.

The study website at this stage (site 1) did a lot better than it had previously, scoring 2.75 from 5 which was above halfway. However Figure 7.8 demonstrates why competitive analysis is so important. 2.75 might be considered quite good if it stood alone, but when taken in context of the four competing sites you can see that it is still a poor score. In comparison to the competition site 1 is still behind.

Averaging both the scores for the competitor analysis gave the following results in Figure 7.9. As can clearly be seen Tapio was much more impressed with sites 2–5 and based on this analysis alone would probably buy from site 3 or site 5 if anywhere as they seemed to cater for more of his needs and be more relevant.

So clearly the competition are doing a better job for Tapio but part of his research method was to check all the major brands (including site 1). This is why a clickstream analysis of site 1, the subject of our study, might reveal more insights.

Keyword	Weight	2.75	3.25	3.75	3.25	3.25
Laajakaista	25%	4.00	5.00	4.00	4.00	4.00
Laajakaista Yhteys	25%	3.00	4.00	3.00	4.00	5.00
Laajakaista Nopeus	25%	0.00	0.00	5.00	0.00	0.00
Laajakaista Hinnat	25%	4.00	4.00	3.00	5.00	4.00

FIGURE 7.8   *Competitive analysis, trigger word relevance*

Website	Weight	1	2	3	4	5
Competitive analysis		**1.80**	**2.30**	**2.73**	**2.15**	**2.58**
Answering the needs of the persona		0.85	1.35	1.70	1.05	1.90
Trigger keyword analysis		2.75	3.25	3.75	3.25	3.25

FIGURE 7.9   *Competitive analysis*

Clickstream Analysis

The next stage of the conversion assessment is to do a clickstream analysis. A clickstream analysis is the simple analysis of the data found in the web analytics tool compared directly against three KPIs. You might think that doesn't measure the engagement of your website well enough, especially if you read Chapter 3 and developed your own KPIs for other reasons. However what a conversion assessment is designed to do is see if there are any improvements we can make from those that have not really engaged well enough to convert.

The three KPIs we're going to use are simply bounce rate (BR), exit rate (ER) and shopping cart abandonment rate (SCAR). BR will be used to score the level of relevance of the landing pages and trigger words used by Tapio in his journey to make a purchase and SCAR will be used to measure the abandonment rate of the shopping cart.

Shopping cart abandonment rate (SCAR) is defined as:

The number of visits that did not finish a pre-defined shopping cart process as a percentage of visits that started the process.

Bounce rate (BR) is defined as:

A visit in which only one page was visited for the duration of the visit.

Exit rate (ER) is defined as:

The amount of visits that exit from the content pages as a percentage of all visits to the content page.

In your assessments you can use as many KPIs as you need and score them accordingly based on the goals you have. For instance form abandonment rate (for lead generation purposes) click depth index, page views per visit or time spent on site could all be used to help you back up the findings and validate your score. However the easiest method is to focus on the fewest KPIs to score and validate.

Clickstream Analysis – SCAR (Shopping Cart Abandonment Rate)

The clickstream analysis scale for our particular case (going back to Tapio) had the following scale for shopping cart abandonment rate.

5 = 40% or less abandonment rate
4 = 50–40% abandonment rate
3 = 60–50% abandonment rate
2 = 70–60% abandonment rate
1 = 80–70% abandonment rate
0 = 81% or higher abandonment rate

As mentioned the business model should drive this score. If by having an abandonment rate of 60% you hit your sales target, score 3. If you exceed your target you score 4 or 5 depending on how well you do. As with all scoring methods the scale depends on your KPIs and your targets. All the scoring method is doing is making it easier to pinpoint problems and produce easily understood dashboards.

Clickstream Analysis – BR (Bounce Rate)

The clickstream analysis scale for bounce rate was defined in the standard three-step process described earlier. Firstly we needed to know the site average bounce rate (overall aggregate). This was so we could see (secondly) whether the subject pages, in this case the broadband pages, were doing better or worse than average. Because we have business objectives already defined in this particular case the business defined the following bounce rates as a good scale on average for both the site average and the broadband pages average.

5 = 10% or less bounce rate
4 = 20–11% bounce rate
3 = 30–21% bounce rate
2 = 40–31% bounce rate
1 = 50–41% bounce rate
0 = 51% or higher

The main point here is that 25–35% bounce rate would be hitting the targets the business had set – a score of 2–4.

Then we need to measure bounce rate across all the sources of traffic and against keywords with reference to the subject pages. By doing this you learn if your trigger words are 'bouncing' or whether the paid sources are underperforming.

The way this bounce rate was calculated was to determine whether the bounce rate was better than the average number you calculated previously.

5 = More than 50% better than average
4 = 40–50% better than average
3 = 30–40% better than average
2 = 20–30% better than average
1 = 0–20% better than average
0 = Worse than average or not measured

So for instance you want to know if Google visits bounce at a better rate than the average bounce rate across all methods to attract traffic to the site. If the site average bounce rate is 30% and the Google bounce rate is 14% (more than 50% improvement over the average) the score is 5. If Google wasn't any better than the site average then it would be an area that needed optimization.

The idea behind this is pinpointing areas of the site that are worse than average from a relevance point of view in terms of landing points around the Laajakaista (broadband) subject.

Clickstream Analysis – ER (Exit Rate)

On the subject pages in the site (in this case subject refers to only pages in the broadband category) you want to know which pages show the highest exit points. The basic premise is that if people are exiting your site from the pages in too high a frequency you're not doing a good enough job. Again you would score every page and take an average but optimize the worst pages first.

5 = 10% or less exit rate
4 = 20–11% exit rate
3 = 30–21% exit rate
2 = 40–31% exit rate
1 = 50–41% exit rate
0 = 51% or higher exit rate

So if one page scored 90% it would get 0 and be in your list to optimize if the purpose of that page was not to make people leave.

Clickstream Sample Scorecard

As can be seen in Figure 7.10 in the example of a clickstream scorecard, once the figures were extracted from the web analytics system and calculated as scores it's easy to see the areas of required improvement.

1.65 out of 5 is bad in anyone's books and the scorecard gives a high level overview of what is on target and what isn't from the clickstream point of view.

The site is not reaching people very well though encouragingly the trigger keywords (3.00) and the paid keyphrase efforts (3.00) are hitting the targets set by the business. The people that visit those pages are on average happier shown by the only scores of 3. This is encouraging because it shows that targeting the persona effectively is working.

The site is engaging very poorly (overall score 1.10).

The majority of visitors aren't happy with the content and leave very quickly.

Clickstream analysis	40%	Section weight	1.65
Reach search	40%	Item weight	2.15
Paid keyphrase bounce rate		20%	3.00
Earned keyphrase bounce rate		20%	1.00
Trigger keywords		40%	3.00
Google bounce rate		10%	1.00
Yahoo! bounce rate		5%	1.00
MSN bounce rate		5%	0.00
Reach referrers	20%		1.75
General affiliate/partner		25%	1.00
Targeted affiliates		25%	2.00
Referral bounce rate		25%	2.00
Direct traffic bounce rate		25%	2.00
Site engagement	40%		1.10
Site average bounce rate		20%	1.00
Subject bounce rate		40%	2.00
Subject exit rate		10%	1.00
Process abandonment rate		30%	0.00

FIGURE 7.10   *Clickstream scorecard*

The exit rates score very low meaning that there are individual pages that need improvement. It has a high process abandonment rate (SCAR).

In the case of the shopping cart abandonment we saw a very big problem that needed fixing immediately in the case of this client.

When we looked at the five-step process there was a big problem with one of the pages (Figure 7.11).

The drop off point between step two and step 3 of the purchase process was an obvious point of optimization for this particular case. If you as an analyst see anything like this it is a **huge opportunity** to begin the quick win process (see Chapter 4).

This insight is showing us that the cart is not working as it should and either an exit survey should be placed on the cart pages to find out why people are leaving or at the very least a heuristic analysis should be carried out.

Heuristic analysis and surveys are part of the final part of the Insight model discussed next.

FIGURE 7.11 *Shopping cart abandonment rate problem*

Experience Analysis

You've seen how the competition is doing, you have examined the click-stream data and now you're ready to look at the user experience overall, in particular our persona Tapio's user experience. The user experience can be gauged in a number of ways. Indeed in Chapter 5 you saw three of them highlighted, heuristic analysis, surveys and lab usability studies. There are many more, but these three are the most common sources of data that help you understand why people do things in the way they do.

Heuristic Analysis

In this case a heuristic analysis combines looking at a number of elements and determining, via the scorecard method, how many affect the experience of Tapio in a positive way or a negative way. Again use a scale of 0–5 where 0 is bad and 5 is great.

The variables follow standard usability practices covering ease of use, efficiency, error handling and satisfaction. We're also looking at psychological methods employed, the visibility of those methods, the level of interactivity and the influence demonstrated by each site.

Does the web presence quickly and visibly show Tapio the authority of the site? How quickly can he see that the site is the right place to be? Are there enough ways to do things that he needs to do to be able to make a decision about whether he wants to continue? Do you treat Tapio like an idiot when he mistypes a URL into his browser or do you take the burden of the blame and encourage him to do it the right way? Is the navigation easy? Is the site efficient? Does it download quickly?

All these things and thousands more affect the user experience. In Tapio's case we scored it like this:

Ease of use	How easy is it to find the product service page price information or a contact for more information?	5 = Within 3 clicks of the mouse and under one minute. 4 = more than 3 clicks of the mouse but under 2 minutes. 3 = more than 3 clicks of the mouse between 2 and 5 minutes. 2 = more than 3 clicks of the mouse between 5–7 minutes. 1 = more than 3 clicks of the mouse between 7–10 minutes. 0 = Anything more than 10 minutes.
Efficiency	Is the user hindered in any way from completing a task by lack of information? Is there a number of ways to complete the task?	5 = 3 easy ways and more than 1 complimentary way to complete the task. 4 = 2 easy ways and 1 complimentary way to complete the desired task. 3 = 2 easy ways to complete the desired task. 2 = 1 clear way to complete the desired task. 1 = 1 difficult way to complete the desired task 0 = No way you could find to complete the task.
Errors	How are errors handled? Does the system try to guide you to the correct location? Look at the internal search engine results page and 404 page to determine result	Web presence receives points for: Error page has search engine 10 points. Error message tries to guess your problem 5 points. Error message provides links to more information 3 points. Informative search engine errors 7 points. Human helpdesk information provided 5 points Human live help provided (chat) 10 points. 5 = 40 points 4 = 30–39 points 3 = 20–29 points 2 = 10–19 points 1 = 5–9 points 0 = 4 or less points.

Scoring the Experience

You would score 5 for efficiency if there were three easy ways to complete a task in more than one complimentary way.

The primary task Tapio has is to research broadband services, so without answering his specific question the heuristic analysis would simply determine whether it was easy to locate the information. If there were three easy ways (top navigation, left navigation and a special offer image saying 'click here for broadband') then you have three clear paths to follow. If there were complimentary ways to also visit the broadband pages such as embedded links in the text using trigger words then that would also count positively for the user experience. Similarly with ease of use, you're simply counting the clicks and time spent and scoring accordingly.

Errors are scored differently and are based purely on how Tapio's errors are handled. Does a search engine and helpful apologetic text appear? If so score accordingly. With errors the more you do to help the user the better. Errors happen a lot and it's surprising how many companies forget this. It's a real opportunity to impress your visitor.

Finally you then need to score the satisfaction overall. This can be done in two ways. You can either ask the analyst doing the heuristic persona test to give their opinion or you can do a survey of your visitors. In Tapio's case his satisfaction overall was rated by the heuristic test.

Satisfaction	Which experience best describes your visit to the website?	5 = The site fulfilled all needs and expectations 100%. 4 = The site fulfilled 80% of my needs and expectations. 3 = The site fulfilled 60% of my needs and expectations. 2 = The site fulfilled 40% of my needs and expectations. 1 = The site fulfilled 20% of my needs and expectations. 0 = The site failed to fulfill any of my needs and expectations.

This should not be subjective where possible. Tapio has ten needs/questions from this website. How many of those questions were answered well?

Take the scores from the competitive testing data. You have a maximum score of 50. Where was the score? Was it 10/50? If so the site fulfilled 20% of the needs in comparison to the competition.

If the site scored highly on Tapio's pain points you might want to adjust the score using the percentages from the competitive analysis. It should be consistently applied.

The scorecard with Tapio's scores show where the action points are (Figure 7.12). The points of improvement here can quickly be spotted. You should be asking questions like, 'why did we only get a 1 for errors?' and 'why did we only score 2 for efficiency?'

Experience analysis	25%		2.49
Usability		35%	2.30
Ease of use		30%	3.00
Efficiency		30%	2.00
Errors		20%	1.00
Satisfaction		20%	3.00
Psychology		35%	2.25
Number of methods employed		25%	3.00
Interactivity		25%	2.00
Visibility		25%	2.00
Influence		25%	2.00
Nurture methods employed		30%	3.00
Nurture methods		100%	3.00

FIGURE 7.12 *Experience analysis scorecard*

7.4 WAYS TO COMBINE CLICKSTREAM AND EXPERIENCE DATA

Survey data is also great for determining why problems happen. It's basically like asking your customers what's wrong in a way that they can answer quickly and easily. The trends you gather and can score from this information are vital to figuring out why things happen.

This kind of data is very easy to score because you simply ask in your survey things like 'Rate your experience 0–5' and then display questions which are non-subjective like 'Did you find what you were looking for?' You could then rate the answer ranging from yes it was great (5) to no it was awful (0).

This is a simplistic example but it explains the theory used in many cases. One example from Nokia (the Nokia N810) shows how using experience data from a survey can seriously affect the product strategy.

A survey of customers was carried out asking a number of questions with a notable result. It was found that 85% of customers didn't think the device was a good tool for Internet messaging, with 65% of them citing a lack of Skype functionality as the main reason for this. Nokia listened. They added the Skype functionality to the device and a few months later the traffic and sales had considerably increased.

A/B and Multivariate Testing

Another area of user experience data is actually measured very well by clickstream data when done correctly. The reason A/B and multivariate testing (MVT) are classed as 'experience' data is because the clickstream data actually reflects a user experience test you're conducting. This is the kind of testing that can drive design. Before discussing this kind of testing you should understand that A/B testing and MVT are great **but only when part of your overall strategy.**

You need to consider what to test before you test. If you get it wrong you might end up testing something that doesn't help you achieve your business objectives or help your personas achieve their goals.

The best situations come from A/B or MVT tests that are part of marketing strategy. You test based on the fact that you have something to say to your target audience as part of your persona design strategy for instance. What you attempt to do when you test is find the best way to say it.

A/B Testing

With A/B testing you either test single elements at a time like individual graphics or you test the entire page. With single blocks this is done with a specific call to action in mind. Your call to action might be a link to another page, a graphic that takes you forward in a part of a process, an email sign up or even something like a purchase.

You measure the effect of a whole new page across engagement KPIs such as bounce rate, page click through rate and time spent on site. Increases in usage of the page are an indicator of success.

In a typical A/B test two versions of a page are created and the results (from clickstream measurements) are compared to see which one works better.

In Figure 7.13 you can see two versions of a home page that were tested as an A/B split test. The first version on the left was the control that had been used for many months in the same manner and had plenty of clickstream KPI data around it. The second version on the right was the tested version and because it showed improvement became the new control.

The way to run an A/B test is to have your designers create the new version of the page. Most web platforms now come with the ability to split traffic between two pages. Showing 50% of the traffic version 'a' and 50% version 'b' is now quite common in content management systems.

If your platform doesn't allow this then it's possible that a developer could look at a switching mechanism made using Javascript and cookies to do the same job, or you could use server load balancing to switch between the pages. The key thing to remember is to name the pages differently so your analytics tool can distinguish between page 'a' and page 'b'.

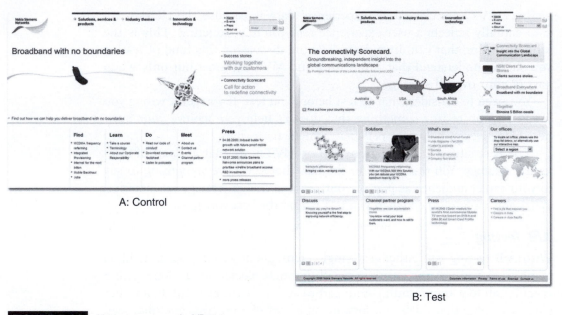

A: Control

B: Test

FIGURE 7.13 *Home page example A/B test*

A/B Testing Page Variables

Another way to test user experience is by testing single parts of a page or 'blocks' using A/B testing if you have for instance two pages that are identical except for one block of text. The key here is to test the calls to action. By doing this systematically over a number of months across many key pages I once improved conversion rates to lead by 800% for one client. For instance see the two text blocks below:

> Wireless and wired M2M connectivity solutions offer reliable data communications to remote devices and systems in a number of industry verticals. In this section, you will find some examples of our products in action. We hope this will make it easier to *choose which product(s) suit best for your own application*

The above text block was the control that had a call to action link as shown above. I read it and didn't understand it, even though I knew what the company was doing.

> We design electronic gadgets that we attach to lifts (for example). It makes it possible for you to control that lift from anywhere in the world via the Internet. It can save a fortune in maintenance costs. *Click here to find out more ...*

The second block of text had a much higher link click through rate than the first mainly because it was much more understandable and portrayed a benefit to the target market. A/B testing the two links was the purpose of the tests and led to similar copy changes throughout the website which eventually improved lead generation by 800%. A €2Million value to the client.

It's worth mentioning at this point that even a small test like the above is something you could develop as a 'quick win' (see Chapter 4). When you have a small improvement (an increase in CTR) like the one above it proves so many of the theories you might have. By producing understandable copy you get more click through therefore more engagement. More engagement eventually leads to more conversion. That means you might be able to persuade previously difficult executives to invest in better copywriting or hiring people.

Single block tests are still A/B tests but when you start testing more than one thing at a time on the page you're beginning to look at multivariate testing, or MVT as it's often abbreviated.

Multivariate Testing (MVT)

Where A/B testing allows you to change one thing at a time and measure the results MVT allows you to test multiple things at a time to help speed up the process. With A/B testing you have blocks as described. The very principle on which MVT is based is splitting up the page into numerous blocks and testing them all at the same time. For instance splitting up the webpage into blocks as shown in Figure 7.14 we can see how the different combinations might be tested.

As you can see from Figure 7.14 I've outlined how you might break the home page up into the blocks or elements you may want to test. Some vendors call these blocks zones. Multivariate testing allows you to test different combinations in each element block. However more excitingly, it allows you to test multiple ideas in each block. You could have three or four tests running in each block showing different offers.

Omniture Test & Target™ is a Multivariate and A/B testing solution that can allow you to run different offers at the same time and measure which one works best.

This kind of user experience measurement is a pretty fast way to test a number of different things at once thus speeding up your optimization.

In Figure 7.15 BT are testing three different offers and three different locations of call to action. The bottom picture is the control with a competition for new visitors. The whole picture is designed to get you to click the part highlighted by the square area in the middle right below the bird. BT is

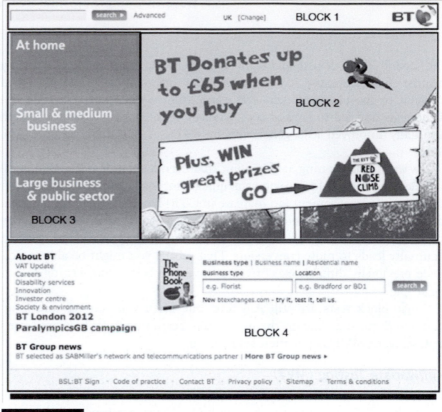

FIGURE 7.14 *MVT blocks*

A

B

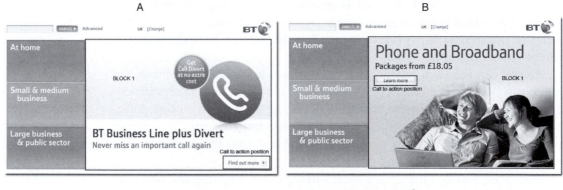

C

FIGURE 7.15 *Multivariate testing and segmenting*

also testing different copy in Block 1 here by appealing to your better nature and offering a donation to the Red Nose fund if you buy. The offers above left and above right have different positions of calls to action and target different personas (allowing better segmentation). One clearly targets a family environment and another targets a Business user.

So there is quite a lot being tested on the home page of BT.com all the time.

This shows that BT test many different approaches to improve their sign-up process and are attempting to uncover where people are most likely to click when they see the offer.

7.5 THE INSIGHT MODEL AND NURTURING/RETENTION

The nurture phase of the REAN model measures how well you retain visitors as described in Chapter 2. While planning the REAN phases you should add the activities you do that potentially retain customers or encourage repeat visitors.

The Insight model works in exactly the same way with retention, however you simply need to upgrade your persona from Tapio the prospect to Tapio the customer and think as you would a customer of your service.

The key to the messaging is the reach sources you use. A customer is reached by email, by direct mail or by phone because you have a relationship with them and permission to talk to them. It's possible also that they will login to your web service out of choice to take advantage of offers you may be communicating to them.

There are entire books dedicated to CRM and eCRM, I would recommend *eMarketing eXcellence* by Dave Chaffey and P.R. Smith to get an idea about how to mine databases and personalize emails to Tapio based on what he does and doesn't do. Also Jim Sterne wrote a great little book called *Advanced Email Marketing* that lightly describes a fictional situation about how an organization could handle email in house.

As previously discussed in Chapter 2 all nurture activities via email can be tracked easily. It's simply a case of planning.

The only major difference with the nurture phase is that you can use it to predict future behaviour. Predicting when a customer is likely to defect needs KPIs that use recency and frequency.

Recency and Frequency

If you have a database of customers for the past 10 years which are the ones that are more likely to buy from you?

Is a sale more likely to come from the customer that bought your product 2 years ago or the customer that bought your product 10 years ago? Recency is based on this principle. The more recently that someone interacted with you the more likely they are to interact again. It's a fact that can easily be proven by looking at your customer data.

Frequency is the measure of how often they interact (i.e. buy). The less frequently they do this the less likely they are to interact in the future.

The basic premise of using the KPIs is to predict when the recency and frequency are at such a time that you need to act. You try to use the numbers to learn when to send the email that reminds your customer you still have something to offer them, or when to offer a discount.

You look at recency to determine that 'x' days after they bought your product is the day that they're most likely never to return again as your customer. Once you define 'x' days is when you send an email.

Another measurement called latency can be used. Latency counts the time (recency) between activities (frequency). For instance:

Time between first purchase and second purchase = 90 days.

Time between second purchase and third purchase = 60 days.

Time between third purchase and fourth purchase = 30 days.

Time between fourth purchase and fifth purchase = 60 days.

Time between fifth purchase and sixth purchase = 90 days.

The above cycle shows a pattern that you can score as average behaviour in a similar way to the way you aggregate bounce rate to get a site average. If you define that the above behaviour is average behaviour based on all the customer data you have then any single customer that deviates from this average should be flagged and scored.

They should be scored higher if they deviate in a positive way like their recency is faster between purchases. They should be scored negatively if they take longer than average. You will then be able to split your customers into level 0–5 customers, where 5 are your evangelist customers and 0 are the customers whom have defected. The defected customers you have lost and are unlikely to ever get back. The customers you want to help get back on track are the ones that score a 1 or a 2.

The other way to use this is to measure out what happens after the fourth purchase to reverse the purchase speed. It could be that your CRM technology needs tweaking or that your messaging is wrong or it simply could be that this is the common lifecycle of your product or service.

We call the subject predictive analytics and it's a whole book on it's own. It's out of the scope of this particular edition of *Cult Of Analytics*. For the time being I would recommend Jim Novo's *Drilling Down* which covers all the techniques used to design RF models and start data mining.

In the next chapter we'll be looking at how to report the Insights you find. Steering groups want one thing, spokes want another thing and the hub deal with the raw data and need to turn it into something useful for the organization as a whole.

CHAPTER 8

Simplified Reporting

Please be good enough to put your conclusions and recommendations on one sheet of paper in the very beginning of your report, so I can even consider reading it

Sir Winston Churchill

8.1 REPORTING – ONE MAN'S REPORT IS ANOTHER MAN'S EMOTIONAL CRUTCH

I did some work for a company once where a marketing manager showed me the reports they were looking at. Their agency had compiled the numbers from a web analytics tool into a Powerpoint show that was 50 slides long. The report had lots of numbers explaining the effect of the campaigns the agency was running, showing numbers like banner impressions, clicks, costs and click through rates (CTRs). The person I was talking to was very proud of the report suggesting that he measured everything down to the last click and could account for every cent of his marketing spend.

Then I started making him feel uncomfortable. I started asking questions like:

- How did you use the numbers? – He kept a list of campaign costs using cost per impression as a gauge of where to spend his marketing money.

- What actions did you take in the middle of the campaign because of the report you got showing progress? – He only got a report at the end of each campaign.

- How did these numbers compare to other campaigns? – He had a list, he could check, he knew the cost information immediately.

- Were these visitors engaging more than all the rest of the traffic to the site or was the campaign engaging less? – He didn't know.

- What was the business value of the campaign? – He knew the cost but not the value.

- If he didn't know the business value how could he truly know which campaigns he was running worked? – He looked like he was going to cry.

The things he didn't know rocked him a little and he challenged me to be able to produce those kinds of insights.

Then I asked him what his primary job was. Still taken aback he explained that he had to make decisions about marketing campaigns and that the numbers he had supported him in those decisions. That's the point. It's not the marketing manager's job to do the analysis, it's the marketing manager's job to improve the business and allocate marketing spend to areas of marketing that works. He is working for a spoke (see Chapter 1) and should have information that helps him make decisions.

My questions had opened his eyes to other possibilities he didn't know he could measure. I quickly reassured him that it's not his job to know what to analyse, that's his analysts' job. I asked him if he would prefer a one-page report that told him how and why to spend his money. He just laughed, said it would never happen and told me I was living in an 'analytics utopia' (his words).

A few months later our team was producing the kind of insights I'd suggested he'd get and we started a process improvement strategy that meant his team could re-produce the same results. Utopia? No, but a step towards it with a strong reporting strategy.

There should only be three types of reports, the numbers, the business insights with associated evidence and the analyst's KPI dashboards from which the analyst derives insights.

Reporting the Numbers

The numbers are important for any business, even the basic ad impressions, visitors, page views are important when you're looking at the very high level of how your business is doing.

The CEO of a huge multi-billion euro enterprise will not care about the tactics. He would want a very high level account of what his business is doing. Taking into the context of the REAN model he might want to know:

We had 4 billion ad impressions (reach), 100 million visitors (engage), 1.3 million sales (activate) and had 30 million repeat visitors (nurture) from customer database activities. This came at a cost of €40 million across all marketing activities. That translates to a cost of €0.40 cents per visitor or €31 per sale. We also know that we currently have 25% market share so we can calculate from that the levels our competition are also reaching.

This gives the CEO an idea of how his business is doing, how much it all costs and how he stands in comparison to his competition. If those numbers are not good enough he can issue the orders to tackle the problem thus involving the business.

Reporting the Business Insights

The spoke managers (the business people and stakeholders) are the people that run part of the business and their unit contributes towards the numbers that the CEO sees. They should only ever receive things that they can act on. The reason for this is simple. It's not their job to become analysts. Your hub should analyse the data and make it easy for the spoke to take action.

Giving these guys a 50-page detailed report on how their online marketing is doing would only help them if they had the time to read and understand it. This is double trouble for the business. Firstly you take the time to compile this information and secondly you have a marketing manager using only a fraction of the data to take any actions.

The business manager doesn't know any better. He will ask for *everything*, so your hub needs to guide him. He will ask because he needs that emotional crutch to fall back on in case his bosses come calling and asked him to justify something. As Mark Twain said, most of the numbers were for support not enlightenment.

The idea of reporting business insights is to condense all the findings and actions required into one easily readable form that can be understood by anyone responsible for the business. What follows are a couple of examples of good business dashboards and the creation process. The first is from a competition run by the Web Analytics Association in 2008.

The Web Analytics Associations' Championship 2008

The following analysis won the Web Analytics Associations' championship in June 2008, a voluntary competition that asked analysts to analyse the WAA website data and tell them what it meant. They could use any forms of data they deemed necessary to give the WAA some insights. ClickThinking, a US based consultancy firm, won the competition:

ClickThinking Business Insight Report (http://www. clickthinking.com/)

The site does not provide for users outside North America[1], mostly relies on people that already know about or have heard of the WAA[2], is not optimized to drive conversion for any industry related keywords that don't include 'web analytics'[3] and while it provides for formal analytics education, it fails to provide analytics help for common analytics problems[4]. The site itself needs some updating to with the most optimal use of Web 2.0 features and best practices navigation (probably should get rid of the Tendenci) as the page reloads when clicking navigational items need to go[5]!

Supportive Data:

1. Singapore and India does three times more searches for the term 'web analytics' than the USA and more than double that of the USA and Canada combined (Google Trends data), yet the WAA site receives 62% of its traffic from North America while India and Singapore only provides around 4%!
2. Almost 19% of direct site visitors' account for 46% of the site revenue with the majority of corporate memberships coming from direct traffic. The search term

web analytics converts 70% better for professional memberships, while *web analytics association* converts 138% better for professional and 63% better for corporate memberships when compared to the overall site.

3. 'Web data' is searched 6.65 times more than 'web analytics' and 'web stats' 1.74 more than 'web analytics', but these keywords don't bring any visitors to the WAA site. (Google Trends)

4. Education is not only a formal thing. Google launching Google Analytics on November 14 2005 brought web analytics into the mainstream. This resulted in more people confronting data anomalies, issues with terminology, etc. The WAA site is not addressing these issues. The only place where this can be addressed is in the Forum and this isn't even hosted within the WAA framework.

5. There is an inconsistency with the cookie trail (aka breadcrumb), the navigation requires page reloads, the blog is stale with old postings and very little comments, too many things link outside of the WAA site like the Social wiki, the forum, etc. and does not seem to contain analytics data.

Our recommendation is a concerted effort to include the rest of the world through copy, keyword optimization, events, help/FAQ and seamless navigation to allow the WAA to truly become the worldwide provider of web analytics education, support, help and jobs in all fields related to web analytics. Localization will be key.

All the other answers are worth checking out and can be reviewed here: http://www.webanalyticsassociation.org/wachampionship/2008winners/

Looking at the winning entry above you have a powerful first paragraph that explains the problem with the website in depth whilst referring to data sources as back up. The first paragraph would wake up anyone in charge of running this website as a business. Of course such bold claims need to be backed up with data and the superscript numbers are then listed, giving strong supporting evidence of the claims and describing in business context what's going on. Finally the most important part is included, a recommendation about what to do next.

8.2 THE BUSINESS INSIGHT REPORT CREATION PROCESS

The ClickThinking example follows the process in Figure 8.1. They wrote a strong lead, they combined it with supporting evidence and they explained what to do next. Simple but effective and therefore a worthy winner of the title.

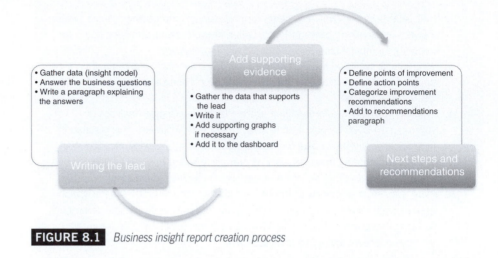

- Gather data (insight model)
- Answer the business questions
- Write a paragraph explaining the answers

Writing the lead

- Gather the data that supports the lead
- Write it
- Add supporting graphs if necessary
- Add it to the dashboard

Add supporting evidence

- Define points of improvement
- Define action points
- Categorize improvement recommendations
- Add to recommendations paragraph

Next steps and recommendations

FIGURE 8.1 *Business insight report creation process*

The full PDF report includes a humorous lead up to how they gathered the data and split the responsibilities amongst their team and is also worth reading in full: http://www.webanalyticsassociation.org/wachampionship/2008winners/ClickThinking.pdf

Developing business insights is a good process for your hub to follow because it makes them think outside of their little world of data. They have to think critically about why they're doing what they're doing and write a lead explaining what their numbers mean instead of just graphs and trends.

Writing the Lead

Writing the lead is the most difficult part of the job for many analysts. People who are used to analysing data are often not that good at getting a powerful message across. Your hub has to learn to do this. Of course they have to do the analysis first which could give them plenty of ideas but the key is to then condense the findings into something that nails the business question the spoke/management is asking. Think of the KPIs in terms of business questions. Why did each KPI get created in the first place? What is the spoke trying to achieve? Remember that not everything that you can measure should be included. Just because there is a list of 20 KPIs doesn't mean that you have to use all of them. In terms of actually writing the lead start with the most painful or most useful piece of information. If you have evidence that your competition is doing a better job than the spoke you might want to start with that. Put each KPI into a sentence that makes sense.

For instance if the bounce rate is 88% say nearly 9/10 of our visitors don't find our website relevant[1]; if conversion is only 1%; say only 1 in 100 people[2] sign up at the moment and we feel there is huge room for improvement. Monetize where possible; Our competitors do three times as much business as we do right now[3] and if we performed as well as they do it would be worth €100 K per month in extra sales[4]. Speak in easy language and get the key points across in your first paragraph.

Add Supporting Evidence

From the above paragraph you can see I added four points where data needed to be used to back up the claims I was making:

1. 88% bounce rate for the last 3 months (source web analytics data).

2. 1% conversion rate steady over the last 3 months (source web analytics data).

3. Average conversion rate industry wide is 3% (source Google Analytics benchmarking and Hitwise data).

4. 1 sale = €1000 and 3% conversion would result in 100 more sales per month at euro value €100 K (source product value).

Keep it very simple, you can add trend graphs to prove the points if required, but often the text is good enough alone. Always include the data sources and back up findings with a timescale you've looked at so that there is some business context.

Next Steps and Recommendations

Adding recommendations depends on what's practical and as a member of the hub you should know what the spokes' limitations are. You can't get the enterprise-wide booking system changed as you would need a lot of evidence that the system was failing 'enterprise-wide'. You could however recommend more study of failing systems on an enterprise-wide level that might help the spoke get the required support from other spokes. You could use a categorization method of changes. I often use three change categories: short-term, mid-term and long-term. Short-term changes are something that can be changed in house without having to seek approvals outside the spoke. Mid-term changes are something the spoke can do but usually with higher approval processes or increased budget. Long-term changes require corporate approval or steering groups decisions and usually affect the entire company. You should focus on the smaller issues first and the larger issues later.

In this above example you might say 'Start A/B testing on high bounce rate pages and keyword campaigns in the short term as well as multivariate testing on our purchase process funnel. We should also carry out other studies with other spokes to see if they have similar problems on the sales side (short term). If there are similar problems we might want to look at a different sign-up technical platform (longer term).'

Case Example

I was consulting with a global team responsible for online sales across the USA, Europe mainland and the UK. I was embedded for a few days each week working closely with the global team developing strategy and doing ad-hoc analysis.

The business question I had from the global manager was whether the money they were due to allocate on campaigns in the USA was a wise use of the resources they had. He had his doubts that the campaigns would perform and wanted my opinion. He supplied me with a projection analysis sent by one of the US online marketing managers and asked me to give me my opinion within a week.

The report I opened from the USA stated clearly that the objective was to increase online sales of the product. The projections were based on previous campaigns. The US marketing manager had projected that they would get 27 million advert impressions by using the media sites they had selected with a 0.25% click through rate to the landing pages. The projections went on to suggest that success from this campaign would be a 1.34% click through rate from the landing page to the e-store. The costs were already worked out based on these figures. You could expect to pay $6 per click to the landing page and expect just over 67,000 clicks to the landing page from the campaign. The total budget for the campaign was $595,000.

To a company of this size running many individual multi-channel campaigns in the $10 M a year bracket $6 a click didn't seem expensive at all. There were no flags raised and the global manager who had asked me to do the analysis was only curious and following a hunch. He wasn't expecting what I told him in the business dashboard that I've broken down into the processes three component parts below.

The Lead

Based on current projections the cost per click is 21.75 times more expensive than search engine marketing[1]. The cost of driving one visit to the e-commerce front door is 2 times more expensive than the product itself[2].

Projections show the estimated cost of driving 1 sale will be $16,107[3] – over 50 times the purchase price of the product[4].

The Supporting Evidence

1. Average cost per click of search engine marketing campaigns €0.30 (source Google for the last three campaigns) as opposed to $6.53 in this projection.

2. Cost of the product is $300 (source website). Estimated visits to the store 1.34% of 67,797 = 922 visits. Cost $595,000/922 = $645 cost per store visit.

3. Average shopping cart abandonment rate (SCAR) 96% for this product (source 3 months' web analytics data). Therefore estimate 4% of 922 will lead to sales (37 projected purchases) 595,000/37 = $16,107.

4. The product price $300. $16,107/300 = 53.69 times more for one sale than the value of the product.

The Recommendations

This campaign is not a profitable use of resources to drive sales. In the short term you should re-allocate the budget to search engine marketing that can be tested and optimized on the fly and has much cheaper entry prices. Currently you can't complain to the Media Agency because you have agreed the 'success metrics'. The point is you CAN complain if you included KPIs that focused on the areas mentioned. Additionally one of the biggest issues is the shopping cart abandonment rate. An abandonment rate of 96% is unacceptable. Longer term a study across all product abandonment rates should be made to determine whether the problem is with this product or with the process. If the abandonment is similar across different product groups then implementing a new process should be considered.

The Outcome

The actions that came from this one report were exactly what I'd hoped for. I have never seen a team ask so many questions of current practices. Not surprisingly they worked very differently in the future.

Budgets were allocated differently, new campaigns were projected based on stronger KPIs and new initiatives to learn from all sources of data were set-up. Marketing managers had stricter controls placed on their campaign budgets. They had in the past concentrated on specialized traffic sources. In this case the manager had been working with online banners and large media agencies, but not with search marketing. This was why he didn't know any better.

The case was turned into a win that was presented throughout the company. They had learned a valuable lesson and they didn't spend the $595,000 on the campaign. Overall this saved the company in excess of $2.5 million because in the first campaign the $595,000 was to be used as a test run for a larger and similar campaign towards the end of the year with a $2 million budget allocated to it.

This report was all about the money and that was why it got so much attention. The company was dealing so much with clicks, visits, impressions and CTRs that it forgot why doing this kind of marketing was important in the first place. Monetization is very important and should be part of any hub analyst's toolbox.

8.3 MONETIZATION

Every business website has a value and it should form an integral part of reporting wherever possible. There is a process (shown in Figure 8.2) that you can follow to monetize sites based on your market size and REAN.

Determine Market Size

How big is the online population by demographic? (i.e. certain country? only of a certain age range?). Once you have this you can do a competitive analysis to see where you stand in comparison to the competitors on the market. We then have the potential size and current market share of the target market group. Data sources: Forrester, IAB, Hitwise, Google Trends, Compete.com, CIA World Library (country populations).

Determine Reach

Determine what percentage is being attracted to the website by all methods per year. The longer the time period is the better, as the length of time will normalize seasonal trends. This gives potential website value based on the amount of visits over the time period and shows the gap between the reality and the market size. Data sources: Web analytics data.

FIGURE 8.2 *The monetization process*

Determine Points of Value

List anything that engages, activates or nurtures the visitor in some way. There are three kinds of value, direct value, indirect value and potential value:

- **Direct value.** Direct value is perhaps easiest to monetize. If you have direct online sales, leads, customer services or advertising revenue then all of these activities can be directly accounted for. A conversion can be assigned a value in the terms of sales or leads. Customer service can have an associated cost saving and ad revenue can be directly attributed to the amount of pages you can serve to an audience.

- **Indirect value.** The vast majority of websites don't sell anything directly. However they all have points of value to the visitor otherwise there would be no point for them to visit. Many websites are educational in nature about a product or service. If that is the case then referrals could be one point of value if such sites are then referring traffic elsewhere. Downloads could be a point of value. Watching a video could be a point of value. Buying a product offline could be a point of value, though tracking it would require survey data or a voucher printed from an online page that would then be a point of value in itself.

- **Potential value.** This is either direct, indirect or a combination of both in relation to the market size. The potential value if you could reach more of the target audience you need to reach and persuade more of them to take action in the way you need them to.

Monetize the Value Points

Direct Value Points

If for instance 500 leads resulted in 50 customers with a profit of €100 each then the value point of a lead is: (€100 × 50)/500 = €10. This means in effect that the lead value is 10€ because on average it takes 10 leads to yield one sale.

Profit per sale (PPS) of the same sale above in an e-commerce operation would be (€100 × 50)/50 = €100 showing that the formula is consistent.

If the cost per support query was €5 and you saved 1000 support requests by website actions then you have just saved €5000.

If you manage to increase the websites capacity for page views and can increase advertising revenue at the same level then 10% more page views means 10% more revenue.

Direct business objectives like these can be easily measured. If however the content had a different purpose than lead generation, sales, service or advertising you would need to use a different calculation to monetize indirect value of content. This calculation would be based on propensity to buy, or customer satisfaction.

Indirect Value Points

Janne Korpi, Business optimization team leader at Trainers' House Analytics Unit designed a calculation in order to work out the value of anything on a website based on propensity to buy. Propensity to buy (PtB) is measured by taking a survey of a sample of the audience who looked at the content in question. You might ask them to fill in a survey after for instance reading a particular article.

The survey would ask something like, 'After reading this article are you more likely to buy product x?' You then compare the people that answered 'yes' to a control group who have not seen the article, they might be asked 'are you interested in buying product x' and then the amount of conversions measured after purchase from those that said yes. You can then use the following calculation to work out the value of the content:

Interest(s) – Interest to purchase on the measured content (%)

Interest(c) – Interest to purchase in the control group (%)

Real(c) – Real purchasers in the control group (%)

PtB = [Interest(s) – Interest(c)] × [Real[c]/Interest[c]]

This would then give a value point percentage of the profit of one customer.

For instance let's say the PtB interest to buy after reading the content was 10% and the control group showed 4% while the real purchases from the same control group was 2%. The content value point percentage is [10 – 4] × [2/4] = 3%. Therefore the PtB = 3%.

We use a control group because without it we would not be able to determine the value of the lift from the content viewed as our subject. What we're trying to do is show what value a specific piece of content is worth therefore we have to subtract the normal level of interest from the new level of interest raised by the content. This makes the valuation of the content fairer.

The second part of the calculation works out the number of people who actually became customers from the control group as a percentage of those that said they were interested. This second figure will never be more than 1

(100%), unless of course your survey visitors mislead you about their intentions saying they wouldn't buy when actually they did.

Once you have calculated the lift in propensity to buy you can then look at the euro value.

In the example shown the content has lifted the propensity to buy by 3% (on average). You would then put this into a final calculation to get the euro value of the content. This would be:

$$\text{€Value of content} = ((\text{Change in PtB} \times \text{amount of visitors}) \times \text{avg profit}) \times \text{market share}$$

So if there were 100,000 visitors to the site, the average profit per sale was €100 with the company only having a 10% market share then in the above case this calculation would be:

$$((3\% \times 100{,}000) \times 100) \times 10\% = \text{€}30{,}000.$$

Following this logic you can comfortably say that this will put a value on the content read.

If the site has bad content then PtB will be negative. This is very useful for sites that are educational in nature but don't sell anything or direct anyone anywhere.

Other indirect measures are less complex. Matching offline sales to website visits can be done with vouchers. Matching retail sales with web based store finder conversions is possible to do in the same way as the lead generation calculations. Visitors should determine the brand value based on their level of engagement. So if you have a brand engagement segment that is 10% of the total visits to the site and you can track how many became customers you have a value on the level of your branding activities.

Indirect values are more difficult to monetize but that doesn't mean they shouldn't be calculated. If based on regular surveys you can determine the value of an educational website, you can determine the level of investment you need in the same way as you would look at an e-commerce website.

There is ALWAYS a customer somewhere and in order to evaluate the value of the website you need to get that average profit of a customer.

(Data sources: web analytics, survey and customer data.)

Calculate the Value Per Point

Once you have the individual value points it's then just a case of adding them up to get the total value of the web property. If you determine PtB lift for indirect content you can take a sum of those numbers per year. If a referral to a partner is potentially worth €300 and there are 1000 clicks then potential value to that partner is €300,000 (then tracking the partner conversion rate is needed to give you a real value). Working this out can lead to advertising revenue from the partner that then becomes a direct addition to the overall value of the website.

Work Out the Potential Value

Finally put this back into the market size by working out the potential value based on the size of the market you can grow into.

If you have figured that your current website value is €1 million a year based on adding up current direct and indirect value points you can firstly work out what your conversion improvements would be on your own reach factors. If 1% conversion overall is equal to a value of €1 million then 2% overall is worth €2 million and 10% overall is €10 million. This is a simplistic example but the point is valid.

By working out the PtB with an increase in market share (20% instead of 10% for instance) you will be able to calculate potential value if you reach your targets. Your KPIs can then be adjusted to match doubling your traffic to the content.

You then could also factor in hitting your KPI target of doubling your market share that would mean also doubling your potential revenues. This can really make a difference when asking for investments.

In short as an analyst you should attempt to monetize wherever possible in order to talk the language of the people reading the business dashboard. That language is all about the money.

It's more than possible that when you show real business numbers that the executives in charge of the spokes will ask to see proof of your findings. This is where the analyst data and KPIs come into play and is what the analyst uses to determine where the opportunities are. The hub analyst can use what he/she gathers in the KPI dashboards and scorecards as proof when he gets asked to show it. This is the really cool part of the analyst's job. It's where he/she gets to show off.

8.4 ANALYST KPIs, DASHBOARDS AND SCORECARD

The analyst/hub KPIs are different again to the business insight reports. They are the data behind the business insight reports. Before you can begin to develop dashboards or scorecards anywhere the analyst has to process all the data prior to reporting on weekly/monthly numbers. Figure 8.3, the hub analysts process for reporting, shows how this works in practice.

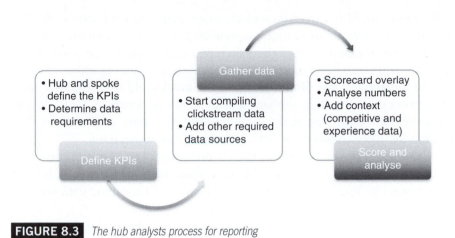

The hub analysts process for reporting

Define KPIs and Data Requirements

Once you have decided what your KPIs are (see Chapter 3) for the particular spoke you're working with you can then determine what kinds of data you might need to compile. You might have data sources from various reach activities like Google, Yahoo, MSN, media agencies running banner campaigns, retail outlets, call centres and countless other methods of reaching the audience. You'd then need to gather the data about what happens on the website. It all goes back to the KPIs and the sources of data required to answer the business questions. Look at Chapter 3 where the process is described more comprehensively.

Gathering Data

Once you have defined the KPIs and the data sources then start the process of gathering this data. If you're doing monthly reports I would compile reports going back for at least 12 months. If you're doing it weekly I would say go back 52 weeks of the year. The reason being you can then quickly build trend data if it's required.

Tools like the Omnitures' Report builder streamline this making it easy to insert data into pre-defined cells so that you can update the datasheets at the press of a button. Doing this allows you to then build graphs and tables on top of the data that can also be automatically updated. If a spoke manager asks you for data about an upcoming campaign you can guarantee that the first thing he will ask when you show him about the campaign effects is how it compares to other campaigns run previously that year. This is why it's always good to have the data to hand so you can quickly answer the questions.

Reporting on KPIs can often include more than one data source. At this time there aren't many tools that integrate all data sources. Omniture do the best job at the moment. Most others do have certain integration possibilities especially with search engines. But when it comes to adding offline data or bespoke integration only Omniture can do it quickly via their Genesis partner network or using their top end tool Discover on Premise (DoP). While Omniture does it the best at the moment even they have challenges in this area and the tools always come with associated cost restrictions.

As the tools get more mature this is one area I see becoming increasingly important and a point of differentiation for the vendors. Cheaper alternatives like Excel or SPSS are very often used to combine data sources at the moment.

Once you have compiled the data sources into weekly, monthly or whatever report datasets you require you can then look at the next steps which is to score, analyse and add context to the data.

Scorecard Overlay

The overlay is called such because it's simply looking at the data you have compiled and scoring it according to the rules you set-up. The way I like to do this is score 0–5 where 3 is the target level. If you hit your KPI target you score 3, if you drop below 3 you're below target and if you go above target you score a 4 or a 5 depending on how much above target you were. The data thresholds are set when you set your targets. For instance you might have a scale of 50% above target scores 5, 25% above target scores 4, hitting the target scores 3, 25% below target scores 2, 50% below scores 1 and worse than 50% below target is 0.

This gives the analyst and anyone looking at the data an instant snapshot of whether they hit the targets across all their KPIs or not. If they aren't hitting the target then the analyst has to drill down and find out why. Another contingency is to build colour into the scale, where red is bad, green is good and orange indicates something you should look at. Something you should look at might be a downward trend but still scoring 3 as it's still above target. In that case you might want to find out why there has been a drop in numbers and how big that drop is.

Going back to the sales business insight example the following KPIs and scorecards were behind the numbers.

KPIs and Analysing the Numbers

Media impressions, CTR, clicks, CPC, landing on e-commerce front door and shopping cart abandonment rate campaigns were all scored.

I had the data set-up in Excel with a data sheet for the impressions and clicks (manually added from media agency numbers), the number of visits and visitors coming from the web analytics tool. In this case I wanted to know how people used the shopping cart and where they left the purchase process. This meant that a scorecard could be compiled against each campaign across all the KPIs over the lifecycle of the campaign that lasted 4 weeks. The scorecard looked like this:

KPI scorecard	Week 34	Week 35	Week 36	Week 37
Media impressions	4	5	5	1
CTR	2	3	3	2
Clicks	2	3	3	2
CPC	2	2	2	2
Landing on e-commerce front door	1	3	3	1
Shopping cart abandonment rate	0	0	0	0

What this tells me is that on the media impressions side the targets were being hit easily in the first three weeks of the campaign and the last week could be explained by the media website reducing the amount of impressions because they had already reached their paid quota.

CTR, the (C)lick (T)hrough (R)ate from the media website to the campaign landing page was below target in the first week, hit the target in the second and third week but fell below target again in the last week. It was a similar story with clicks. This meant that the media site was serving a lot of ads but there wasn't enough click through and therefore the clicks to the landing page target was down.

The (C)ost (P)er (C)lick target was $6 and this was also below target due to the lower amount of clicks resulting in an actual CPC of $6.53. The amount of clicks landing on the e-commerce front door were also below target for two of the four weeks and the abandonment rate was below target over the entire period.

Putting the Scores into Context

From the above scorecard I knew I had to drill down on the shopping abandonment, and the cost per click first as these were the two consistently underperforming KPIs. I also had to put this into context. I knew that search marketing for this kind of product would work out a lot cheaper and drive many more visitors. I then also looked at all the other numbers around the campaign. Was a 1.34% click through to the store going to be enough to be profitable? A quick calculation told me that even if all the visitors hitting the store bought the product (922) that they wouldn't cover the cost of the campaign. This was a massive oversight from a sales point of view. Marketing managers put more emphasis on the media impressions and clicks than the sales figures. That was their biggest problem and was why I zoomed in on the potential cost per sale in my insight report.

The other major thing was the shopping cart abandonment. It was 96% every week for the past six months. This needed action from company. I would spend the money they were going to spend on campaigns fixing the shopping cart and product placement problems they were having.

I could have added other things like how the competition were selling the products on other sites or heuristic analysis, but at this stage the company had enough problems caused by their own poor campaign management that could quickly be fixed in the short term. I therefore zeroed in on the things that they should look at first before worrying about how the competition was doing. Overall this was a very poor campaign and I had to write the strongest lead I could in order to get the points across.

The data was all there if anyone needed it, but actually no-one asked to even see the scorecard such was the urgency instilled in the business insight report.

Dashboards

Primarily I used scorecards but we had dashboards with the data going back for over a year showing general performance and targets. I would argue that while dashboards recording performance are useful for the analyst, everyone has to understand them if they are going to be shared throughout the organization. For that reason I haven't made a big deal about them here. They are useful for the hub to monitor performance but in my view the hub should use a good lead rather than a good graph when reporting business insights.

CHAPTER 9

The Proliferation Process

You can't build a reputation on what you are going to do.

Henry Ford

CHAPTER CONTENTS

9.1 FROM GROUND ZERO TO THE CULT OF ANALYTICS

The executive steering group (see Chapter 1) won't build a culture by talking about it, they have to plan then make other people act to make the changes happen. However where you start depends on where you are in the adoption model.

Figure 9.1 is my own adaptation of a graph created by Jari Salojuuri of Trainers' House Analytics unit showing the level of adoption that web analytics typically has in most organizations.

In Figure 9.1 the arrow going left to right represents time. The arrow pointing upwards represents organizational readiness. The idea here is to show that it takes time to reach the five levels of organizational readiness. That time depends on your organization but 2 years would be the minimum time between level 1 and level 5.

Level 1: Analytics Ground Zero

Ground zero means that your organization doesn't have a web analytics system. It may be that some IT staff know that they can get log files but no one understands the data they produce correctly. The need for analytics may stem from some random campaigns that someone is asking to measure. It could be that the CEO has decided it's time to move into the twenty first century and start measuring performance, a good catalyst for change, but currently your organization has not yet started any activity.

What to do Next?

Your first milestone should be to generate internal awareness about what web analytics is, how your competition is doing it and the tools they use. You may at this stage consider outsourcing to a consultancy to run a workshop. At this stage you might not have executive backing. You need to get backing from the executive level at some stage. It may be that your executive level don't know

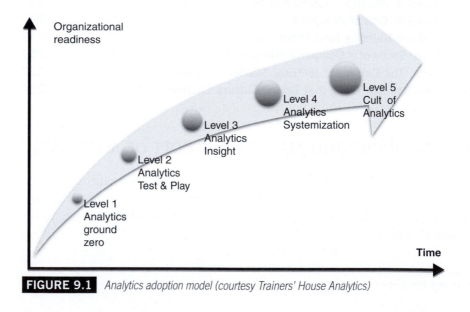

FIGURE 9.1 *Analytics adoption model (courtesy Trainers' House Analytics)*

the importance of analytics. In this case you need to convince them by show-ing them the outcomes of the awareness workshops and where your business opportunities lie.

If at least some of the executive level buy into the idea and start to create an internal vision about how to use analytics for your business then you're ready to take things further. If you don't have backing you can still move to the second level without them and try to prove business benefits by producing some quick wins (see Chapter 4) but it will be harder to achieve anything more than level 3 without executive backing.

Level 2: Analytics Test and Play

Level 2 means that at least a few of the people in the organization realize the potential that using analytics can bring them and they're starting to make a noise about it. You might find a tool like Google Analytics in place and some enterprising individuals that are trying their best to make sense out of their campaigns. The reports your enterprise might use tend to be scattered and sporadic, perhaps campaign specific. Little actual action happens because the information is in the hands of so few people and usually it's the wrong kind of people. Basic level implementation of tools means potential analysis and reporting capabilities but so far you haven't gone down that road.

What to do Next

If you have buy in at this stage from the top management you might now be ready to determine roles in the business by using the hub and spoke model (see Chapter 1), designing a REAN model (see Chapter 2), doing some KPI work-shops (see Chapter 3) for your spokes prior to finding out what tool specifica-tion you need (see Chapter 5). At this stage you need to build awareness that these models exist and try to encourage management to take the next step.

If you don't have buy in at this stage you need to continue the awareness push either with previously mentioned awareness workshops or, because you have a tool, you might want to plan some quick wins (see Chapter 4) to help convince your management. If you don't have the analysis know how then ask for help from a consultant who is competent with the tool that you're using and learn from them.

You're still not ready at this stage to start building incentives into daily working practices, especially without executive buy in.

Level 3: Analytics Insight

You've gone beyond simple experiments with tools and are now using the tools and fully understand the potential of analytics to your organization. You are using web analytics tools to deliver basic reporting and random analysis happens across the business as key people start to learn how to use the tools. These 'analytics stars' are starting to really get to grips with things but the majority of people still haven't enough time or training to understand analytics intricacies.

Information reaches a lot of people through company communication channels such as intranets, emails and newsletters.

Because of web analytics you're beginning to compare campaign performance, have seen the benefit of SEO to your organization and may even be developing content to be search engine friendly because of this. Wins are slowly forming. There is basic measurement in place across the entire organization and in certain key areas you may even have advanced implementation with good KPIs measuring performance.

You may even be combining data already as suggested in the Insight model (see Chapter 7).

Management is almost certainly backing the initiatives but if they're not you should now have ample evidence that they need to continue the process building. Make them well aware of all the gains to the business.

What to do Next

The hub should be formed (see Chapter 1). It's vital to get the right people in this key area, the 'analytics stars' should be part of the hub and you need to utilize their knowledge and build processes around them that allow knowledge to be transferred, otherwise if the star leaves the business you're back to level 2.

KPIs may already exist in some units and in others they may not. The hub and spoke model along with REAN should be clearly explained to all concerned (by the hub) and used as underlying strategies to everything they do in the future.

The strategy should ideally come from within the hub or within the business. You can bring consultants in to help with the practical things but you should own the hub and spoke concept and REAN. It's your business and your strategy. These models should be applied to your business, if REAN doesn't work as an acronym call it something else but use the concept. Nokia, where we first introduced REAN in 2006, have developed variations around Acquire, Engage, Convert, Retain (AECR) because their business uses these terms. HP have their own variation. NSN use REAN because we introduced the ideas there.

It's better if you have words that your business is already using so that they see the point faster.

KPIs should be developed in units (spokes) that aren't already measuring them. The ones that are measuring them should have their KPIs placed into the context of the REAN model.

Once you have implemented the thinking so that it becomes used more commonly you can then start thinking about pay based incentives but right now while it's great that analytics is being used it's still a long way off being embedded into the business.

Level 4: Analytics Systemization

You have developed a hub and spoke model and have an underlying strategy like REAN in place. You've developed advanced KPIs for each spoke and have a scorecard or dashboard system that monitors business performance.

You have a REAN scorecard reported to the executive management and tactical business insights regularly being sent to the spokes. Actions are being taken based on the information in most cases rather than reports being filed and forgotten.

Regular analysis is carried out when it's needed and not before.

Your hub plans quick wins to share with the spokes that still need the most help to understand analytics. The hub is really becoming a functioning measurement organization helping to provide intelligence for the entire company and you have advanced analytics measurement coming from your tools.

All the data sources are utilized and data abundance doesn't frighten you.

What to do Next

You're almost there and you should keep up the momentum. This is the perfect time to start rewarding good analytics practices internally. We'll cover that a little later in this chapter. You might also be at the stage where you want to automate more of the data coming into your hub. It won't be long before the spokes understand quite a lot about analytics and you need to gear up for that. They will start asking more and more difficult questions that need more of the hub's time so look at automation wherever its possible.

Data integration is also a big question for level 4 analytics. Streamlining customer relations management (CRM) and business intelligence (BI) data to truly combine it with web analytics data is the next thing to tackle and start predicting what people will do.

Level 5: Cult of Analytics

Web Analytics data is fully integrated with all marketing systems and measures on and offline marketing/sales activity to a reasonable level of accuracy. You're doing everything you did at level 4 but you're doing it every day. Your hub can predict how your customers will act in a given situation to a certain level of accuracy. Your spokes are now basing the vast majority of their actions on what the data tells them they should be doing, while the hub quickly finds out the answers to key business questions. Investment decisions are made at the executive level based on analytics data in most cases.

Your customers can tell you something through their online behaviour and you can react on the fly to help them and nurture them. Your lead generations systems drop hot leads into the email inboxes of your sales people. Your e-commerce systems are integrated to react to who your visitor is based on behavioural or customer segments.

You can really start to measure the ROI on your analytics expenditure and you're finding out that while the cost of implementation and systemization was high, it was most definitely worth it.

What to do Next

It would be easy to say, do nothing different because you're already at 'Analytics utopia'. However you've only just begun (Figure 9.2). Amazon probably hit the analytics cultural level around year 2000 and they are still at it, constantly improving their services, increasing their revenues and proving the doubters of the 'dot bomb' completely wrong. You need to consistently do the things that work and consistently stop doing the things that don't work. Because you're measuring everything that matters that shouldn't be a problem.

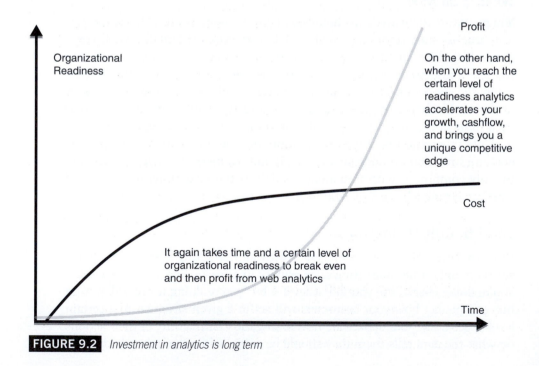

Profit

Organizational Readiness

On the other hand, when you reach the certain level of readiness analytics accelerates your growth, cashflow, and brings you a unique competitive edge

Cost

It again takes time and a certain level of organizational readiness to break even and then profit from web analytics

Time

FIGURE 9.2 *Investment in analytics is long term*

Culture Building Best Practices

You now know where you stand in the adoption model. You now know what you have to do next. One of the things you may start doing is help your employees to embrace the culture and to do the right things. This is sometimes called empowering employees.

Incentives, rewards, competitions, prestige, all of these things will help people to start taking the courses of action you need them to take in order to get your analytics to the next level. The spokes are full of people that have been taught how to do their job in university and then had years of working experience, they now need to learn to understand why analytics is important.

Finding people to populate your hub is a different story. The first hard job is getting them in there and finding ways to train them in the right way, the second is then keeping the people in the hub because they will be head hunted for opportunities elsewhere if they are any good.

In order to keep good people you need to keep building your culture so that the money they're offered doesn't become the only issue.

Culture Building Tip 1: Reward Passion

Anyone with good people and business skills who demonstrates passion for the job should be promoted. In an analytics culture the key is to get people in charge who understand why analytics is truly important and have a passion to follow that. If a guy in the spoke starts talking like a web analyst with real passion ask him/her if they would like a job leading their spoke. If you hear people groaning about a high bounce rate or cheering about a 5% improvement in abandonment rate you have a potential candidate as an analyst in the hub.

Only people who have really got a passion for the work should be promoted to positions of authority in the hub or the spokes. It's important for the business that both the hub and the spokes have people leading the staff that truly understand why they are doing all this extra work. Without real passion in this field and a lot of patience you will fail to do a very good job.

Culture Building Tip 2: The Hub as the Analyst's Prize Job

You should promote the hub as the centre of analytical excellence, the centre of business intelligence, the place where only the talented can survive. It's true so promote it as such.

Culture Building Tip 3: Hub Incentives

Pay people in the hub more when they win for the company. Pay them more when they really win big. Individuals can be paid bonuses by showing the spokes things that contribute to direct cost savings or improvements. The team as a whole should also be rewarded so that when one of the hub do well they all get a piece of the action. For example if the hub spots that a funnel process has high abandonment and suggests to the spoke that they run a test (as well as help them by telling them how to do it) that increases conversion rates; the hub should be rewarded.

Culture Building Tip 4: The Spoke as a Business Optimization Role

People in the spokes are really the ones who will actually make business optimization happen and they should be treated as the core business teams ultimately responsible for business results. They have high pressure roles and the people in those teams should understand their value.

Culture Building Tip 5: Spoke Incentives

Where the hub is looking for opportunities the spokes are taking actions to capitalize on the opportunities that they find. Reward the actions with incentives. If an action is taken that works then the whole spoke gets a piece of the action. For instance if the hub tells the spoke a test needs to be carried out and the spoke does the testing that eventually leads to improvement the spoke should get the reward. Individuals in the spokes can be rewarded for suggesting 'tests' that can be taken.

Culture Building Tip 6: Prestige

When someone in the hub or spoke does something that is particularly insightful, out of the box, innovative or just plain clever reward him or her with a prize of some nature. Put the idea on a pedestal for all to see and make sure that the awareness is spread. Use communication tools at your disposal to sing the praises of the idea or innovation. Try to find small wins everywhere to reward.

One example of this is the Stinky award covered the book *Always Be Testing* By Bryan Eisenberg and John Quarto-vonTivadar (http://www.testingtoolbox.com/)

Intuit's Stinky (http://www.intuit.com/)

When it comes to companies that embrace a culture of testing, we have to take our hats off to Intuit. You see, Intuit has this small, cute, squishy toy skunk – the Stinky. It's an award, but it isn't given to the testing winners who achieve positive returns on investment through their testing successes. Testing losers earn the right to display the Stinky with pride.

Thomas Edison once quipped, 'Results! Why, man, I have gotten a lot of results. I know several thousand things that won't work.' When you test, you always learn something: You learn from what went right; you learn from what went wrong. Usually you learn more from the failures, but whatever the outcome, you've got a lesson.

What you choose to do with it defines your TCR — your Testing Culture Rating. The Always Be Testing culture at Intuit recasts every negative as a positive. Intuit groks testing. Intuit has an extremely high TCR. We acknowledge there are often impediments to developing a culture of testing, but these are not insurmountable. As you'll see in multiple examples throughout this book, Amazon.com is by no means the only company to make a commitment to testing. It is by no means the only company that could sing the praises of testing's value. And it has obviously dealt successfully with the obstacles that discourage many companies from leaping wholeheartedly on the bandwagon.

Culture Building Tip 7: Remove Barriers

Make it easy to do things inside the hub and spoke system. Paperwork and red tape should be kept to a minimum. Access to analytics systems should be quick and controlled by an effective administration system from the hub.

Hold regular meetings with open communication encouraged. Discuss any problems that might exist in terms of how the hub works with the spokes. Take action on problems raised and fix issues. Managers in the hub and spokes have the responsibility to lead these discussions.

If people aren't immediately sharing the vision take their ideas and show them how analytics can help them back up their arguments, earn them more money and bring them a lot of internal prestige. Show them how they fit into the hub and spoke model and ask them to try their new role, don't simply expect them to 'get it' immediately.

People are complex creatures and they may 'toe the line' for a while, trying out what the management are telling them but without seeing 'wins' (see Chapter 4) they will lose heart and start grumbling about the good old days when they weren't measured by a scorecard. Show them why this isn't the point. Make sure enough 'wins' happen. Make sure they understand why performance measures are there.

Make sure that spokes are independently measured for success. If one spoke is failing they should try to copy what the other spokes are doing not hold back everyone.

Culture Building Tip 8: HR Should Replace Problem People

With any vision there are some people that simply won't share the idea. Offer these people an easy way out of the hub and spoke model either by moving them to somewhere where they will be better suited, offering them early retirement or, worst case scenario, let them go.

This may sound controversial but if you're trying to change to a data driven company and someone in a particular area doesn't like the idea then they will breed contempt of the new ideology. This kind of person can cause a lot of damage, especially if the person is well liked. Well liked people that can't manage change are possibly the worst problem you might find. Politics in big enterprises often get in the way. This is one of the reasons why it's vital that the management vision is strong.

I've seen individual people jump on reports that are 50 slides long with little value unless you're an analyst and use the same arguments that I have shown in Chapter 8 as a weapon against analytics. They might argue, 'All these numbers and for what? I get sent these reports every week, I am supposed to be using them to help meet my quotas yet they take weeks to read and understand. This will never work!'

It could be that they aren't educated enough in which case you need to lower the barrier and find ways to get them on board. But if they persist that this new analytics drive is just one big waste of time then they have to go or you'll never get anywhere fast.

Culture Building Tip 9: HR Should Hire Good People

Just as you let people go that don't fit with the new cultural approach you have to bring in people that do. They don't all have to understand the intricacies of web analytics but they should understand the data you're using is very important for the success of the company.

Also make sure that HR (human resources) is in line with the new policy. It's no good allowing new hires to come through that are being screened (formerly or informally) in old ways that don't match the new hire requirements. In interviews people will tell you what you want to hear in order to get a job so new employment practices should be considered that screen people in an appropriate manner.

9.2 CASE STUDY OF A COMPANY THAT GET IT

In their 2008 SEC filing, Amazon describe the vision of their business as to:

> *Relentlessly focus on customer experience by offering our customers low prices, convenience, and a wide selection of merchandise.*

The vision is to offer Earth's biggest selection and to be Earth's most customer-centric company.

How 'The Culture of Metrics' Started in Amazon

A common theme in Amazon's development is the drive to use a measured approach to all aspects of the business, beyond the finance. Marcus (2004) describes an occasion at a corporate 'boot-camp' in January 1997 when Amazon CEO Jeff Bezos 'saw the light'. 'At Amazon, we will have a Culture of Metrics', he said while addressing his senior staff. He went on to explain how web-based business gave Amazon an 'amazing window into human behavior'. Marcus says: 'Gone were the fuzzy approximations of focus groups, the anecdotal fudging and smoke blowing from the marketing department. A company like Amazon could (and did) record every move a visitor made, every last click and twitch of the mouse. As the data piled up into virtual heaps, hummocks and mountain ranges, you could draw all sorts of conclusions about their chimerical nature, the consumer. In this sense, Amazon was not merely a store, but an immense repository of facts. All we needed were the right equations to plug into them.'

James Marcus then goes on to give a fascinating insight into a break-out group discussion of how Amazon could better use measures to improve its performance. Marcus was in the Bezos group, brainstorming customer-centric metrics. Marcus (2004) summarizes the dialogue, led by Bezos:

'First, we figure out which things we'd like to measure on the site', he said. 'For example, let's say we want a metric for customer enjoyment. How could we calculate that?'

There was silence. Then somebody ventured: 'How much time each customer spends on the site?'

'Not specific enough', Jeff said.

'How about the average number of minutes each customer spends on the site per session', someone else suggested. 'If that goes up, they're having a blast.'

'But how do we factor in purchase?' I [Marcus] said feeling proud of myself. 'Is that a measure of enjoyment?'

'I think we need to consider frequency of visits, too', said a dark-haired woman I didn't recognize.

'Lot of folks are still accessing the web with those creepy-crawly modems. Four short visits from them might be just as good as one visit from a guy with a T-1. Maybe better.'

'Good point', Jeff said. 'And anyway, enjoyment is just the start. In the end, we should be measuring customer ecstasy.'

It is interesting that Amazon was having this debate about the elements of RFM analysis in 1997, after already having achieved $16 million of revenue in the previous year. Of course, this is a miniscule amount compared with today's billions of dollar turnover. The important point was that this was the start of a focus on metrics which can be seen through the description of Matt Pound's work later in this case study. (Full case study can be found here: http://www.davechaffey.com/E-commerce-Internet-marketing-case-studies/Amazon-case-study)

9.3 THE ONE BIG THING THAT DRIVES CULTURE CHANGE

The one big thing that all successful cultures have at their heart is the vision. Not a grand vision statement or some difficult to grasp concept but something simple and easy to understand. A great vision has the power to inspire. But at the very least the vision should be believable and conceivable. Like Amazon, The vision is to offer Earth's biggest selection and to be Earth's most customer-centric company.

Analytics is never likely to be the vision itself. It simply isn't interesting enough to inspire everyone to change daily routines. The reasons for using analytics should be the core of the vision. In order to build a culture of analytics or a data driven company you need to have a reason to be 'data driven'. This should be where the vision statement lies with the analytics strategy from hub and spoke to reporting being part of the overall roadmap.

This isn't to say I don't believe that analytics is important enough on its own to be the reason for a company to change. In many ways I think analytics should be the foundation of all business activities, however I don't think you can inspire the people on the front lines of the business with a statement like 'We will become data driven'. People would ask the question 'Why?'

I'd like to share if I may what I consider a simple believable vision communicated with urgency by a true leader. This was a vision that when implemented used more data, intelligence and analysis than any other campaign that had gone before it.

He utilized competitive intelligence, analysed his own situation and drew upon human endeavour (just like the Insight model) in a time when computers were the size of houses. He never mentioned this in his 'vision statement' but before he released the vision he had already started on gathering data and finding new data sources.

It was 4 June 1940. It was his fourth speech as Prime Minister. His accession to the position had been controversial and was in fact a default ruling. Members of both the major political parties in Britain openly criticized him.

His speech opened with a factual account of the French collapse, the evacuation at Dunkirk, and preparations for home defense. It was a brutal wake up call for the British Empire. We'd been hit and hit hard. But he then said his government was determined to 'ride out the storm of war, and to outlive the menace of tyranny, if necessary for years, if necessary alone'. This single sentence hushed the entire House of Commons. He went on:

> *Even though large tracts of Europe and many old and famous States have fallen or may fall into the grip of the Gestapo and all the odious apparatus of Nazi rule, we shall not flag or fail.*

We shall go on to the end, **we shall fight** *in France,* **we shall fight** *on the seas and oceans,* **we shall fight** *with growing confidence and growing strength in the air,* **we shall defend our island,** *whatever the cost may be,* **we shall fight** *on the beaches,* **we shall fight** *on the landing grounds,* **we shall fight** *in the fields, and in the streets;* **we shall never surrender!**

His immediate audience was stunned, and then erupted into a prolonged standing ovation.

The entire nation heard it, understood it and more importantly believed it, we were to fight, defend and never surrender. A vision that had analytics at its core, turned Britain into one of the finest counter intelligence agencies in the world, bred exceptionally talented analysts and helped defeat one of the greatest tyrants to walk the earth, was started when Churchill said 'We shall fight on the beaches.'

That in my view was his finest hour. Now it's your turn.

Index